GRACE TRIUMPHANT

The Triumph of God's Grace in the Philippines

GRACE TRIUMPHANT

The Triumph of God's Grace in the Philippines

An autobiography
By
CYRIL H. BROOKS

Walterick Publishers © 1985

Scripture taken from the HOLY BIBLE: NEW INTERNATIONAL VERSION. Copyright © 1973, 1978 by the International Bible Society. Used by permission of Zondervan Bible Publishers.

ISBN: 0-937396-66-4

TABLE OF CONTENTS

1. Where it all Began 9
2. Boyhood Days 13
3. Life in Canada 23
4. Service in World War I 31
5. Call to the Mission Field 39
6. Preparing for the Mission Field 47
7. Guidance Regarding the Field 57
8. Beginning Our Missionary Work 65
9. Back to Manila 77
10. Our First Furlough 87
11. The Beginning of Work in San Juan 97
12. A Decade of Activity 107
13. War Clouds Gather 117
14. The Japanese Occupation 127
15. Life in an Internment Camp 135
16. Liberation from Internment 143
17. Homeward Bound! 153
18. Home at Last 163
19. Post-War Religious and Political Conditions . 171
20. Rehabilitation in San Juan 179
21. Church Growth 189
22. More Church Growth 201
23. The Bible School of the Air 213
24. Camp Work 225
25. Fellowship in the Gospel 233
26. Fellow-Workers in Christ 243
27. The Progress of the Gospel 255

INTRODUCTION

Two years of combat duty in France in World War I—deliverance in moments of danger. In hospital with pneumonia and pleurisy—the doctor's verdict, "He won't live through the night!" Years of missionary service in the Philippines including facing starvation during Japanese occupation and internment camp. Dramatic rescue shortly before planned assassination by the Japanese. Experiences like these have made up a full life, a life full of God's goodness and grace.

Folks often have said, "You should write a book!" The stock reply was, "When I have nothing more important to do!" Now as an octagenarian, my strength and ability for some of the important tasks is limited and it seems there is time to record this testimony to God's faithfulness.

If possible, I would like to avoid the frequent use of first person pronouns as I don't want to be that kind of an "I-specialist." But to write in the third person seems a bit devious. If there is any value in this testimony, the honor and glory belongs entirely to God. Like Paul, I can only say, "By the grace of God, I am what I am." Had I only been more submissive to the Lord's leading and power, His grace could have done greater things in and through me. Oh, the wonder of His patience and longsuffering in displaying His love and grace to one so undeserving of it! Like Jacob of old, I say, "I am unworthy of all the kindness and faithfulness You have shown your servant" (Gen. 32:10 NIV).

Many years ago, it was my privilege to spend a day with two godly servants of the Lord, Mr. and Mrs. Jansen, at the Culion Leper Colony. When I thanked Mrs. Jansen for her kindness and hospitality, she remarked, "Don't rob God of His glory by thanking me." So to any who may read this story I want to say, "Please don't rob God of any glory by attributing any credit at all to us."

1
WHERE IT ALL BEGAN

"The righteous man leads a blameless life. Blessed are his children after him. . . . Her children rise and call her blessed." (Prov. 20:7; 31:28)

Lingfield is a pleasant Surrey village with quaint, old timbered cottages. It lies about 25 miles southeast of London, England; its only attraction to the world being a race course. But the activities there did not interfere with the placid life in the village as both race track and railroad station were outside the village. In the center of the village was a pond and as a young boy I thought that it was there the saying originated, "You can lead a horse to water but you cannot make him drink." Across the street was the blacksmith's shop where we watched with fascination the horses being shod. In later years when I had to memorize Longfellow's "The Village Blacksmith," I would think of Mr. Huggett, the burly blacksmith. I also knew him as the Sunday school superintendent at the Mission Room.

This chapel was just behind the day school and had been opened for services on June 9, 1875. On Sunday mornings after the children were dismissed from Sunday school, the older folks would gather and quietly take their seats around the table on which had been placed the bread and the cup for the Lord's Supper. The benches had been made for adults and the back rest was just a bit high for a small boy. He either had to sit up very straight or was in danger of sliding out the back of the seat. Across the fields was the Anglican church. It still has one of the few extant chained Bibles. When Bibles were first printed some were chained to the pulpit so they could not be borrowed by eager parishioners! When the church bell stopped pealing at eleven o'clock a brother would rise to announce the opening hymn. The reverence and devotion in those meetings left a lasting impression.

During the summer months an open-air meeting was held beside the pond. At one end of this pool stood an old stone building under the shade of a large tree. This small building was called "The Cage" and had once been a prison. It was there the Gospel was preached and on a quiet summer evening the preacher's voice would ring out over the whole village. There was little need for a sound system when there was no noise of traffic or radio. Among those active in the local church meeting in the Mission Room were Harry and Ellen Brooks.

Harry was 25 and Ellen 23 when they were married on December 20, 1886. At the turn of the century they lived on a large estate called Felcourt some three miles from the village. Harry was head gardener and their home was part of an ivy-covered house that was round in shape. They had four children. Ethel Annie, who after she married Richard Weller in 1911, lived in Western Canada: Florence Lillian who never married but also went to Canada and for 25 years worked in the Dept. of Agriculture of the government of British Columbia; George Arthur Stanley remained in England where he took up horticulture and was for several years in charge of a large seed-growing company. He was named after two of his uncles, George and Arthur, but the third name was taken from a great pioneer missionary in Central Africa, Frederick Stanley Arnot. There was a gap of seven years before their fourth child was born on December 11, 1898, and named Cyril Harry. The second name, of course, was after my father but the first name was from Cyril Bird, a missionary who died from fever in Angola in 1896. Many years later I became well acquainted with his widow and her second husband, Dr. Andrews.

Naming their sons after missionaries would indicate that Harry and Ellen Brooks were very missionary minded. At one time they had a desire to be missionaries themselves in Spain but the

Where it all Began

Lord did not open the way. Instead they did missionary work in Surrey. For some years in Lingfield, baptisms were held in an iron tank in a field beside the Mission Room. In 1901 the brethren worked together to install a baptistry inside the Mission Room. Harry Brooks was one who helped in that project.

Looking through his small diary for 1905, his last year here on earth, it seems that quite often he was away preaching on Sundays in small assemblies that he could reach on his bicycle. It was in that missionary spirit that they offered their youngest son to the Lord for missionary service even before he was born. I only learned of this after I had personally responded to the Lord's call.

Naturally my memories of those early years in Lingfield are vague. Walking through the garden with Father and being given a small ripe tomato, popping it in my mouth to get all the delicious flavor as it broke open! Lying down to rest after lunch but sneaking out the front door with my sisters in hot pursuit. One day when Mother was baking I sat on a loaf of bread; it had to be reshaped before it could be baked! There is still a scar on my knee, the result of a fall. . . . Seeing an automobile for the first time. Evidently it was in the fall because I was amused to see the leaves chasing the car in its excessive speed—probably 20 miles an hour!

A tree near our house had been cut down, and a cross-section of this placed beside the kitchen stove was my favorite seat, especially for family devotions each morning. Even before I learned to read I had my own Bible, like the big folks. Such daily family devotions have been maintained all through life. At the Mission Room they had Sunday school both in the morning and in the afternoon. However, in the afternoon I stayed home with Mother to hear Bible stories and learn Bible verses. It was easy to learn Isaiah 53:6 for all around were flocks of sheep. I knew how they would go astray in their own way. So at a young age I learned that Jesus bore the iniquity of us all. I can't remember a time when I didn't believe that.

Many Bible teachers and missionaries visited Lingfield and were entertained for a meal in our home. I soon learned that little boys are to be seen but not heard! Most of these men had beards and, to me, seemed such good men. I was sure that old people had no difficulty living a good life and staying out of mischief. They seemed to be very strict when they frowned on any misbehavior on my part. To my childish mind God the Father was like those men and I was scared to pray to Him. But Jesus was my Friend who loved me and had died for me, so it wasn't hard to pray to Him. On one occasion, so I was told, I was seen riding on a wooden sawhorse and lustily singing the chorus of a missionary hymn, "Speed away, speed away on your mission of light."

The last entry in Father's 1905 diary was for October 24, but for the next day Mother had written, "His 44th birthday. Annual tea at Staffords Wood, good time, his last meeting." It was no doubt fitting for he had often preached there. Right after that he was not well and Dr. Austin was sent for. The good doctor was a leader in the assembly and a close personal friend. I still have a book that he gave to Father. A specialist was called in from London and an operation performed. I really don't know what the trouble was. Possibly his life might have been prolonged had modern medical knowledge been available.

Thursday evening, November 30, I went in to kiss Father goodnight. The next morning when Mother awakened me, she said, "Jesus has taken Daddy to heaven."

During his illness someone sent a card with this simple message, "Your Father knoweth." It was a great comfort to Mother in her sorrow. She wrote in the diary, "Dearest H. fell asleep in Jesus. The Lord gave and the Lord hath taken away. Blessed be the name of the Lord." Mother told someone that in almost twenty years of married life there had never been an angry word between them. They loved each other but even more they loved the Lord Jesus Christ.

I heard some older folks say, "He's too young to understand." I don't recall shedding any tears. In childlike faith I believed he was indeed with Jesus in heaven. Yet I did miss my Father for I knew he loved me. Looking back over my life, I realize I missed a great deal by not having a father during my formative years. He was laid to rest in the cemetery near the Anglican church on December 6, just a few days before my seventh birthday. It was a double funeral for a close relative was buried close by at the same time.

2

BOYHOOD DAYS

"A father to the fatherless, a defender of widows, is God in his holy dwelling." (Psa. 68:5)

What is a widow with four children to do when, the day after she has buried her husband, she receives notice to vacate the house they had lived in for years? Of course, free rental of the house was one of the perquisites that went with her husband's work on the estate. So the owner was within his rights. Nevertheless it was a situation in which the widow proved the truth of the above verse.

The two girls, Ethel and Florrie, were away in domestic service. Ethel was working for Mr. Scott in Dorking, a partner in the Christian publishing company of Morgan and Scott. Florrie was working in a house where her cousin was cook. George had received a scholarship and was boarding at Reigate Grammar School. So at the age of seven, I was the only one left with my Mother. Because of these circumstances I was not only without a father but was also deprived of the usual companionship of my sisters and brother. It was almost the same as being the only son of a widowed mother. Apart from schoolmates, I had few playmates. No doubt life would have been different if my Father had lived, but God makes no mistakes.

I was shy and rather timid and not too robust in health. One day coming home from school, a rough boy from the slums knocked me down. He got some fun out of it, but I didn't! He also took my cap. I was scared of him, but I was more scared to go home without my cap. So I followed him at a discreet distance until he left my cap on a gate post and ran off.

Mother was in her early forties and needed to find a way of supporting herself and providing for me. God again proved to be a "defender of widows." In a short time she obtained a position as a housekeeper for a gentleman bachelor. Mr. A. C. Knight was a director in a large soap manufacturing company. As a Christian who attended the Congregational Church, he was interested in boys and an active leader in the Boy's Brigade. Thus, it was possible for me to remain with my mother in his home. In World War I Mr. Knight served as an officer and was killed in the ill-fated Gallipoli landing. By that time we had moved to Canada.

Early in 1906 we moved to Blackheath, a suburb in southeast London. A large heath or open space for sports activities lay between Blackheath and Greenwich Park. I became well acquainted with that park in which was the Greenwich Observatory, the place of zero longitude and source of Greenwich Mean Time. Nearby was a Naval museum and the Thames River.

About the time of my eighth birthday there was a fall of snow. As my Sunday school teacher escorted me home, she asked, "What is whiter than snow?" That really puzzled me! I thought of white things—writing paper, sugar, salt, mother's laundry (no tattle-tale gray for her!)—but snow was whiter than all these. Mother dropped a hint that I should think in another direction. So I finally learned what the hymn said, "Wash me in the blood of the Lamb and I shall be whiter than snow." I could rely on the word of God, "Though your sins are like scarlet, they shall be as white as snow" (Isa. 1:18). I am sure that I was saved then for I cannot remember a time when I didn't believe that Jesus died for me. However, I didn't have complete assurance.

There was a lot of emphasis those days on the second coming of Christ and I had learned about the Rapture. Sometimes I would look out of my bedroom window at a gorgeous sunset and wonder if Christ would come before morning! But sometimes I was not so sure. One afternoon I came home from school to find the door locked. Mother was out shopping, no doubt. No problem! Just sit on the doorstep and wait. But it seemed to be an awfully long wait. Then the thought—maybe the Lord has come and I am left behind! How can I find out? I know! I'll watch the people walking down our street. If I see one person I believe to be a Christian (that, of course, would have to be someone from our chapel!) then I'll know the Lord hasn't come yet. Even then I was well-indoctrinated—no partial rapture theories had come my way. To my great relief the first Christian I saw was Mother entering our gate.

From time to time I was bothered by this lack of assurance. One Sunday evening (I can't remember when it was) I determined to do something about it. It may have been something the preacher said in the service, I really don't recall. Anyhow, as I kneeled to say my usual bedtime prayer, I added something. "Lord, if I never really trusted in you before, I do now believe and accept you as my Savior." Immediately I was assured that I was really saved and that assurance has never left me. No doubt I was truly saved before but it needed that definite act to assure me. Later on I learned that assurance of salvation is not based on our experience but upon the promises of God's Word.

About a quarter of a mile from where we lived in Blackheath was Alexandra Hall. In some ways the assembly there was different from others. Most of the members were upper-class people and only a few of the poorer class. There was one woman who was a charwoman but rather outspoken and uncouth when she poured out her scorn on the snobbery of some ladies there. Mother's ministry was to befriend some of the old ladies and I was not enraptured over such guests! She also took an interest in young women in domestic service who were away from home.

When we first moved there, the congregation at Alexandra Hall was quite large. Some two to three hundred would meet each Sunday morning to observe the Lord's Supper. Without fail one brother, a Mr. Luck, would read a chapter from the Bible without comment and Easter Sunday it would surely be Luke 24. There would be some five hundred at the evening service. Dr. Robert McKilliam was the recognized leader in the assembly and always preached when he was home. Though a medical man, he was a great Bible student and also editor of a monthly magazine, "The Morning Star," which emphasized the Second Coming. The choir, mostly of older persons, sat on the platform. One gentleman had his favorite seat by the railing and during the sermon he would lean on this railing and enjoy a little sleep.

The assembly regularly held a brief 15 minute open-air service on the steps before the evening service, summer and winter. Then in the summer there was an open-air meeting in the center of the town after the service. Later when numbers were dwindling they held an evangelistic campaign. The invited preacher was an eccentric man by the name of Hodson. His zeal for the Lord was accompanied by a sense of humor and a quick repartee. On one occasion, so I am told, he carried on a tent campaign in an English village. Sunday morning he went to the Anglican Church to hear the parson. Being sadly disappointed by the sermon he asked the parson, "Do you call *that* preaching the Gospel?" It seems that in retaliation the reverend gentleman persuaded two village thugs to beat up Mr. Hodson and burn down his tent. When they accosted Mr. Hodson in front of his tent and stated their intention, he, being a big husky man, picked them up one by one and tossed them over the hedge. The parson who had been standing at a distance, approached and haughtily asked, "Mr. Hodson, do you call *that* preaching the Gospel?" To which Mr. Hodson replied, "No, I call *that* casting out demons!"

Perhaps the dwindling attendance was in part due to the fact that there was no Sunday school and very few young people at Alexandra Hall. After we left there Dr. McKilliam passed away which further contributed to the decline. During my war service in World War I, visiting Blackheath one evening I found about twenty believers meeting in a much smaller hall.

As there was no Sunday school there, I went on Sunday afternoons to a Sunday school in a rough area of Lewisham. My chum, Willie Peacock, went with me and our teacher was a fine man, Mr. Bernau. In that slum neighborhood the windows were protected by heavy wire screens. Almost every week some boisterous boy was forcibly evicted for making trouble, but they would invariably return the following week.

My schooling started in Lingfield with a year or so in Primary School before Father died. When we moved to Blackheath I went to Northbrook School at Lea Green, a 20 minute walk each way. There was no such thing as school buses in those days. I enjoyed the teachers there but very much disliked the principal. For me, Mr. Fluke had an appropriate name: For one thing

Boyhood Days

he smoked! One day in class he misunderstood an answer I gave (deliberately I suspect) and made fun of me before the class. It seemed to have been due to my stand as a Christian, even though that was a weak one. During one vacation I was waiting to get a haircut. Mr. Fluke came in and took his place in the barber's chair ahead of me, with some snide remark to the barber.

Coming home from school one afternoon, one of my two companions found a shrivelled up potato in the gutter. It looked quite rubbery and my chum said, "wonder if it would bounce!" No time was wasted speculating on the "bounceability" of an old potato; regardless of surroundings, at a busy crosswalk where three streets met, my chum flung the potato to the ground. And oh, did it bounce? On the rebound it struck the bonnet of an old lady who was approaching and would have completely dislodged it but for the ribbons by which it was tied. (In those days little old ladies wore bonnets which were high in front above the forehead and were fastened with ribbons tied under the chin.) I caught a glimpse of hands raised to retrieve the bonnet and heard a scream. We did not linger to hear the tirade about juvenile delinquency in that "modern age." Three boys decamped in three different directions with speeds that surely could be in the Guinness Book of Records had they been recorded.

Later I was transferred to Greenwich Central School, the equivalent of High School. It was a 45 minute walk from home but we didn't think anything of that in those days. The headmaster there, Mr. Wood, was strict but considerate and well-respected. Monday morning assembly was devoted to Scripture reading and prayer. These schools were for boys; none were co-educational then. Each Monday morning the two class monitors had to arrive early and fill all the inkwells on the desks (no such things as fountain pens or ballpoints!). One morning my classmate and I were carrying a tray of inkwells down the stairs when a latecomer dashing up the stairs collided with us. At the next assembly there were some caustic remarks from the headmaster about the carelessness of boys who spattered ink on the stairs!

Somehow I managed to stay out of trouble so was never sent up to the headmaster's office for misbehavior. A notation in his black book meant no recommendation when leaving school. I doubt that I deserved what he wrote on April 25, 1912—"that he is a lad of excellent character, that his conduct, industry and progress have been very satisfactory and that he leaves the school after having gained the esteem of his fellow pupils and of his masters." This recommendation was given shortly before I left that school to go to Canada. The teacher and the class kindly gave me a monetary gift as I was leaving.

Vivid in the memory of my boyhood days are the summer holidays. Mother and I usually visited her relatives and since there were many of them it meant going to different places each summer. Mother's family was so large that her youngest sister was an aunt already when she was born.

Cromer is a seaside resort on the east coast of England. A Japanese Lantern was thrust into my hand so I could participate in a lantern procession and I won third prize. Any inflation of my ego was dissipated a few days later. While digging in the sand, one of my shoes was buried and lost. Scolded by Mother I was mortified to have to walk home barefoot.

One of Mother's brothers lived in Cardiff in South Wales where he worked in the drydocks. I was fascinated to see a ship in drydock. One of my cousins also worked there and later was killed by a fall into a drydock. One day we went on an excursion steamer across the Bristol Channel to visit picturesque spots like Clovelly. This small place in Devon was then only reached by boat and the houses were perched on the steep hillside beside the sea. A stop at Ilfracombe for a lunch that for a boy was memorable—roast lamb with young potatoes (cooked with a sprig of mint) and fresh green peas. The dessert was a dish of raspberries topped with Devonshire cream, a very thick, rich cream.

Littlemore was a village a few miles from Oxford where Mother had been born and where her oldest brother had a blacksmith and carriage building shop. It was interesting to see how they fitted an iron rim on a wooden cart wheel. A trip on a small boat through some locks on the upper Thames river took us to a garden party for residents of the area on the large estate of the Earl of Harcourt. Another day we went through Oxford University without absorbing any knowledge from that noted place of learning.

Boyhood Days

One summer Mother and I went different ways and I stayed with the family of Ethel's fiance, the Wellers. Dentures were new to me then. I was amazed that Richard who was to become my brother-in-law took his teeth out at night. It was impossible to remove mine, I found. Sixty years later in 1969 Anna and I visited Rich's two surviving sisters living in the same house. Naturally they had aged but the house seemed to be just the same.

Mother's youngest sister, Aunt Millie, lived in Folkestone on the south coast facing the English Channel. Her husband was a retired army man and they had two daughters about my age. On one of our visits there the Red Cross and Ambulance Corps were holding some sort of maneuvers. They called for some boys to volunteer with a promise of sixpence. We were taken out of town on a truck and told to lie down scattered over a grassy field. Tags were placed on us to describe the kind of wounds we had supposedly suffered. Then the nurses came to bandage us and take us back to school which was to be the hospital. Many of the boys were "ambulatory patients." With bandaged heads or arms in slings they had to walk back to the school. As one of the more seriously wounded I had the good fortune to be trundled back on a stretcher. Housewives seeing the procession of wounded and not knowing it was a maneuver came out to commiserate with the unfortunate victims of an accident. For their benefit I tried to look as miserable as possible under the circumstances. At the "hospital" a treatment of lemonade and cookies effected some "miraculous cures" so our bandages were removed and we were sent off home.

Mother thought there would be better opportunities for me in a young country like Canada. World events didn't concern me then but there was already talk of war with Germany. My sister Ethel left for Edmonton, Alberta, the day after her marriage on June 1, 1911. A year later, Mother, Florrie, and I were to follow. George had obtained a second scholarship to the College of the Royal Horticultural Society and so decided to remain in England.

At the age of thirteen the matter of baptism arose. There was no baptistry at Alexandra Hall and I don't know what position the assembly there took on baptism. However, with considerable trepidation I went to Dr. McKilliam for an interview. He was very gracious as he talked with me about my faith in Christ. So I was received into fellowship at Alexandra Hall shortly before leaving. It was arranged that I should be baptized at Lingfield in the baptistry which my Father had helped to construct. That was on the 7th of May, 1912, and was for me a very happy occasion. The Lord impressed upon my heart, John 13:17, "If you know these things, happy are ye if ye do them." So, though I was very nervous, I was also very happy. There was much about baptism that I didn't understand, but I knew it was something the Lord wanted me to do.

Even in those days I was keenly interested in missionary stories. I don't recall a great deal of missionary interest at Alexandra Hall but more than once I would walk to King George St. Hall in Greenwich to hear some missionary, especially if he was from Africa. One of the thrills was to be allowed to go to the annual missionary meetings in London in October, 1911. They were held then at Devonshire House which was packed for the evening meeting. I sat on a step up in the gallery and listened to Dan Crawford, then home on his first furlough in over twenty years.

A few days after my baptism on May 16th we left Southampton on a Cunard ship, S.S. Ausonia, definitely not one of their best. We were traveling with an emigrant party arranged by the Salvation Army, mostly of women. First morning out I was one of the few brave souls that showed up for breakfast. The menu in steerage class was Irish stew or boiled eggs. Irish stew for breakfast—perish the thought! and the stew too! So I had two hard-boiled eggs which I soon regretted eating! I was seasick for a week and for years wouldn't touch a hard-boiled egg. Years later we learned from our good friend, George Maslen, that he traveled on the Ausonia on the previous voyage. The food was so terrible, the steerage passengers almost rioted!

Out in the middle of the Atlantic we were surrounded by icebergs and moved forward very cautiously, with good reason for just a month before that the Titanic had been sunk. I remember the news headlines, "The unsinkable ship sunk." This ship had been built with watertight compartments to make it unsinkable in theory. On its maiden voyage with many celebrities aboard it struck an iceberg with a loss of hundreds of lives. We thanked God for a safe trip.

Boyhood Days

Landing at Quebec on Sunday evening, bells were tolling. I thought they were church bells until I discovered that every train engine had a bell and also a cow-catcher in front. For some days we journeyed by train to Calgary. The train would stop at intervals to change engines and crew, while the passengers made a wild dash to the station restaurant for a quick snack. Trains there were quite different from English trains and different too from present day train travel.

In Calgary we stayed overnight before proceeding north to Edmonton the next morning. The Salvation Army took us to their citadel where a testimony meeting was in progress. Various members there took us home for the night which was very kind of them. I was rather amused by the testimony of one man as he told of his new joy in salvation. In his elation he was jumping up and down on the platform, and rubbing his stomach exclaimed, "I have such a good feeling down here!" Remembering the misery of our seasickness a week before, I rather disrespectfully whispered to my sister, "If he had been where we were last week, he wouldn't have such a good feeling down there." It is to be hoped his assurance of salvation was not resting merely on his physical feelings.

A train ride the next day brought us to Edmonton, the capital of Alberta, then more like a growing frontier town. There we were welcomed by my sister and her husband.

3

LIFE IN CANADA

"He led them by a straight way to a city where they could settle." (Psa. 107:7)

Life in Canada was quite different in many ways. Before leaving England I had become the proud possessor of my first (and only) bowler hat, that very typical Englishman's headgear. It didn't take long to learn that in Canada a bowler hat soon became a target for things more solid than ridicule.

Our home in Edmonton consisted of two tents, with rough board floors and boarded sides. A large canvas covered both tents and provided further protection from the weather. One tent served as parlor, dining room, and kitchen while the ladies slept in the other. A small shack served as a bedroom for my brother-in-law and me until winter came. Then we moved into the living tent and slept on the table near the kitchen stove. The shack then became cold storage for sides of beef and pork. One day my sister went to cut off some meat in the shack. Without thinking, she put the key in her mouth for a moment. In that excessive cold it lifted the skin from her lips. Walking down the main street one day, a man stopped her and said, "Excuse me, but is your nose frozen?" She hadn't realized it!

We lived on the flats beside the North Saskatchewan River and so had running water nearby. In summer we also found some edible berries to vary our diet. In winter we had to cut a hole through two or three feet of ice to get our water. Just downstream from our tents the high-level bridge between Edmonton and Strathcona was being built. During the winter a lot of scaffolding was built on the ice. Then in the spring came the break-up as the ice broke and began to drift downstream. Huge chunks of ice as big as the side of a house would be toppled one over another, carrying everything before it. Earlier in the winter, ice was cut in blocks and stored away in large warehouses for use during the summer.

Money was scarce for us in those days so on arrival in Edmonton we had to find work. Florrie got a job in domestic service and Mother did odd jobs of practical nursing. That summer Ethel had her first baby, a girl Beatrice (Tricie). Ethel's husband Richard was a house painter in England but had to take different jobs in Canada. Thirteen years old, my first job was as a messenger in a jeweler's store. It also included being the janitor. Saturday nights the store stayed open till ten. As I made my way home one Saturday night there was a terrific thunderstorm. Getting off the streetcar I walked the rest of the way, past the new Alberta Parliament buildings under construction and past an old Hudson's Bay Fort. Between the flashes of lightning it was impossible to see anything. The road turned to the right to go down a hill to the flats. If I missed that turn I would tumble down a steep embankment onto railroad tracks below, which could mean broken bones or possible death. As I groped my way in the dark there was a brilliant flash of lightning. Just before me was the edge of the embankment. I was aware that the Lord was watching over me as I made my way down the hill.

That summer there was a succession of jobs. The jeweler was not satisfied and fired me. To me, it was a terrible blow. But then a sister in the assembly gave me a job of putting insulation on water pipes in the basement of an apartment block she owned. For me it was a good job while it lasted and for her it was cheap labor! During the annual fair at the fairgrounds I worked as a busboy in a restaurant, hard work but plenty to eat. Next I worked as a messenger in a dress shop. It was managed by a man and his wife who were constantly bickering. Getting tired of being caught in the cross-fire, I quit.

Then I went to the Canadian Pacific Railroad to work as a telegraph messenger. I didn't have a bicycle but I could move

Life in Canada

fast and I knew all the empty lots and short cuts around town. When I discovered that the other boys didn't want to take the morning delivery to the west end of town, I volunteered. Offices in the Parliament Buildings were opening up so there was always plenty of messages to be delivered there and all close together. We were paid according to the number of telegrams delivered. On that run I was able to go home for lunch before going back to the office. I averaged a dollar a day which wasn't too bad then. I could get a good substantial meal in a clean restaurant for 25 cents! One day I found a meal ticket from a better restaurant. People would buy a ticket for a lump sum at a discount. Most of the slots in this ticket were not punched out. I had visions of scrumptious meals—for free. At noon I made my way to the restaurant. Funny! Nobody inside at noon! Then a sign on the door caught my eye, "Gone out of business." I learned that in this world you don't get something for nothing. So typical of much this world offers—bitter disappointments and unfulfilled promises.

Winter was hard. Plenty of opportunities for skating but I wasn't athletically inclined and never took to ice skating. One night in a blizzard I escorted Mother home from work, at 30 below zero Farenheit. As we struggled through the snow I wondered if we would make it. Another morning down by the river the temperature dropped to 52 below. I used to pick up our milk in bottles at the Fort on the way home. It would be frozen with the caps resting on frozen milk an inch above the top of the bottle. One evening I had a bottle cradled on each arm. At a little slope on the road both feet shot out in front of me and I sat down suddenly and sorely. I saved the milk at the expense of some pain and effort in getting back on to my feet.

Often I wished that I could go to a place where it was always summer. Not that I ever expected my wish would be granted for then I had no idea that I would spend most of my life in the tropics. Those days I was not doing very well spiritually. I was a weak Christian, not only because I was young but mainly because I hadn't been taught to feed upon the Word of God. We attended the assembly regularly but there were not many young people. There was little help for young people because of the sad condition in the assembly. Shortly after our arrival in Edmonton, the hall was moved to a new location. It was something new to see such a building being slowly moved down the street!

There were two factions in the assembly. One older brother who owned the hall had a few friends with very rigid views about fellowship with other believers. On Labor Day there was a conference at which many gathered, including quite a few preachers. The two factions had each invited preachers favoring their own views. It was an open platform, no pre-arranged program. On the hot afternoon meeting, crowded together in a rented building, one brother droned on endlessly. In politics it would be called "filibustering." He was trying to keep the platform from a preacher with more open views on fellowship. Finally an old brother who had pioneered in the Lord's work on the prairies, got up to read 1 Corinthians 14:30 and told the speaker he should give place to his brethren.

Then one Sunday soon after that episode it was announced that the assembly had been given notice to vacate the hall. However, word had been passed by the owner to his cronies to stay on. Thus the assembly was split with a good deal of bitterness and hard feelings. Such an atmosphere and such unchristian spirit didn't tend to foster spiritual growth in a young believer like myself.

Those days there was a real estate boom on the Pacific Coast. Agents were extolling the claims of British Columbia, which is indeed a beautiful province; but not all the agents' claims were credible. Some friends bought farm land very cheaply due to the glowing report they received, only to discover later that their farm was on the slopes of a steep mountain! Nevertheless, we decided to move away from Edmonton to a milder climate. In April, 1913, Richard, my brother-in-law, went ahead to Victoria on the southern tip of Vancouver Island. The rest of us followed a month later to the small house which he had purchased. In the Oaklands district, close to a new school, we found congenial neighbors. Out of ten homes in that block where we lived, there were at one time believers from the assembly in nine. Next door was a missionary family that had served the Lord in South India. Two of the boys were slightly older than I, and I became very chummy with Frank Maynard. Through the help of another neighbor I got a job in a large department store, David Spencer's.

Shortly before our arrival a new assembly had been formed in the Oaklands district, a hive-off from the large assembly down-

Life in Canada

town, Victoria Hall. They were then meeting in a rented hall above some stores at the corner of Hillside and Cedar Hill Road. One evening at prayer meeting, we boys saw a barn burning down the road a mile or so away. We thought the brethren would never close that meeting so we could dash out to see the fire!

In 1914 the Oaklands assembly was able to purchase a piece of land next door to where they were meeting and start building. A lot of the labor was volunteer, and some of my spare time went into that project. In August of that year Frank and I had our holidays and decided to hike part way up Vancouver Island. The war clouds were looming but that was no concern of ours then. By the first afternoon we were starting the climb up the Malahat. Today the Malahat is a scenic drive north of Victoria. Then it was a one-way gravel road with places here and there for the occasional vehicle to pass. It was a steep climb, and a few bragged they could make the climb in high gear. That was extremely unlikely! Evening was approaching and we were beginning to look for a suitable place to sleep out for the night. A motorist in a model-T open Ford offered us a lift. Frank climbed in the front seat beside the driver and I clambered up on some baggage in the back seat. Then the driver took off on one of the most exciting rides I have ever had. Up and down, round the curves along a cliff-hanging gravel road, he didn't let up until he pulled up in front of a saloon in Duncan. He promised to be out in a few minutes, just long enough to fortify his spirits with liquor. A few miles further on he stopped again at the saloon at Horseshoe Bay. We decided not to imperil life and limb any longer with such a driver. Anyway, it was getting dark. So we hiked off the road, made a bed of pine branches and bracken fern, and curled up in our blankets.

Next day we hiked a few miles further north and then retraced our steps. Frank had a friend at Cobble Hill with whom we spent two delightful days boating and swimming. From there we went to Shawnigan Lake (very few houses there then) and after a night there hiked to Goldstream by way of Sooke Lake. It was a lonely trail but very beautiful. We didn't see a soul all day but did see footprints of bears and panthers.

While we were on that hike, World War I had been declared. The department store where I worked was between two newspaper offices. The latest war bulletins were posted in the windows so people would stop to catch up with the war news. I was not much involved with such things as I was only 15.

My Christian life was quite nominal; I still hadn't learned to feed on the Word. Going to meetings, to Sunday school, and in summer attending the open-air meetings downtown was the extent of my spiritual activity. But there was no real spiritual growth nor any clear witness for Christ. I was saved but was not being challenged, or else ignored what challenges there were.

By 1915 the call for men to volunteer for military service was more insistent. I wasn't really interested in going overseas and my family certainly didn't encourage any such thoughts. There was a difference of opinion in the assembly about military service. Some joined up but others took the stand of conscientious objectors and suffered for their stand. One brother was very outspoken in his criticism of those fellows who had enlisted. For me, his criticism carried little weight because he was earning good wages making war supplies. What was the difference between making bullets and firing them?

What did attract me was the possibility of enlisting in a local regiment guarding the Pacific Coast. This regiment was part of the regular Canadian army and different from the Canadian Expeditionary Force preparing to go overseas. This would afford me a bit more money than I was earning, and I would be stationed near home. There was also a youthful desire to get away from home and see a different side of life. There was no thought of praying about such a step or asking the Lord about His will.

Changing my age from 16 to 18 was dishonest but I rationalized it was for my country. Recruiting officers were only too anxious to build up their quota and I was big for my age. So I became a private in the Royal Canadian Garrison Artillery and was stationed at Signal Hill, overlooking the Naval Base at Esquimalt. Being regular army we were issued dress uniforms in addition to the regular uniform. Arrayed in my bright red uniform I supposed I would make some impression on young ladies when I was on leave on Sunday. Troops training for war service got no such uniforms but they saluted my uniform, supposing only an officer would dare to wear such regalia. In a few months I was promoted to lance-corporal and got my first stripe. That added more to my pride than to my efficiency. Certainly I was not doing well in the Lord's service and was not

Life in Canada

a good soldier of Jesus Christ. Looking back I marvel at His grace—I deserved a dishonorable discharge from His service. How amazing is the longsuffering and patience of our wonderful Lord and Savior, Jesus Christ.

The winter I was stationed at Signal Hill was unusually severe for Victoria. Usually there are only a few inches of snow during the season but that year there was about three feet in one storm. I was in town when it started and before long the streetcars were not running. That meant plodding three miles through a foot or two of newly fallen snow. Next day the troops were called out to help clear the snow from the streets but that did not include our regiment. Victoria is famous for the tourist slogan "Follow the birds to Victoria," because of the sea gulls. That winter the birds were hungry. Some of the fellows tied pieces of fat bacon on opposite ends of a string and had fun watching the tugs of war between flying birds.

We had a trumpeter to sound calls. He was never in uniform in time to sound the call half an hour before parade each morning, so he would open a window and raise the trumpet through it to sound that call. One morning one of the fellows climbed up on the roof with a jug of water which he poured into the trumpet just as the call was beginning. There was great amusement as the call died out in a gurgle and a splutter!

Increasingly there was talk about going overseas. Some men deserted to join outfits headed for action in Europe. Very foolishly I agreed with one of my chums to be absent without leave. Over in Vancouver we enlisted with a construction company that was going to France. We even went back to Victoria to say goodbye to our families. But on our return to Vancouver we were arrested by the M.P. and sent back for courtmartial. We were sentenced to 30 days in military prison. One evening there I picked up the Bible and read Psalm 51 and on my knees confessed my sin to the Lord. A day or so later our Commanding Officer offered us a reprieve if we would volunteer for overseas service with a detachment being sent from the Battery. On my release I asked my family's forgiveness and also went to confess to some of the elders of the assembly. It is an episode of youthful folly that I would like to forget but I take comfort that when God forgives, He forgets. It is no pleasure to record it here except that it does magnify the grace of God.

4

SERVICE IN WORLD WAR I

"What benefit did you reap at that time from the things you are now ashamed of?" (Rom. 6:21)

The answer to that question is so obvious! NONE! If it were not for the wonderful goodness and love of our gracious Lord during the experience of military service, it would be better to draw a veil over those years. One of the most unhappy people in the world is the believer who is not living for God. He gets no joy out of his Christian experience for he is out of fellowship with his Lord when he is disobedient. He is not allowed to get any happiness out of the world because of his guilty conscience and the working of the Holy Spirit in his heart. As I was one of those weak and sad Christians, I did many things of which I am now utterly ashamed.

Some years later, after the Lord graciously restored me to himself, I found much comfort in the prophecy of Joel. While the interpretation refers to Israel, there was an application that I could and did appropriate. "I will repay you for the years the locusts have eaten" (Joel 2:25). An earlier chapter tells of the havoc and destruction caused by a plague of locusts. How much better it would have been if there hadn't been any locusts in the first place. Yet the God of all grace has restored what the locusts ate. Though assured of my own salvation, I was a weak believer, so weak that those around me didn't know I was a believer.

The military authorities decided to form a battery of artillery from among the Royal Canadian Garrison Artillery. So I was one of the detachment from the West Coast. A journey of 3000 miles took us across Canada from the Pacific in the West to the Atlantic in the East. In Halifax, Nova Scotia, we joined detachments from other outfits and were stationed in the Citadel. This is an old fort on the top of a hill overlooking the city and Bay of Halifax. One of my buddies had a brother who, in the Navy, had charge of a launch there. Once or twice we went on the launch for a cruise around the harbor. It is a spacious harbor; in fact, it is two harbors connected by a narrow channel. Some months later, while we were in France, an ammunition ship collided with another ship in the channel. The resulting explosion destroyed a large part of the city.

One night while there we were called to fight a fire at the docks. We dashed down the hill, through the town to the docks. A ship was on fire but we could do nothing as we had no firefighting equipment. One man was trapped and tried to wriggle through a porthole. He died before a torch could be brought to cut a larger hole. Often I wondered why portholes on ships were not made a little larger.

Church parade on Sunday mornings was compulsory. Our colonel suggested that the whole battery march to a different church each Sunday, rather than going off in small groups to the church of our choice. Since I didn't know of any assembly in Halifax, I went along. It was a standing joke that after the parson welcomed the battery to their midst that morning, he would announce, "We will now take up the offering."

A huge Newfoundland dog was our mascot. He marched down the dock with us when we embarked for the Atlantic crossing but was not allowed on board. The dog did not intend to be left behind. At midnight when everything was quiet he started up the gang plank. The lone sentry could not restrain such a large dog, so he stowed away. He got out of quarantine in England just in time to rejoin the battery when it crossed over to France. The mascot disappeared when we first went into action and we heard reports that a large dog had been seen up in the front lines.

In the south of England we were moved to different camps for various stages of our training. Occasionally I got a weekend

Service in World War I

leave and was able to visit my brother and his wife and some of our old friends. In the depth of winter we were at Lydd, a bleak spot on the south coast. There we were trained in building gun emplacements. One night with snow on the ground I attempted to jump over what I supposed was a narrow creek. While still in mid-air I realized it was wider than I thought! I went through the ice up to my hips in cold water! A breathtaking discovery! But it had its compensations—I was ordered back to barracks to get hot soup and dry clothes and was excused from further duty.

At our last camp on Salisbury Plains we were supplied with our guns—six-inch (155M) howitzers—and other equipment, including steel helmets, which had been introduced the previous year. One chap entered the barracks wearing his helmet. Behind the door was another soldier with a push broom which he brought down on the steel helmet with a resounding whack. He almost knocked the fellow out but pleaded, "I just wanted to see how good they are!"

An overnight trip on a smelly cargo ship took us from Southampton to Le Havre in France. On the previous trip, it had carried horses and mules, much used for carrying supplies to the front lines. Nobody seems to have bothered to clean up afterwards. After a short while in Le Havre we traveled north by box cars to the front. Our guns were in place just in time for the opening barrage for the battle of Vimy Ridge on Easter Sunday, 1917. Being quite far back (befitting greenhorns as we were) the Germans were soon pushed back beyond our range. Vimy Ridge overlooks the coal mining district of Lens and the Douai plain. On a clear day Douai can be seen, the place where the Roman Catholic version of the Bible was published in 1609 A.D. The Canadian infantry soon cleared the ridge of Germans and pushed forward to the plains beyond. They probably could have broken through the German lines and gone on to Douai, but the generals were not prepared for a fluid war. For them it was a static war of armies in trenches facing each other. It was not long before the walking wounded were filtering back through the village where we were. From one of them I learned that my chum, Frank Maynard, had been killed in the first assault that morning. It was quite a shock because I was hoping to see him again soon.

During the summer of 1917 we saw considerable action as we were located in a village at the north end of Vimy Ridge. German planes knocking down our observation balloons, a disabled plane skimming over our heads to a crash landing, dog fights as those planes did barrel rolls and loops. One day we saw a red plane which we guess may have been the famous German Red Dragon ace, Baron von Richtofen. When I see our modern planes I wonder how the contraptions they flew then could stay together.

My job as signaller involved mostly repairing and installing lines between the guns and headquarters. During two years of combat I never once fired any kind of a gun. Our quarters were in the basement of a ruined house. One day in the next village we saw a stove which had been removed from a house and was evidently destined for some officer's mess. That night we "acquired" it for our own use. As I was reading by the light of an oil lamp one night, my buddy knocked it over. I jumped up to beat out the flames from the kerosene on my bed. My buddy roared with laughter as he said, "Look at your hair!" I couldn't see my hair but I rubbed my hands vigorously to extinguish the flames shooting up from my hair. He thought it was a hilarious sight! Fortunately no damage was done apart from a free hair singe; it was just the kerosene that burned. I got even with him a little later. One day he said "I smell something burning." With a laugh I replied, "Yes, it is your moustache." He was burning his cigarette to such a short butt, it was singeing his moustache.

Soon after arriving at that village it was my turn at noon to collect our food from the cookhouse. The cooks were in a ruined house. Since I was busy on a job one of my chums from Victoria offered to go in my place. The Germans had evidently been watching men gathering at that spot. That day a shell struck the cookhouse killing seven of our fellows, including my chum. Another fellow from Victoria lost his leg at that time. I realized that God was taking care of me, even though I didn't deserve it.

That same afternoon two of us signallers were ordered to accompany a lieutenant to a forward observation post. The road we had to take was one of those French hard cobblestone roads, and the Germans were dropping a shell on it every minute. Our lieutenant never thought of taking a detour apparently. We start-

Service in World War I

ed up that road. A shell landed and as the fragments flew overhead we ran as fast as we could, loaded down with equipment. Then the whistle of another shell coming! We dived into a trench beside the road long enough to avoid its fragments. Then up and on the run again. We were very expert in judging the size and approximate destination of any shell by the sound it made. A leisurely hum could be ignored but not a sudden rush. The problem was that the nearer the shell was coming, the less warning time.

One September night the Germans shelled the village with small shells. We called them "whiz-bangs" because there was a whiz, then a bang. Among these were some gas shells. The gas sank into the hollows so we avoided the ditches and shell-holes. We had gas masks which we seldom used. It was impossible to communicate with a mouthpiece, and the eye pieces were of mica which clouded up. (That was before clear plastic had been invented.) A lot of our lines were broken so we were out all night repairing communication lines.

With daylight the shelling stopped and it was a beautiful sunny clear morning. Before getting some rest, Martin and I volunteered to go to the cook house for our day's rations. Returning to our billets we were approaching the main intersection in the village. We heard the screech of a large shell coming fast and close! I dropped and flattened myself on the road as the shell landed and fragments flew. Sometime later I found a small piece the size of a split pea had penetrated the leather patch on my riding breeches and just slightly scratched the skin. Relieved that I had not been hit I jumped to my feet and called to Martin to come on. He was lying face down on the road and didn't move. I turned him over—a fragment had torn into his chest. Already his uniform was soaked in blood. I rushed to get help but knew it was no use. He was a fatalist and venturesome, so I doubt that he even tried to fall flat. For a while my nerves were a wreck. Again the Lord had graciously delivered me. Yet I didn't change my ways. Strange but true, that often the fear of men has a stronger hold on us than the fear of God.

Soon after that episode we were transferred north to the cathedral city of Ypres in Belgium. The cathedral and most of the town lay in ruins. We were billeted in the basements of ruined houses. Our guns were located about five miles out of the city towards Passchendale Ridge which our forces were trying to take from the Germans. Every other morning we walked out to our battery position for a 24-hour duty; we passed through places where there had been villages but not a brick remained. Off the main road it was nothing but mud, knee-deep and thigh-deep. The mud had its compensations for it smothered the fragments of bursting shells.

At that time I was teamed up with a typical old soldier, usually grumbling and complaining about everything. However, we seemed to get along well together. One day we were sent to check on telephone connections installed in an old German gun emplacement. The doorway faced the German lines and the door was a wet blanket soaked with mud. Ever thank God for a wet blanket? I had just entered, trying to adjust to the candle-light inside, when a German shell burst just outside the door. The blanket smothered any fragments but the candles were all extinguished. I was shook up and the fellows inside were cursing me for attracting that shell. What about Brown who was just behind me. I called to him. He shouted back, "I've been hit!" I dashed outside—he had been thrown 20 feet to the other side of the emplacement. He was feeling himself to find out where he had been hit. Actually he wasn't, but was badly shaken and that ended our duties for that day.

The Canadian infantry captured the ridge with much loss of life. We were pulled out for a rest over Christmas. The Canadian Commander, General Currie visited us on the farm where we were resting. Before the war he owned a real estate agency in Victoria and I often delivered packages to his house. In his speech he said the capture of the Ridge afforded us a jumping off place for the spring offensive. That spring of 1918, the Germans took the offensive and pushed our troops off the Ridge back almost to Ypres.

At that time we were in position on the southern end of Vimy Ridge. We didn't get news but we knew by watching the positions of the observation balloons that the Germans were advancing both north and south of us. We were in a dangerous salient. Our officers were edgy for they knew it would be difficult for us to retreat. The code word was "Ottawa." That meant blow up the guns and get out as best you can. Fortunately we didn't have to run for it. With the arrival of American reinforcements on the Western Front, the German drive was halted and turned.

Service in World War I

That summer and fall we were out of trench warfare and more constantly on the move as the Germans were being driven back. We would hardly get into position before orders came to move again. We were advancing through terrain which had not been so badly destroyed. We stopped in villages that had only recently been evacuated by the inhabitants. The danger here was booby traps left by the enemy. A soldier entered a home where there was a piano; as he struck the keys it blew up. During that advance we ran into some poison gas but it was fairly well dispersed. Apart from runny eyes and noses it didn't seem to bother us much. Not wanting to be thought of as a malingerer, I didn't bother to report it. Later I realized it would have helped me to have a sick call on my record. Also I reaped some consequences after discharge.

One evening one of our buddies killed a rabbit with a lucky throw of a stone. We gathered some vegetables from some Frenchman's garden and had a good rabbit stew, a welcome variation to bully (corned) beef and hard biscuits. Then in November came the glad news of an armistice. I still have a message form that came to our battery, "Hostilities will cease at eleven hours on November 11th . . . there will be no intercourse of any description with the enemy." In a village in Belgium at the eleventh hour of the eleventh day of the eleventh month, we embraced each other and rejoiced that at last the fighting was over. Sometimes it had seemed as if it would go on for ever! We moved into a town near Mons and were there for some months. This was where the British "Ol' Contemptibles" first faced the Germans in 1914.

Some of us got a pass to visit Brussels just ten days after the Germans left that city. We splurged on an expensive meal in a hotel on the main square. On our way there we passed through Waterloo, reminder of an earlier war. The army set up some practical courses which would be a help in returning to civilian life. Early in 1919 I went on a pass to visit my brother in England. On my return I passed through Folkestone to get my boat across the Channel. Some Canadians were demonstrating, demanding an immediate return to Canada. The delay gave me an opportunity to visit with my uncle and aunt there. When I got to France I was again delayed at a base camp but finally got on a train, riding a freight car. It was headed for Cologne, Germany, and I was tempted to go all the way. However, since I was already AWOL I decided to hop off near Mons. I feared if I stayed away too long it might delay my return to Canada.

In the spring we transferred to a camp in North Wales to await our departure for Canada. At the beginning of May we boarded the S.S. Mauretania at Southampton. It paid off to have a name beginning with "B"—I was assigned to a cabin, instead of a hammock in the hold. The Mauretania was a sister ship to the ill-fated Lusitania which had been sunk by the Germans early in the war. For years it was the fastest ship across the Atlantic. Our trip was no exception. Leaving Southampton on Sunday evening we arrived in Halifax early Friday morning. Disembarkation went off without a hitch. Those going to the West Coast disembarked first on to a waiting train. Thousands of men were off the ship that morning and at noon it left for New York for a return trip.

At many towns on that 3000-mile journey welcoming crowds greeted the returning veterans. Only on the last part of the journey did the authorities foul things up. We had to have just one more experience of the army's "hurry up and wait." From Vancouver to Victoria they chartered a slow boat when we could have easily been accommodated on the regular daily sailing.

The inner harbor of Victoria is one of the most picturesque in the world. It never looked better than on that evening in May as we filled the forepart of the ship. As the ship approached the dock, right ahead was the beautiful Empress Hotel, ivy-covered and surrounded with lawns. To the right were the stately Government Buildings with trim lawns and beautiful flower beds. But the best sight of all were the loved ones waiting on the pier and waving frantically as we came in sight. Home again safe and sound! "But where sin increased, grace increased all the more." It surely was only because of super-abounding grace that I was back from the horrors of war.

5

CALL TO THE MISSION FIELD

"I will instruct you in the way you should go; I will guide you and watch over you." (Psa. 32:8)

During the months prior to returning home I faced up to the need of a change in my lifestyle. Getting out of the army and away from army life seemed like a good time to get right with the Lord. Anyway I was tired of the way I had been living, tired of treating the Lord so despicably in spite of all His wonderful grace in keeping me safe through years of combat. After the armistice I had given up cigarettes and had switched to a pipe. Even then, long before warnings about lung cancer, cigarettes were called "coffin nails." Crossing the Atlantic I tossed pipe and tobacco into the ocean. I had cleaned up my life but was not yet getting into the Word.

Soon after arriving home I was invited by Brother Fisher to spend some time with him at Deep Bay. He was a brother of one of the pioneer missionaries to what is now Zambia. Mr. Fisher had a few acres of land on the waterfront where he grew asparagus and black currants to augment his retirement pay. Working in the garden and going fishing was a restful change from war experiences. He gave me a Scofield Bible which was a help as I started the habit of daily reading of the Scriptures.

Also, soon after my return it was announced that C. A. Swan would have three meetings at Victoria Hall in downtown Victoria. As one of the pioneers in Central Africa he had thrilling tales to tell. He first went to Africa in 1887. In 1904, for health reasons he went to Portugal and during the war had worked with Portugese troops in France. This was of interest to me because for some time we had had some Portugese attached to our battery in France. In boyhood days I had been keenly interested in hearing missionaries, especially those from Africa; but at this time I was going more out of curiosity, little dreaming the impact those meetings would have on my own life.

I remember very well where I was sitting at the third meeting. Before giving his address, Mr. Swan prayed. He prayed for those who had been bereaved during the war—for those women whose men would not be returning. More than 60,000 Canadians died in World War I. Then he thanked God for those who were returning and said, "Lord, show them what they have been spared for!" I have not the slightest idea what else he prayed for nor how long he prayed. His request was instantly answered in my case. The Lord spoke to me. It was not an audible voice; no one else heard it. But it was as real to me as the voice of the preacher. "I have spared you to go to the mission field!" Foolishly I tried to argue with the Lord—that is always a wasted effort. "But, Lord, I have just arrived home after being away three years. I don't want to leave again right away. I have a widowed mother and I need to stay here, build a home, and provide for her." Again I heard His voice, "You left home for king and country, are you not willing to leave home for Me? Don't you believe I can take care of your mother?" What is the use of trying to argue with the One who has all the answers? Before Mr. Swan finished his prayer I also had prayed, "All right, Lord, if that is what you want, I am willing."

God is a God of infinite variety and He uses different methods to call His servants. It is not often that He speaks so directly, but I am thankful to Him for that definite call. During our first furlough, I met Brother Swan again in Victoria and related to him how God had instantly answered his prayer that night.

One of the first priorities before going to the mission field was to build a home for my Mother and sister Florrie. We were able to buy two lots, L-shaped around my sister Ethel's home. One of the jobs I had was working for a brother who was a builder. In my spare time I dismantled a small house on the lots we bought. With the help of our builder friend, plans were drawn and a

Call to the Mission Field

start made on building a house. Good progress was made during the summer of 1919. Many evenings young fellows from the assembly would come and help build.

I had found a new joy in walking with the Lord and feeding upon His Word and in realizing His grace in calling me to be a missionary. Often I was singing while I was working. One day up on the roof laying shingles, I was singing and suddenly realized I had just sung, "Some day this earthly house will fall." The humor of it struck me. As far as I know that earthly house is still standing after over sixty years. After Mother passed away, Ethel and Richard sold their house and moved into that house, and after Ethel's homecall it was sold.

The Canadian government was offering educational opportunities to veterans, especially for those who, like myself, had enlisted in their teens. I submitted an application for the Bible Institute of Los Angeles, but it was turned down because it was not in Canada. At that time I didn't know of any Bible school in Canada though there was one in Vancouver. So I applied for a commercial course in a business college in Victoria.

Through the fall and early winter I was working hard, studying days and working on the house at night, unless it was a meeting night. Dr. Harris Gregg held a series of Bible lectures which I attended at noon and in the evenings. These were a great blessing in my spiritual life, but the pace was beginning to take its toll.

Early in January, 1920, we had a very cold spell. I was getting dressed one morning and saw flames reflected in the mirror. I dashed out to see a neighbor's house on fire and rushed over to see if I could help. The owner was coming out of the basement and said no one was in the house. While I was about to see if any of his belongings could be saved, the roof caved in and nothing more could be done.

Shortly after that, I had bronchitis which developed into pneumonia and pleurisy. When I was admitted to the Jubilee Hospital I didn't realize how serious the condition was. All I could think of was the stabbing pain in my rib cage every breath I took. About eleven that night the veteran's chaplain came in to pray with me. I wondered why he came at such an hour. I appreciated his concern though I don't think he was a saved man.

That evening a business man from India was booked to give a

Bible study at the Oaklands Chapel. Just before he spoke it was announced that I was seriously ill in the hospital and that the doctor didn't think I would last until morning. I didn't know that until later. The guest speaker suggested that instead of a Bible study they give themselves to prayer. "The church was earnestly praying to God for him" (Acts 12:5). "The prayer offered in faith will make the sick person well" (Jas. 5:15). That doesn't require instantaneous healing—in my case it was a long process.

The doctor tried to draw off the fluid in the pleural cavity by inserting a needle. This was unsuccessful because the fluid had turned into pus. That called for an operation, cutting between the ribs to insert a drainage tube. Mother came to see me before going into the operating room and said, "If anything happens, it is all right, isn't it?" "Of course," I replied, "but nothing is going to happen. I am going to the mission field and this must be part of the training." Dr. Wace, one of the best surgeons in Canada operated, but my confidence was not in him but in the Lord.

Coming out of ether (what a wretched smell!) I was greeted cheerily by the head nurse on the ward, Miss Harman. She was a keen Christian and later was a missionary in the Congo and was martyred in the rebellion there. The Matron of the hospital was a very different type. The nurses were terrified of her as they heard her storming down the hospital corridors. Mother had brought me a few violets, the only flowers in the garden. They were too small for any available vase so the nurse had put them in a small salt dish. Miss McKenzie came into the room, spotted the violets and with an indignant swoop carried off my violets, saying, "Violets in my salt cellar!" Weak as I was, I just had to laugh, though the nurse saw no humor in the situation.

My roommate was Mr. Enoch from Ladysmith. He was not like his Biblical namesake for he was not a believer. My visitors and I had many opportunities to witness to him about the Savior. He seemed to be near the point of decision but one day said, "I don't have the kind of faith you have." I replied, "What do you think faith is, something that comes in 57 varieties?" It is not the kind of faith nor the quantity of our faith that counts— what is vital is the object of our faith. When he left the hospital he had not put his faith in Christ.

Two or three months later pus accumulated again and so

another operation was scheduled. This was done by Dr. Russell Robertson, who was also a very fine surgeon. He was a tall, dignified man with penetrating eyes. He would stand at the foot of a patient's bed, read the chart, and look at the patient. Some of them said he didn't need an X-ray for he could look right through you. The physician in charge of my case was Dr. Baillie with whom I developed a fine rapport.

That summer I was transferred to the military hospital in Esquimalt, overlooking the harbor. The surroundings there were much nicer but it was a long way for my visitors to come. The Matron there was very different. She maintained strict discipline but never raised her voice and never corrected a nurse in front of the patients. She was a lady who won their respect by her fairness.

There it was discovered that my kidneys had been affected and I had nephritis. That meant sweat baths and a restricted diet. It was strawberry season and I didn't object to a dish of strawberries every meal. The doctor prescribed a bottle of Guinness Stout as a tonic every day. I didn't object on conscientious grounds since it was prescribed as medicine, but I didn't like the stuff. All the other patients wanted the same prescription!

One of the orderlies there was a short, stocky man with long arms. The guys called him Tarzan. He wrecked more than one bedside table which did not easily adjust. The nurse at that time was an unusually large girl, almost six foot and well-proportioned. One evening Tarzan brought in the supper trays without the dessert which was stewed apricots. The nurse ordered him to take out the trays and add the dessert in the ward kitchen. To Tarzan it was simpler to bring in the large bowl of apricots and ladle them out on the trays. It was a battle of wills. She ordered him to take out the trays. He threatened to throw the apricots at her. She had the authority but he had the power! He hurled the bowlful of apricots, right on target. She was apricots from her cap all down her uniform. She ran out in tears to change. Tarzan hastily departed amid the indignant shouts of the patients. He didn't return!

In October the Matron kindly arranged for an ambulance to take me for a day with my family. It was an act of kindness that was greatly appreciated. Towards the end of November I was discharged from the hospital—almost the entire year spent there. My application for a new course was turned down because the Board said my illness was not service related. If only I had gone on sick call when I got that whiff of gas in France!

The first Lord's day back at the Lord's Supper after all those months of absence was a precious occasion. Someone gave out the hymn "Awake, my soul, in joyful lays." I asked them to repeat one verse:

> "When trouble, like a gloomy cloud, has gathered thick and thundered loud, He near my soul has always stood, His loving-kindness, oh how good!"

A few months after my release from the hospital I was offered a job which afforded a wonderful opportunity for recuperation. Our friends, the McGee's, were in charge of a small leper colony on D'Arcy Island, a few miles from Victoria. Mrs. McGee was going to England for a few months and her husband needed companionship and assistance. It was really like a vacation for the work was minimal. Besides five lepers, all Chinese, there were just the two of us. We lived on Big D'Arcy and we could walk all around it in half an hour. Nearby was Little D'Arcy which was uninhabited. It had a cove which was an ideal spot for bootleggers to hide. Those were Prohibition days in the U.S. and we were only a few miles from the border. Since we had no means of communication nor protection, it was prudent to ignore what was going on around us. There was time to think about the future and pray about being a missionary. One day the Lord showed me very clearly that wherever He sent me, I would have to learn to love the people, even if they seemed unlovable in some ways. Then I had no idea where He wanted me to go. I had some thoughts of Africa and also of Portugal to help Brother Swan.

During those years of waiting for the Lord to open the door, I received great help from Brother Duncan McKerracher. He taught a class of young fellows and we drew upon his knowledge of the Scriptures. Sometimes after prayer meeting we would stand under a street lamp with our Bibles looking for answers to our questions. He introduced me to good books and helpful writers, like Sir Robert Anderson, Dr. A. T. Pierson, and others.

Call to the Mission Field

One evening we called on Mr. Cecil Hoyle, then an old man, who had been a missionary in Spain from 1876 to 1907.

Sometimes I thought about the elders at Oaklands. Some of them were still in their thirties, but ten years or so older than myself. In ten years would I have the ability in preaching, teaching, and leading an assembly? It was another challenge to apply myself more diligently to the study of the Word of God. One of the older men, Billy James, a bachelor, was a bit eccentric. But he really loved the Lord and was exuberant with the joy of the Lord. He was a chimney sweep and never seemed to get all the soot off his face. But at the worship service his grimy face would just beam with his simple-hearted love for Christ. Mother would often invite him home for lunch on Sunday, in spite of her feeling that he could do with a good bath!

Saturday evenings there was an open-air meeting on Government Street outside a mission called "Stranger's Rest." Billy would come straight from his work, his face black with soot, and declared to whoever was in earshot, "My face is black but my heart is white, cleansed by the blood of the Lamb." One day he said to me, "Did you notice the Greek owner of the candy store across the street. He sat in his upstairs window listening all evening. Let's pray for his conversion." On our first furlough we were visiting in a home in Long Beach, California. Our hostess had a Christian lady help with her laundry. As the latter was ironing I learned that she was from Victoria. It turned out that her husband, Mr. Phillips, was the Greek owner of the candy store. He had been saved, had given up his business to go into full-time work among Greeks in the U.S.

Billy James would often eat a simple noon lunch at the Stranger's Rest. He invited me to join him there and spend some time in prayer together which I was happy to do. I learned that previously John Lamb had met with him for prayer and went to Venezuela where he served the Lord from 1920 to 1932. He was followed by Dan Baillie. Dan was from Ladysmith, up the Island, but was living in Victoria. He spent five years (1921-1926) in Manchuria as a missionary. It was my privilege to follow and to kneel in prayer in a corner of the mission with this dear brother. He never went to the foreign field himself but helped pray others out.

6

PREPARING FOR THE MISSION FIELD

"The Lord will fulfill his purpose for me;
Your love, O Lord, endures forever—
Do not abandon the works of your hands."

(Psa. 138:8)

In the early months of 1921, Mr. Tom Baird visited Victoria. He had formerly been a missionary in Malaya (1893-1906) and was a forceful speaker, much addicted to alliteration. One of his sayings (quoted from memory)

"Oh! will my will to will God's will, then willing will be well. The willing will that wills God's will, within God's will will dwell."

Through him I learned about the Missionary Training School in Brooklyn, New York, under the direction of Mr. and Mrs. Richard Hill. (The daughter of Mr. & Mrs. Baird was married to Rowland Hill, a brother of Richard.) The Richard Hills had been missionaries in Persia and Turkestan from 1908 to 1918, and had started the school to help prospective missionaries.

It was very naive for me to pray that the elders at Oaklands Chapel would be unanimous in their willingness to commend me for missionary work, and primarily to spend some time at the Missionary Training School. Now that I am wiser in the ways of elders I would not have the faith to pray such a prayer. But very graciously they did commend me, and if there were any dissenters I was not informed. The counsel of Duncan McKerracher was a great help and blessing those days. In August I finally received a reply from Mr. Hill welcoming me to the School. After receiving his letter I read Psalm 138 with great blessing, assured that the Lord would fulfill His purpose in me. Still I had no guidance on the field of service though my thoughts turned toward Africa or possibly to Portugal, realizing that Mr. Swan needed help there.

On my way from Victoria to New York, I stopped for a day in Port Hope, Ontario, to visit my Aunt Millie and two cousins. She was my Mother's youngest sister and had married a retired army man. He was a professing Christian who regularly attended a Baptist church. The members there were probably not aware of how shabbily he treated his family. Shortly before my visit he had been working on the railroad and had been in an accident. It was really a relief for my aunt to be spared his meanness.

Approaching New York on the train from Montreal, I was getting shaved. In the mirror of the washroom, I saw a passenger open his case and lying on the top was a Bible. Supposing he was a Christian I was wondering how I could strike up a conversation. He was evidently a travelling salesman acquainted with another passenger in the washroom. The latter remarked, "What's that—a Bible? I didn't know you believed in that stuff!" The man replied, "I don't, but it helps getting through customs!"

Landing in Grand Central in New York and trying to find the way to Brooklyn is quite an experience for a stranger. As I grabbed my suitcase, a fellow offered his help which I declined for I suspected ulterior motives. I found a subway train marked "Brooklyn" but got off too soon, still in downtown Manhattan. Up on the surface in the square at City Hall, I asked a man how to get to Seventh Avenue, Brooklyn. He replied, "See that tall building? That's the Woolworth Towers, the tallest building in the world (at that time)." I wasn't interested in a tourist spiel, I wanted to get to Brooklyn. He continued, "Go over there and below that building you will find a subway for Flatbush, Brooklyn. Seventh Avenue runs off Flatbush."

Preparing for the Mission Field

So before noon I located the school but the only people there were a family of missionaries home on furlough, Mr. and Mrs. Asa Moore. She was a sister of Richard Hill. They shared their lunch with me and told me that everyone was at the conference at Sea Cliff, Long Island. So by mid-afternoon I had found my way to the conference at Sea Cliff. A meeting was in progress, a question and answer meeting with C. F. Hogg and Harold St. John on the panel. One questioner wanted to know why believers from various assemblies could fellowship together there but when they went home, there was no fellowship between some of their assemblies. Mr. Hogg raised his hands and replied, "The inconsistencies of brethren!" Another question was that old perennial about baptism for the dead. Both Mr. Hogg and Mr. St. John said they had seen many interpretations, none of which satisfied them. They didn't know the meaning. After the meeting I approached a group around a brother who seemed to think he had the answer!

After the evening service I located a cot on the upper floor of the chapel, the regular meeting place of the assembly in Sea Cliff. The young men billeted there were rather noisy and boisterous. No one seemed to be in charge. I was tired after a long exciting day full of new scenes. After eleven o'clock I thought it was a poor testimony for the assembly among the neighbors. So I went to the head of the stairs and over the din demanded they quiet down. Next morning I noticed furtive glances in my direction. None of them, of course, could identify the stranger—and I didn't enlighten them.

Since I was handy at carpentry and had some of my tools with me, after the conference I was asked to help with repairs at the Sea Cliff Yacht Club. This building, facing on the shores of Long Island Sound, had been purchased by the conference committee. After work on Saturday afternoon I went down to the pier for a swim with George Fraser who was preparing to go to Venezuela. He dove in with his glasses on and lost them. Repeated dives failed to locate them, and he was sorely handicapped. Next morning early, after praying about this need, he went down to the shore as the tide was out. There he found his glasses intact without a scratch in spite of the tossing of the water on the pebbly beach.

There was also work to be done on the school building in

Brooklyn as we were settling in. The fellows were on the top floor and I roomed with Leonard Bewick from Kansas City. Horace Davey from Ottawa and Tom Mornan from Buffalo were in another room. Also on that top floor were the only married couple in our class, William and Margaret McKellin from Paterson, New Jersey. On the floor below were the girls, Carrie Saunders from Peterborough, who in later years married Horace, Margaret (Peg) Fleming, later married to Mr. Kramer of Guatemala, Margaret (Meg) Dryden of Seattle, later married to James Buckley, and Irene Stedman, Len's fiancee, and Anna Carson from Buffalo, who roomed together.

Soon after classes started in September there was a Saturday conference at the Richmond Hill assembly on Long Island. Several students planned to go but one by one dropped out so that only Anna Carson and I went. In the meeting, Scott Aspinall, an elder from Brooklyn, was sitting a couple of rows ahead of us. His head was nodding but not in agreement with the long-winded preacher! Gently I nudged Anna's elbow to call her attention to his vain effort to stay awake. There was no platonic interest in that nudge. Actually then I thought she had a boy friend in Buffalo. Back at the school, I happened to mention the incident to the fellows, and it was their subsequent teasing that did arouse my interest. Later they told a joke about a black man who was buying a cigar, but wasn't sure what brand to buy. He was also uncertain which girl to marry. The salesman suggested "Havana," to which the customer replied eagerly, "That's what I'll do—I'll have Anna." However, I wasn't seeking that kind of guidance! But before telling how the Lord guided, let me digress to tell about Anna Carson's background.

Early in the 1890's, a young carpenter, Samuel Carson left Ballymena in Ulster, N. Ireland, for Buffalo, New York. He was disappointed to find only one assembly there since he was acquainted with Belfast where there were many. In Buffalo he met an Irish lass, Rose Logan, who came from a village about twenty miles from Ballymena. They were married and had two children in the U.S. before returning to Belfast. In fact they crossed the ocean more than once. Of their nine children, the two eldest and the two youngest were born in Buffalo, the rest in Belfast. The middle one of the nine was Anna who had two brothers and two sisters, both older and younger than herself.

Preparing for the Mission Field

When Anna was four or five, they left Belfast to return to Buffalo and Mother Carson refused to make the trip again.

Anna was a bit of a tomboy who would eagerly leave her dolls at the chance to play baseball with the boys. A visiting friend asked her how long it took her to walk to school. She didn't know as she never *walked* to school. "I can make it in three minutes when I jump the back fence and go through the vacant lots."

Brought up in a Christian home and attending Sunday school regularly, Anna knew the way of salvation. Her Sunday school teacher was Jeannie Mowat and one Sunday she asked the girls if they were saved. Anna replied, "Yes—I think so." Later on, Gavin Mowat, Jean's husband, was the speaker at the Sunday evening service. On the way home he asked Anna, "Anna, are you saved?" This time she was able to answer with confidence, "Yes, I know I am now." She had believed before but had lacked the assurance of salvation.

So Anna spent her school days, elementary and high school, in Buffalo. Her interest in missions was stimulated by her friendship with Gavin and Jeannie Mowat. Jean's brother George Gibson married Sarah, Anna's eldest sister. The Mowat's went to Central Africa (1911-1927) and then to South Africa (1928-1950). No one could attend Assembly Hall in Buffalo for long and not be made aware of missions. Edward Fairbairn, a leading brother, was a dynamic missionary enthusiast even though he was a businessman in Buffalo.

When Anna expressed her desire to be a missionary, Mother Carson could not bring herself to be willing to part with her daughter. She was a very dear Christian but found it hard to face such a sacrifice. Meanwhile, Anna was teaching a Sunday school class of little boys, among whom were Lyndon and Laurence Hess and William Oglesby, who all went into the Lord's service in later years. Anna refused to go against her Mother's wishes, confident that if the Lord wanted her to be a missionary, He would incline her Mother to give her consent. The delay of a year or two was a testing time, part of God's preparation. Finally in 1921 Mother gave her consent and Anna went to Brooklyn. She has often commented since that if she had had her own way and gone earlier, we probably would not have met.

As interest in Anna deepened into love, I realized the need to be very sure of the Lord's will in this matter of a life partner. When I first arrived at the school someone gave me a leaflet on "The Will of God." What impressed me in this leaflet was the truth that God had a plan and purpose for the life of every believer. I determined to study what the New Testament taught about the will of God. With the help of a concordance I looked up every reference. Not an easy task because often "will" is used as an auxiliary verb. One of the great lessons I learned was concerning our Lord Jesus Christ. In the four Gospels, only about three times did He mention His own will and each time it was for the blessing of others.

So I began to pray earnestly that the Lord would show me His will regarding Anna Carson. Naturally the more I prayed and thought about her, the more intense became my desire for her. But there was no green light from the Lord, no assurance that this was His will for me. Weeks passed by—times of spiritual struggle. Once I decided to try something that I knew was not right. I would let my Bible fall open and see what verse came up. Naturally the Bible fell open near the middle, at the book of Job. Before my eyes were these words, "I made a covenant with mine eyes; why then should I think upon a maid?" (Job 31:1). That was *not* what I wanted! It was even more discouraging as I read on, "If mine heart have been deceived by a woman" (v. 9). However, as I prayed about this, I was convicted of the error of handling God's Word in such a way. The guidance I then received was not about a life partner but on how to apply the Scriptures to my present circumstances.

Several weeks went by in this heart-searching, seeking to know the Lord's will. Then in our class one morning as we studied the life of Christ, there was a sentence at the bottom of the outline. "They forsook all and followed him" (Luke 5:11). It challenged me! Four fishermen had just made the biggest catch of fish in their career—what a price they would fetch in the market! But they forsook *all*, fish, friends, fortune, and family to follow Him. Then I realized I had not forsaken all, even in my earnest desire to know His will. Deep down in my heart was the unexpressed wish, "Lord, I want your will but please let it be what I want." I was not fully yielded; I had not forsaken all. As the class closed with prayer, I prayed my own prayer, "Lord, if you want me to go to the mission field alone, I am willing to do your will."

Preparing for the Mission Field

It was not an easy lesson to learn. There has to be complete surrender to His will without any mental reservations. "If any man will do His will, he will know. . . ." (John 7:17). We must be willing to do God's will *before* we know what His will is. (To know God's will we must be prepared to do the very opposite to what we desire.) Then I learned how wonderfully gracious is our God! It seemed almost immediately after I reached that point of full surrender (and really meant it) that the Lord granted me my desire. The assurance came to me that it was the Lord's will for me to ask Anna to share my life.

For appearance's sake in the neighborhood, students of the opposite sex were not allowed to go out in pairs. We were not circumventing that law when we met later. So on December 3, 1921, Anna and I went out and rendezvoused. Then I told her for the first time that I loved her and found it was reciprocal. Sixty years later we are still telling each other of our love! We went through Prospect Park (it would probably be unsafe now) where I told her how the Lord had been leading and that I wanted her to have first place in my life *after* the Lord. Miss Annie Hill had asked Anna to get some argyrel for her but in our excitement we asked for arsenic! The look on the face of the drugstore clerk made us realize our mistake. Miss Hill never learned how our romance had endangered her!

Our class did a lot of things together, and there was a good spirit of fellowship. We often went together to conferences, to farewells for other missionaries, and to our weekly medical lectures by Dr. Baldwin. Most afternoons were spent helping in a hospital outpatient department. The mornings were devoted to Bible lectures. John Hill was a favorite instructor with most. Formerly a business man he had a methodical mind and his outlines were a help in our studies. He was interested in the students and arranged trips to such places as museums or the 42nd Street Library where we were shown some rare Biblical manuscripts. Richard Hill was different than his brother in that he was more of a devotional speaker. Everyone had a great respect for George Aldrich because his rich spiritual teaching was backed by a godly life. His reading of part of I Corinthians 15 was unforgettable—this was at the funeral of Mr. Faulkner, father of Mrs. Richard Hill. Brother Aldrich had formerly been an Anglican clergyman and his diction was beautiful.

A Wall Street businessman, Charles Bellinger, came in one

evening each week to teach Galatians. He asked questions which forced us to think for ourselves. Even if our answers were correct he would sometimes oppose them to see if we would hold our ground. Some of the students were awed if not terrified! But he was a real friend of the students and keenly interested in missions. We also benefited by the visits of other preachers and missionaries. We shall not soon forget the visit of Charles Kramer from Guatemala. He spoke little English but would lustily sing in Spanish, until one day the police informed us the neighbors were complaining.

School life was not without its lighter sides. There were some who seriously doubted our fitness as prospective missionaries. But I pity the missionary without a sense of humor. Harriet the cook was a sister from the Black assembly in New York. Her room was immediately below our bathroom on the top floor. Coming in one evening, Anna and I discovered water dripping in her room. Harriet was away for the weekend. I ran upstairs and saw the bathtub was overflowing so I turned off the water. In Tom's room a discussion was in progress as usual, on election or predestination. Casually I inquired who intended to take a bath. Tom raised his hands in horror—he had completely forgotten he had left the water running. Not long after that we repainted the rooms upstairs. Len Bewick did the bathroom. Since it was hard to get behind the tub he moved one end slightly and broke the waste connection. Again Harriet's room got an unwanted shower.

In some ways the conditions at the school were not ideal. We were made to realize that we were "only students" and learned to accomplish the lowly task. However, there were benefits in the teaching we received and also in the many contacts with people and assemblies, particularly in the New Jersey area.

Another advantage was getting to know many of the Lord's people in the assemblies in that area, especially over in New Jersey. It was our privilege to get to know some of the leading men of God, and we still treasure the memories of those men, most of whom are now at home with the Lord.

Usually we fellows would pair off to visit some assembly on Lord's Day, very often by invitation. It was our mutual arrangement that one fellow would pay both fares going and the other would pay coming home. One Sunday Len Bewick and I set out

Preparing for the Mission Field

for New Jersey. As I was short of cash I let him pay the way going there. What money I did have went into the offering. Quite often someone would slip some money into our hands on such occasions. But that day I had received nothing and I doubted that Len had enough to pay our homeward fare. Secretly I was praying about this—not even Len knew about my predicament. One of the brethren drove us to the train station, but how would we buy tickets without money? Then as we got out of the car I felt a bill left in my hand as I parted with the brother—more than enough to pay our fares. We learned many lessons of faith and of what it meant to trust God in those days.

7

GUIDANCE REGARDING THE FIELD

"Show me your ways, O Lord, teach me your paths."
(Psa. 25:4)

During the year at school we were much in prayer for guidance as to the sphere of service the Lord planned for us. Anna's thoughts had been towards South America while mine were toward either Africa or Portugal. One morning in December, the student body were in prayer together as was the daily custom. It seemed as if the Lord said to me, "Go to the Philippines!" I didn't even know where the Philippines were but I guessed they were somewhere off in the Pacific like Hawaii. To my best recollection I had only once heard of those Islands. Just previous to that in a letter from John Thomson, one of the elders at Oaklands Chapel, he had told about the visit there of Mr. and Mrs. George Wightman. They had formerly been serving the Lord in Mexico and were then on their way to the Philippines. When I stopped by a second-hand bookstore in Brooklyn a few days later I found a book on the Philippines. Usually I haunted such stores to look for Biblical books but that time I was looking for something different.

That Christmas I had been invited to visit an old Victorian friend who was farming in New England. It was a mild winter so I really enjoyed the opportunity to get away from the city and from studying. There wasn't much I could do to help Joe on the farm so I went for long walks. One afternoon I arrived at a sandy beach and walked up and down beside the sea. It was my prayer that the Lord would bring the Philippines before me again if that was the place He had chosen for us. That evening sitting before the crackling fire, Joe and I chatted together. He mentioned John Lamb in Venezuela, remarking that they spoke Spanish there. Then he said one of his neighbors spoke Spanish, having picked it up in the Philippines when he was in the army. Joe knew nothing of my exercise about that country. However, the mention was so casual that I asked the Lord for further confirmation.

Back in Brooklyn, I was at the watchnight service held at the school. The next morning, I went to the 13th Avenue Gospel Hall for the Lord's Supper. On the table were several copies of a new issue of "Voices From the Vineyard." Glancing through this missionary magazine, I noticed a letter from George Wightman. But what caught my eye was the editor's note in bold type right above the letter. It stated that for almost a quarter of a century the Philippine Islands had been under United States rule and yet so far there was no missionary serving the Lord there, commended from a U.S. assembly (Wightman's were from Scotland). That was the answer to my prayer for guidance. Further confirmation was that the same issue told of A. G. Ingleby (going to Portugal) to help Mr. Swan. It was as if the Lord was telling me he had someone else picked out for Portugal.

On my first furlough I related this incident to Richard Maclachlan, editor of Voices. He remembered that editorial note and said he could not recall doing such on any other occasion.

There was no doubt in my mind that we were to go to the Philippines but Anna wanted her own assurance as to the Lord's will. She was not satisfied with my argument—if it was the Lord's will for us to be married, then He wouldn't send us to different fields. Basically she was fearful of the criticism that she changed the choice of field of service for my sake. There was one student who had signed an autograph book "Yours for India" but at a later date another entry said "Yours for China." Eventually she went to Central America! One night Miss May Van Dine stayed with Anna and Irene as an overnight guest. While having her devotions next morning, she turned to Anna

Guidance Regarding the Field

and said, "Anna, have you ever thought how sometimes we allow what people may say to divert us from what God wants us to do?" She too was unaware of what Anna had been thinking. That convinced Anna that she could accept going to the Philippines as the Lord's will for her too.

Many times through the years we have been most thankful for the conviction we had that the Lord sent us to the Philippines. Our first term was particularly difficult with unforeseen discouragements and repeated financial trials. Once it was suggested to us by a fellow missionary that we were in the wrong place and should seek another field of service. It would have been easy to become a missionary drop-out! But we had this assurance that the Lord sent us there with clear and definite guidance. Therefore, we would need equally clear guidance if he should want us to leave.

As our first year at school drew to a close the question arose whether we should return for another year. We were not altogether happy with the situation there so questioned the advisability of returning. Another question was whether we should be married before going to the field. There were some very strong views about this. Responsible brethren in Great Britain and America were insisting that engaged couples should spend a year or two at least on the field before getting married. This would give time for cultural adjustment and language study before assuming marital responsibilities. The one exception would be when the missionary on the field recommended marriage first.

In our correspondence with Mr. Wightman, he suggested we should go as soon as feasible and that we should be married first. Since they were the only missionaries of our group there, it would be difficult to arrange suitable housing for singles. Naturally we were happy with his advice and the elders in Buffalo agreed to this. The next question was what to do in that summer of 1922 in further preparation for missionary work.

A good friend arranged for Anna to take a course in midwifery in Buffalo, believing that this would be of service on the mission field. So her summer was spent with medical studies and assisting a Christian doctor who lived across the street. Thus, she was able to get the required number of delivery cases, along with the lessons. Actually she rarely used this training in the

Philippines. It was not needed since there are medical facilities available to most of the people.

Leaving the school in Brooklyn we travelled to Buffalo where I was introduced to her family. I don't think they were greatly impressed until I preached one Sunday evening at Assembly Hall. That was an ordeal for me and I really worked hard on preparation. The Lord graciously helped. Whether the hearers reaped spiritual benefits I don't know, but I do know there were favorable reactions in the family. During the three weeks there I also helped in open-air meetings, visits to the City Mission, and in tract distribution.

Then I headed for northern Ontario. On the way I stopped at a Dominion Day conference in Hamilton where my old friend Tom Baird was one of the speakers. He kindly introduced me as an out-going missionary. After an overnight stop in Peterborough I went on to Haileybury. There I found my way to the home of Mr. Sam Taylor, an evangelist working for the Lord in that area, who was heading up a special campaign there. He was a hard worker who disciplined himself and expected others to do the same. As he opened the door I introduced myself and he greeted me, "Welcome, if you have come to do the *work* of an evangelist." The emphasis on work did not escape me and I found there was indeed work to be done.

Other members of the team arrived a little later: Tom Baird spent part of the summer there. His messages and Bible studies and private conversations were a real help; Arthur Smith was a beloved member of the team with his winsome ways. He was one of the outstanding violinists in Canada and had played in some top-rate orchestras. It was always a thrill to listen to his playing though he never played just to entertain. Going into a small village for an open-air meeting, a man would look out of the saloon and shout, "Is Smitty there with his fiddle?" The saloon and pool hall would empty to listen to Smitty and his fiddle and also his attractive way of presenting the Gospel. Without "Smitty" we preached to unseen audiences—if there were any!

Then there was a young school teacher with his bride, Mr. and Mrs. Horace Lockett. It may have been there that he got some ideas which lead in later years to the summer Bible school in Guelph. Miss Hartshorn came from Peterborough as pianist

Guidance Regarding the Field 61

and soloist. To our surprise a romance started between her and Sam Taylor. We thought he was a confirmed bachelor! Sam was no singer! One day at lunch he said to Muriel Hartshorn, "When I get to heaven, I'll have one more joy than you—for the first time I shall really be able to sing." Among our group also was Horace Davey who had been at Brooklyn with us and Alvin Sauer of Buffalo.

The mornings were devoted to Bible study. In the afternoons we went out in tract distribution covering the whole town of Haileybury and also in open-air meetings in isolated villages. Usually these would consist of a saloon and pool hall, a general store with a post office, and a dozen houses. It was not easy to preach when we didn't know if anyone was listening. Saturday evening we helped in an open-air meeting in Cobalt, noted then for its cobalt mines. Sundays we would visit New Liskeard and help with the Sunday school and assembly meetings there. Haileybury is on the shore of Lake Temiskaming, a good place for swimming until some of us got sick from algae on the water.

Early in September I returned to Buffalo, but some of the workers carried on. Less than a month after that summer campaign ended a disastrous fire swept through that area. Haileybury was practically destroyed and there was great loss of life. That no doubt included many who had heard the Gospel in that summer effort. The workers lost their possessions but were able to get out after helping others to evacuate.

On September 20th there was a quiet wedding in the Carson home with a reception afterwards in the Gibson apartment upstairs. None of my relatives were able to attend, and I was really too excited to remember much of what took place. We were married by Mr. Hugh Kame from Erie, Pennsylvania. He had formerly been a Baptist minister but had left that denomination to serve the Lord with the assemblies. Some of the young folks planned to chase us when we made our getaway. However, we climbed out a bedroom window and got in a waiting taxi and so eluded our pursuers. After a night at the Statler Hotel, we had a one-day honeymoon at Niagara Falls. We couldn't afford a longer stay!

The day we left Buffalo, October 4th, was a hectic time, especially for Anna. She needed one more delivery to make up the required quota and Dora Murset had her baby early that morning, very conveniently. Her board examination for midwives was that afternoon while I was home finishing up the packing. She got home in time to change and leave for Assembly Hall for our farewell supper and meeting. From the Hall, we were escorted to the station by many friends to leave on the night train for Chicago. Reservations had been booked two weeks before, but to my dismay the conductor said the berth was already occupied. The ticket agent had put the date of sale instead of date of departure on the ticket. While I was discussing this with the agents, one man noticed my Canadian veteran button. He too was a Canadian veteran and persuaded the conductor to put us in a better berth that was vacant. It was the Lord's provision when Anna was so tired.

On arrival next morning in Chicago our hostess, Mrs. William Trotter, noticed how tired Anna was and sent her off to bed to sleep until time for dinner. We had dinner with Mr. and Mrs. Tom Bendelow and there learned about the fire in Haileybury. I spoke in the Austin Street Hall that evening and the next two nights we had meetings in Minneapolis and Duluth through arrangements made by Tom Baird. After a couple of more stops we arrived in Victoria.

It was not an easy situation for Anna, having just said goodbye to her family and then to meet my Mother and sisters for the first time. They gave her a royal welcome and received her as a sister. However Florrie, I think, had not quite forgiven Anna for taking away her brother. Florrie had an unhappy experience with a fellow who claimed to be a Christian. They broke up when it was discovered that he was only pretending to be a believer in order to woo her. After that Florrie and I had been very close, often walking to work together each morning. However, Florrie never let her feelings interfere with her support of us in her prayers and by her gifts.

We spent six weeks there visiting the assemblies in Victoria (two at that time) and some up Vancouver Island. Through the years these assemblies have been loyal in their support through their gifts and prayers. Naturally there have been many changes. Of those who signed my letter of commendation, all are now at home with the Lord, the last of these, Mr. John Thomson, passing away in November, 1980. Yet the succeeding generations have been faithful in maintaining the interest in us and the Lord's work in which we are engaged.

Guidance Regarding the Field

We were booked to sail from Victoria on the "S.S. Empress of Asia" on November 30th. It was hard on my Mother because the next morning was the 15th anniversary of Father's home-call. It was a chilly evening as friends gathered on the pier to see us off. As the ship began to move away from the pier, I called out, "Cease not to cry unto our God for us" (1 Sam. 7:8). Our cabin was full of flowers and boxes of chocolates and candies, some from friends in Vancouver where the ship began its journey. Dinner was being served but we preferred to go to bed.

The chief steward was surprised to see us at breakfast; he thought we had been left behind in Vancouver. An old lady there had been looking for us. There was a group of Scandinavian Alliance missionaries on board bound for China, so we enjoyed their fellowship even though their knowledge of English was limited. One afternoon another missionary told us she heard an elderly lady of that group crying in her cabin. Anna went to see if she could offer some help, but as she listened she realized the dear sister was on her knees pleading for lost souls in China.

Skirting the Aleutians it was bitterly cold and stormy. Some times the deck was covered with ice and passengers were not allowed out. In Yokohama some of us went for a day of sightseeing in Tokyo. On our return we got off the train at a station marked Yokohama but soon realized it was not where we had entrained that morning. We made an effort to find our own way, walking back to the ship. Soon we were lost, wandering narrow streets and being eyed curiously by Japanese preparing their evening meal. Even then there was some anti-American hostility so they didn't appear too friendly and we were unable to find one who could speak English. Finally we came back to the station where we started our walk, evidently having gone in a circle. In the station were other passengers with a similar experience. Together we found someone who could give us directions in English. Less than a year later most of Tokyo and Yokohama were destroyed by a great earthquake and fire.

Stops were also made in Kobe and Nagasaki; the latter was a coaling stop. As the ship anchored in the bay, barges loaded with coal pulled alongside. A bamboo scaffolding was quickly erected on the barges and on the side of the ship, which was soon swarming with men and women who passed baskets of coal from one to another to be dumped down the chute. By afternoon the job was done and the crew was busy removing the layer of coal dust from the decks and sides of the ship.

The next call was Shanghai where the ship anchored at the mouth of the Whangpoo River. The passengers were taken up river to the city in launches—a bitterly cold ride in the middle of December. We had the address of Dr. Parrott and his wife and were thankful to see her turn on the heater. No wonder Chinese wear padded garments in winter! We enjoyed the fellowship with them that Sunday and also with Mr. Eldridge of the British and Foreign Bible Society who had formerly been the agent in Manila.

The ship left Shanghai Sunday evening and arrived in Manila on Wednesday morning. A quick jump from the cold of winter to the heat of the tropics. We made frequent trips to our cabin to change to cooler garb. We were up early Wednesday morning to catch our first glimpse of the Philippine Islands, the land of the Lord's choice for us. It was just over a year since the Lord said, "Go to the Philippines." We praised Him for the way He had been leading us forth.

8

BEGINNING OUR MISSIONARY WORK

"I am with you and will watch over you wherever you go. . . . I will not leave you until I have done what I have promised you." (Gen. 28:15)

Landing for the first time in a strange land is always an interesting experience. As soon as our ship cleared quarantine a stream of people came aboard. Among them was Mrs. Wightman (Mr. Wightman was abroad just then) and Mr. Jesus Alvarez, a young brother in the assembly in the Walled City. He had previously been a law student, but after he really came to know the Lord he decided to give his life to the Lord's service. He was helping in the work at the Walled City when we arrived. Later he went to seminary and returned to his previous denomination in which he finally became a bishop.

The first evening, December 20, 1922 (which would have been my parent's 36th wedding anniversary), we went to the prayer meeting at the hall in the Walled City. There we were warmly welcomed by the believers and for us it was a great joy to meet them. When we complained of the heat, they informed us it was winter! So we dreaded the hot season, but it wasn't so bad for we became acclimated as the temperature rose. Really the difference is not so great for the temperature does not vary much more than thirty degrees Fahrenheit throughout the year.

Perhaps this would be a good place to digress in order to tell about the beginning of the work here among those known as Brethren. I quote from an "Echoes Manual" that I wrote in 1929.

"More than one has had a part in the commencement of the work here along Scriptural lines, but the first who started such an assembly was Mr. William Averyt, who writes of his coming to the Philippines, thus, 'On July 8, 1911, in my room about one o'clock in Jonesboro, Arkansas, God, through His Son, spoke peace to my soul. . . . He soon thrust me forth away from human props out into the harvest field. To the Philippine Islands I was sent to be stationed in the 13th Infantry at the Cuartel de Espana and afterwards at Ft. McKinley. . . I was very definitely led by the Holy Spirit among the high school students in the Walled City.' Soon after his arrival, or early in 1912, he began to visit these students in their rooms. Among the first to be saved was Sulpicio Guillen and his cousin. (Mr. Guillen was for many years a linotype operator with the Manila Daily Bulletin. After his retirement he moved to Kapatagan, Lanao del Norte where he had some farm land. He passed away a few years ago but we still correspond with his widow who is now in her mid-eighties and quite frail.)

"A little later a Bible class was started in a room on Calle Victoria, Walled City, and about that time Major (then Capt.) Moses T. Barlow was temporarily transferred from Albay and met Mr. Averyt. They enjoyed much fellowship together over the Word of God. Later, in 1913, Major Barlow was again in Manila and here I give his own account of those days: 'Bro. Averyt was a great help to both Mrs. Barlow and myself. He convinced Mrs. Barlow that she should obey the Lord in believer's baptism and baptized her in Manila Bay. He also helped me to understand many truths.

" 'Bro. Averyt informed us that he had been teaching these students, and that practically all of them had made a profession of being saved and had been baptized. He told us that he had been working up to a point where he hoped to begin a regular assembly, meeting in God's appointed way each Lord's Day, around His table in faith, knowing that He is in the midst in fulfillment of His promise. It was while we were in Manila that the meeting was begun. Mrs. Noronha and daughter were also convinced that that was the proper place for them and used to

Beginning Our Missionary Work

gather with us. Our understanding was imperfect, but we just took the Scriptures, and the Lord honored our request for understanding and graciously opened his will to us as we trusted him to do so. Those meetings in that student's room on Calle Victoria were the most godly meetings any of us attended. There was a spiritual warmth there, an earnest seeking after God and a certain, unmistakable presence of the Holy Spirit as the result. I doubt if I shall ever attend more spiritual meetings until we have the Great Meeting with our Savior in the air. The assembly at that time numbered eight or nine in fellowship.

" 'I left Manila for the U.S.A. on December 15, 1913, and returned June 2, 1914. While in the United States, I had been admitted to fellowship in the assembly at San Francisco and had learned many things. The little meeting was still in existence, but meeting in the home of Mrs. C. H. Noronha, Malate. I was surprised and thankful to find that my company was stationed right in the city of Manila. It was only a little over a month until it was moved elsewhere, but I frequently went into Manila, and the meeting continued in Mrs. Noronha's home after we finally left the Philippines on June 19, 1919.' "

Mr. & Mrs. George Wightman, having been compelled by certain Mexican laws to leave their work in Tehuacan, Mexico, were exercised before the Lord about another field of service. Having been put in touch with Major Barlow, they learned of his prayers for someone to carry on the work after his return to the United States. Mr. Averyt had also returned to the U.S. where he took employment on the staff of the Chicago Tribune. In March 1929 it was my privilege to have lunch with him there on our first furlough. He went home to be with the Lord three years later. Believing it was the Lord's will for them, the Wightman's came to the Islands in May 1919 arriving just a month before Major Barlow and his family left for the U.S.

Realizing the opportunities afforded among the students in the Walled City, and the absence of other work there, they rented a hall. This hall, directly opposite the Roman Catholic Cathedral, was opened in July 1919 and used for two years. Then a move was made to the corner of Victoria and Magallanes Streets, also in Intramuros. These buildings had to be renovated to make them suitable for meeting places. There were then about 14,000 people living in that section of the city.

Many of the old-style Spanish residences were occupied by large numbers of students. But there was a strong Roman Catholic influence with several of their churches and institutions in that area of a little over a square mile.

Major Barlow was an active worker, and he encouraged the holding of services in the barrios around Fort McKinley. This was where the Filipino enlisted men and their families lived. In the spring of 1920 a simple bamboo structure was purchased in Masilang and the Wightman's continued the work there. This was about six miles from the city but easily accessible by an electric streetcar.

There were two problems opposing building up a permanent work in both the Walled City and Masilang. One was that both students and soldiers are transient. The students would move away from the Walled City generally when they had completed their studies and started to work in other places. The soldiers were either transferred to other places or were discharged. The other problem was that of language. Both of these groups came from different parts of the Islands and from different language areas. The services in the Walled City were in English as students were studying in that language. At Masilang it was mostly Tagalog that was used, though many who attended were not fluent in that language.

Upon our arrival in Manila, while I was clearing our baggage through customs, I was approached by a Filipino in plain clothes. He surprised me by asking if I had a license to carry a gun. "No," I replied, "I never owned a gun in my life!" He then wanted to know what I had in my hip pocket. With a smile I said, "That is not a gun—it is a sword!" He was rather nonplussed when I produced my pocket Bible. Of course, he wouldn't have understood what I meant by a sword. He still entertained his suspicions for when I went to another building to get my hold baggage, he showed up again and insisted on opening the cases. Perhaps he still hoped to find some weapons!

Since the services were in English I was immediately put to work. The last day of 1922 was a Lord's day, just eleven days after our arrival. As I was asked to preach that morning, I prayed that the Lord would bless that first Gospel message in my new field of service. It was my request that in His will He would grant the salvation of a soul to confirm that He had called

Beginning Our Missionary Work

us to the Philippines. How good of the Lord to graciously answer that prayer. After the message a young man by the name of Joaquin dela Cruz accepted the Lord as his Savior. He had had some previous knowledge of the Scriptures, but he surprised us by asking to be baptized that day. The senior missionary was not there; it was up to me to make a decision. My training and experience had never included examining a candidate for baptism. It was my idea, however, that converts should wait awhile in order to prove the reality of their conversion. Joaquin was not to be put off in that way. He clinched the matter for us by saying, "Tomorrow is New Year's Day. I want to start the New Year in newness of life." So that evening a group of us went to the waterfront at the site of the present Manila Yacht Club. In the bright tropical moonlight we had a little service and I had the joy of baptizing the first Filipino convert in my service for the Lord.

The Gospel Hall was the only Protestant work in the Walled City. The services were in English and attended mostly by young men who were students. Besides the missionaries there were only two married couples but no young women. Being newlyweds, Anna and I felt that was not a satisfactory situation. Those young men would look for female companionship elsewhere and we would lose them. But getting young women into the services in those days was no easy matter. They were carefully chaperoned and did not go out alone. A young man and young woman never went out together without someone else with them. The girls who came to the city to study would promise their mothers to remain true to their church. They lacked the venturesome spirit of the young men.

We talked with a missionary friend about this problem. He felt that there was a weakness in student work in regard to building up a permanent work. It was necessary to reach the families, for when the parents were won the children would probably follow. Our efforts to attract young women to the services proved rather futile.

Since there was no Sunday school, we began one and got some of the children of the neighborhood to attend. In this, Tagalog was needed so our part was limited to teaching the children to sing choruses and to memorize verses in English. Others helped us with the teaching and one of these was Joaquin, even though he was a Visayan. The Lord worked in the hearts of some of the older children, and we had the joy of seeing some of them trust in Christ for their salvation.

Somewhat later we invited two teenage girls to spend a few days in our home. One night they had gone to their room and I was working at my desk on the other side of the thin wall. The girls were having a discussion. One said that after you are saved you will not sin any more and the other was disagreeing. I couldn't help overhearing them. To prove her point, one girl pointed to me as an example saying that I was saved and I didn't sin! In our devotions at the breakfast table next morning, we endeavored to straighten them out on that theological matter!

Very soon we realized that we needed to learn Tagalog. While English is widely spoken because all education then was based on English, a knowledge of Tagalog, the principal Philippine language, was essential to get closer to the people. However, there was no language school and very few grammars or dictionaries. Mrs. Guillen, one of the believers, helped us with conversational Tagalog. For a while we paid an elementary school principal to give us lessons on Saturdays. It was not very satisfactory as she was not prepared and did not understand the problems facing a non-Filipino in learning the language. One day after she had given us some rules and some vocabulary, we asked her, "Can you give us some rules on the formation and structure of sentences?" After pondering it a bit, she said, "Whichever way sounds best!" None of it sounded best to us! Yet she was right, for Tagalog is a euphonious language and there are ways which do sound best.

We were fortunate to have acquired a couple of old grammars and an old dictionary which had been left behind by Major Barlow, but a language cannot be learned simply through books. We needed to get away from Manila where English was widely spoken and where there was a multiplicity of languages. Though Jesus Alvarez was a Bicolano from Camarines Sur, he arranged for us to go to Camarines Norte, the southern limit of the Tagalog-speaking area in those days. First we rented the house of a Chinese merchant in Daet, the capital, for two months. This gave us a base to look around for another place in that province. During our two months there, a fire nearby burned down a number of houses. Awakened by the shouting

Beginning Our Missionary Work

we saw the fire was across the street at the back of the property. Hastily we threw most of our few belongings into trunks and suitcases and loaded them on a carabao cart in the yard. We were ready to evacuate if the fire leaped across the street. Beside the cart was a warehouse made of galvanized iron. I wondered why the Chinese were putting wet sacks on the roof. Later we learned it was where they stored their stocks of gasoline and kerosene! The fire was brought under control by tearing down some shacks in its path and by a vigorous bucket brigade bringing water from the river.

We located a house in Indang (now Vinzons) and rented the upstairs floor for ten Pesos ($5.00) a month. We hoped to be able to rent the lower part for a Gospel Hall but the owner had rice stored there. Soon we learned that this attracted rats, and we got used to seeing rats running along the rafters over our heads at night. A mosquito net wasn't much protection but fortunately the rats were sure-footed! Traps didn't do much good, but one evening a rice snake disposed of one rat.

There was no evangelical work in Indang and to our knowledge only one man who claimed to be a nominal Protestant. The community was under the control of the parish priest. Every day the church bells tolled for either a wedding, a birth celebration, or a funeral. A minimum charge of P25.00 for any of these was a burden to poor people. So often we were asked for a contribution to help. One day our laundry woman wanted to know where I had gone. Anna told her I was out in the barrios selling Bibles. The illiterate woman said the priest told them the Bible was a bad book and they shouldn't read it. She also averred that the priest had made himself rich at their expense but still they went to him to confess. Yet she admitted he was not a good man because he had daughters of his own living in the church house.

We didn't have enough Tagalog to conduct services but we did have classes for children in our home, where we taught them verses and choruses. One evening as we went for a walk, just as we passed the priest we heard children's voices in a home singing, "The best book to read is the Bible." We had a large blackboard on which I wrote a Gospel verse each day and placed it on a rack in front of the house. It could be seen by all passersby and yet was out of reach of children.

The first Good Friday we were there the procession passed our house. On every other house a candle was burning; we had the light from God's Word which everyone read as they slowly passed by. Among the various images carried in the procession was the town's lone hearse. It was the burial of Christ! In the hearse was a coffin and in the coffin a life-sized image of Christ. For a moment the incongruity of Christ (even as an image) in a coffin appalled us. Then led by the Spirit, I said to Anna standing beside me, "He is alive!" The truth of the resurrection became very real at that moment.

Itinerating on foot with a bag of Scriptures had a two-fold purpose. It was one way of spreading the Word of God, and it afforded an opportunity to hear and use Tagalog. We not only went through the town of Indang but covered other towns. What we particularly enjoyed was travelling through the coconut groves or across the rice paddies to isolated hamlets. We would carry a sandwich for lunch and buy a green coconut, a drink safe and sterile, bottled by nature. After a while Anna had to stay home as she was expecting our first baby. Outside of Labo was a river, so at noon I would go out of town a little to take a dip in the river and eat my lunch. The school principal in Indang lived across the street, and he warned me there were crocodiles in that river.

It was also a way to learn about the culture of the people. I learned that often the women held the purse. More than one man was convinced to buy a Bible until he asked his wife for the money—then the sale was off! Sometimes they didn't have money so I accepted some fresh eggs or a few ears of fresh corn instead. The people laughed at the mistakes of this crazy Americano but were good-natured and, as is customary in the Philippines, most hospitable. They would look at the four Gospels—San Mateo, San Marcos, San Lucas, and San Juan—and want to know if I had San Geronimo or Santa Maria. I sold more than one New Testament by showing the letters of San Pedro!

Living was primitive. We had *running* water when we ran with it from the well just outside our door! Just as we were getting up one morning I heard the boy from across the street drawing water. The first plunk was the bucket but then a second plunk must be the boy! Sure enough the boy was down the well. The neighbors quickly gathered and were discussing how he fell into

Beginning Our Missionary Work

the well. "Never mind," I said, "let's get him out." So a long bamboo was put down and the boy climbed out and stood, dripping wet, in their midst while they scolded him for his carelessness. Our neighbor told our helper that Americans were dirty people—he never saw them taking a bath beside the well! She told him we had made a corner of our kitchen into a bathroom—with bamboo slat floors there was no trouble with clogged drains! He was not impressed—seeing is believing!

One afternoon we sat in our house studying Tagalog and munching on finger-size bananas when suddenly it seemed to cloud over. Strange, because it was not the rainy season. We heard sounds of people shouting and running about; they were quickly covering the well. A swarm of locusts was coming. They covered the ground and roofs when they landed and some people scooped them up in sacks. Some ate them but others didn't. The locusts had evidently fed elsewhere as we heard later they had ruined crops and even coconut palms in other places. I was watching a long low building across the street, when for a split second it seemed the roof was levitating but really it was the mass of locusts lifting off simultaneously.

Some months later a devastating typhoon passed over that area. In one place I later saw an area of abaca plants which had been sheared off as with a giant scythe. In the early morning the wind was strong, lifting up the nipa thatch so the rain was soaking us. Thinking it might be more secure on the ground floor, I investigated. I could hardly hold my ground against the wind. The front wall downstairs had fallen outwards, so with difficulty we took refuge there, with the rice and the rats! Soon our roof was "Gone with the wind." In mid-morning the wind and rain stopped quite quickly—we were in the eye of the storm. Knowing that soon the storm would hit us again but the wind blowing in the opposite direction, we took refuge with crowds of others in the bakery down the street. It was a substantial low building and his stocks of baked goods were soon sold out. We all huddled together there until mid-afternoon.

The storm was over. The only dry thing in our house was Leonard's crib which we had covered with a piece of oil cloth. At least the baby had a dry bed. The wooden parts of the sewing machine lay in a heap below the iron frame. Letters from velvet texts were plastered in odd places on the walls. A box of Scriptures which had just arrived was blown open and its contents soaked and scattered. Not the ideal way of scattering the seed of the Word! A friendly storekeeper allowed us to stay temporarily in a room over his store, where he also lived. The priest was angry with him about this, thinking this was a way to get us out of town. He also persuaded the owner not to repair the roof, until I told the owner that his rice was starting to sprout. Then he put his own interest ahead of that of the church. That was the only time we ever had what has been called "$1000.00 salad." A mentally deficient man in the town brought us the heart of a coconut tree which had blown down. It was very delicious. It was expensive because to take the heart kills the tree.

We had some amusing problems with language study. There is a word in Tagalog which is used when quoting what someone else has said. People would ask me the price of a Gospel. "Two centavos" I would reply. Then someone would tell the others "Two centavos *daw*." I didn't know what "daw" meant but when I used it they would roar with laughter. Then we repeatedly heard a word "Kwan."

Every time we asked what "Kwan" meant we got a different answer. It was utterly confusing, until one afternoon the light dawned and I said to Anna, "Kwan" means "what-you-may-call-it" and can be used for people as well as things. Very often we would try to talk in Tagalog (with an American accent) and it was frustrating to get the reply, "I don't understand English." It was a great achievement when one day a person replied in Tagalog—he understood what I was trying to say!

Some Sunday mornings I would go to the Presbyterian church in Daet as we had gotten to know them there when we lived in Daet. They would often ask me to preach. I found that sometimes interpreters would sometimes not repeat what I had said but what they thought I should have said, according to their ideas. So it was there that I made my first stumbling attempts to preach or rather read a sermon in Tagalog. Sunday afternoons, Anna and I would simply remember the Lord in the Lord's Supper, just the two of us. One day after our little service I had an unusual sense of the Lord's presence. Leaving the table I knelt at a camp cot which we used as a couch in the living room. In a few moments Anna joined me there as we silently contin-

Beginning Our Missionary Work

ued our worship and praise to God for all His grace. We were overwhelmed by a realization that the Lord was with us, even though we knew of no other believer within miles.

During our stay in Indang we had to go to Manila for the birth of our first child. There were no adequate facilities then in Camarines Norte. On our way, we had to pass through Naga, the capital of Camarines Sur. Fortunately there was a hotel of sorts there because we were delayed there almost a week. The ship that was to take us from Pasacao to Aloneros was in drydock. In Manila we stayed with Mr. and Mrs. G. B. Cameron, agents of the American Bible Society. Anna had rather a hard time with the birth of Leonard. We went to the Mary Johnston Hospital shortly after five in the morning and the baby was born shortly before midnight. Dr. Rebecca Parish was in charge of this maternity hospital—a very fine doctor and also a fine Christian. Nowadays Mary Johnston Hospital is several blocks from the water's edge, surrounded by slums and a harbor area. Then it was on the waterfront of Manila Bay and the fishermen would spread their nets to dry on the sea wall of the hospital. A lot of land has been reclaimed from the sea.

Leonard was a good baby and rarely woke up at night. He was a source of attraction in Indang as he was the first white baby in that community. The children loved to watch him getting his morning bath, and he delighted to splash the water over them. When we took him out for a walk in the late afternoon, old ladies would say, "He has no hair." Then as they gently stroked his head and blond hair, they said, "Oh, yes, he does have hair—it's like hemp."

9

BACK TO MANILA

"But God chose the foolish things of the world to shame the wise; God chose the weak things of the world to shame the strong." (1 Cor. 1:27)

The time came for a decision as to our place of service for the Lord. Should we continue in Camarines Norte and endeavor to establish an assembly work there? Or should we return to Manila and help build up the work in that area? It was evident it would take some time to establish an indigenous assembly in Indang. A few individuals had sought us out but they were from other places. Indang seemed to be too much under the influence of the priest for the adults to quickly respond to our message. We were rather isolated as travel to Manila was sometimes uncertain. We were alone and it didn't seem likely that any work there would stand on its own when it came time for furlough. So we decided to return to Manila.

At that time Brother Wightman had gone into business to support himself while he continued to carry on the work in the Walled City. We rented an apartment in Ermita within walking distance to the Gospel Hall. There were many tests of faith in those days. Before going to Camarines there had been trials. At one time we had a book of tickets to buy bread but we could only afford a few cents on a tin of guava jelly to put on the bread. On January 9, 1923, I wrote, "Funds low—promises great." That was before the days of blaring radios, but next door the neighbor had a phonograph and a few records which were used from morning till night. Many an evening we walked to the waterfront and sat on the rocks to watch the famed Manila sunset and get a little quiet.

When we lived in Ermita there were severe testings. More than once I would go out selling Scriptures in the morning to get enough cash to buy some dried beans for our meals. One morning we had only some bread in the house. But as we were getting dressed, one of the Filipino believers arrived from the province with a "pasalubong" (a greeting gift) of eggs and fruit. He never knew how he provided our breakfast! We knew the Lord had a purpose in allowing such trials which seemed so difficult at the time but there is always an "afterwards" of blessing. "No discipline seems pleasant at the time, but painful. Later on, however, it produces a harvest of righteousness and peace for those who have been trained by it" (Heb. 12:11).

It was some years later that I realized the Levites who were recipients of the tithes of Israel were required to give a tithe also. Since we had been giving to the work of the Lord all that could be spared above actual living costs, we had not thought of giving a share of what we received. Indeed was not all we received being spent in some way in serving the Lord? However, we can testify that from the time we began to give a special portion to the Lord, we have never been so severely tested as we were before. Of course, some would say that this was because by that time we were better known and no doubt that was a contributing factor.

One Saturday evening we received a letter from a friend in Victoria with a postscript expressing sympathy with us in the homecall of my Mother. It came as a shock because we had not heard that she was even sick. My sisters thought that rather than giving me the shock of receiving a cable, they would write a letter giving all the details. That was before the days of airmail, and the friend's letter just happened to catch an earlier boat. I was booked to speak the next morning and the lesson was on the martyrdom of Stephen. It was not easy under those circumstances. Some time later Anna received word of the passing away of her younger sister Mae. However, this did not come as a sudden shock because she had been ill for a long time. Nevertheless it was hard to think of that beautiful young woman taken

Back to Manila

away in her youth; but the comfort was that both of these were "at home with the Lord."

It was shortly after Mother's homecall that Kenneth was born on May 2, 1926, at the Mary Johnston Hospital. In memory of Mother we gave him the middle name of Sheldon which was my Mother's maiden name. He had bronchitis quite early and, though he got over it, it seemed to affect his sleeping patterns. He would resist our efforts to put him to sleep in the evening, even to the extent of rubbing his eyes.

Another discouraging problem of that first term was difficulties with our fellow workers. This caused a great deal of heartache. We were young and inexperienced, and there was no one else in our group with whom we could confer. Looking back over the years we now know we should have reacted differently, but then we needed counseling which was not available. The experience has taught us the need for patience and love even when faced with what we then saw as wrongdoing.

Yet there were bright spots too as we resumed work in the Manila area. In addition to the regular services at the rented hall in the Walled City, I helped out in a book store we had there which afforded a number of contacts. Also at that time I began a campaign of canvassing all the homes in the Walled City. It took some time for scores, if not hundreds, were living in the old Spanish houses, several in each room in very crowded conditions. Some lived in screened-off places on landings and stairways. Almost all morning might be spent in just one large house. One day I was talking to a group in a courtyard when a basin of water was dumped on us from above. It was apparently unintentional—the person threw the water and then looked! Later this coverage with Scripture was extended through almost all the districts of Manila, south of the Pasig River.

The work at Masilang near Fort McKinley (now Fort Bonifacio) continued. However, the bamboo and thatch chapel was so dilapidated that we decided to abandon it. On the main road leading into the camp at Guadalupe we found a storefront to rent and the work of children's classes and Gospel preaching continued. This area was also canvassed with literature and invitations, but the response was quite meager. People were slow to investigate some new religion, as they viewed it. During our furlough in 1929 this work was dropped.

While I was taking care of the bookstore one morning, a

young man who had been attending the services came for a talk. Simeon Endaya was a quiet man, a postal clerk. He told me that he had been brought up a Roman Catholic and served as an altar boy. Then the family switched to the independent Aglipayan Church, a break-away from the Roman Church. When Simeon was a high school student in Manila he wandered into a Methodist Church. There he was received as a member and baptized by sprinkling for the second, maybe third, time. Through the testimony at the Gospel Hall he was now a believer in Christ. Did he need to be baptized by immersion? I gave him some references to study and told him to see what the Lord wanted him to do and not take my word only. He was back the next morning asking to be immersed.

One evening in his work at the registry division of the post office, he receipted for a large amount of money to be sent to the Culion Leprosarium. The ship that was going to Culion failed to sail the next morning as scheduled. On his return to the office Simeon checked and finally found the bag, empty of its contents. Outside detectives were called in and they suspected Simeon seeing he had not only received the bag but also discovered it empty. All day they grilled him but he maintained his innocence. Towards evening one detective accused him of hiding some information from them. Simeon replied, "Yes, there is one thing I haven't told you." They shouted, "Come on then, out with it." He said, "I haven't told you about my Savior. Because of my faith in Him I could not steal that money." He was released but kept under surveillance. Some months later a janitor at the post office suddenly seemed to have a lot of money—he was the guilty party.

In giving his testimony at the prayer meeting, Simeon said something like this. "Throughout this experience I realized the peace that keeps our hearts and minds. You will say, 'You had peace because you knew you wre innocent.' But that was not the case. A co-worker of mine, who also was innocent, had no peace. He went to the Quiapo church to pray to the Black Christ (a famous image) but still had no peace." Simeon had an opportunity to witness to him about the source of real peace in Christ.

Often at the times of services at the Hall some of us would stand outside and try to persuade passers-by to come in. One of

Back to Manila

these was an elderly man, Lutgardo Ramos. Having been addicted to drink and gambling he was dressed very poorly and was quite reluctant to enter the hall. Soon his life was drastically changed when he trusted Christ as his Savior. His wife was very much opposed. She stopped the children from coming to the Sunday school and took his Bible away from him. Even when we visited their home she practically ignored us. This was most unusual for Filipinos are customarily hospitable. Brother Ramos continued faithfully in spite of the difficulties. The change was evident even in the way he dressed. He often mentioned this when giving his testimony. In later years he helped us a great deal when we began the work in San Juan. He loved to preach the Gospel and invariably from the Gospel of John. He went home to be with the Lord during our second furlough.

About the same time a very different type of man began attending the meetings. He was chief clerk of the Bureau of Health and well educated. In his search for the truth he had some contacts with Seventh-Day Adventists but was not satisfied. He found the truth in Christ as he came to the hall and soon was active for the Lord. A meeting was started in his home in Paco district along with the help of David Shepherd. David was a self-supporting missionary from Paisley, Scotland, managing a plate-making concern which prepared plates for printing Bibles for the American Bible Society. As the work in Paco grew, they rented a storefront in 1931. Geronimo Mercado was burdened for the need in his home town of Tanay, Rizal. He would leave his office at noon on Saturday and go directly there. Meetings would be held there Saturday evening and Sunday morning, often in the open air when weather permitted. Later on this testimony was extended to the neighboring towns of Pililla and Guisao. A small bamboo chapel was built in Pililla, and one of the converts baptized there was an old man at the age of 96.

Sunday afternoon Geronimo would return to Paco for the services there. Another who helped for a while in these efforts was George Burns. He was a New Englander, a veteran who was partly disabled in World War I. He lived on his pension and had a zeal for distributing tracts and personal witnessing. Brother Mercado later donated a lot for the building of a chapel in Tanay. He passed away during the latter part of World War II and his widow some years later. His daughters and their families are active in the assembly in San Juan. Geronimo Mercado had a gift of translation and translated several worship hymns and also wrote some original Tagalog hymns which are included in hymnbooks we are using still.

His younger brother, Sergio was saved in later years and after our return to the Philippines in 1949, often went with us to Tanay to help in the work there. He also worked for the Bureau of Health, in malaria control. His work often took him away from home, and it was on one of these trips that the bus he was riding on was ambushed by dissidents. Brother Sergio Mercado was one of the casualties. It was a great loss because he was a keen student of the Word and a gifted speaker like his brother.

In 1927 serious communist disturbances in Central China led two missionaries from there to join us for a time. James Buckley was from Ottawa, Canada, and Fred Pucknell was from England. Jim bought an old Model-T Ford. Only oldsters will remember those vehicles by which Henry Ford put cars within the reach of the working class. They lacked the conveniences of modern cars, but they were simple enough that most repairs could be done by a mechanically minded owner. We took out the back seat and installed boxes to carry supplies, equipment, and a stock of Scriptures.

We would leave early Monday morning and be on the road till Friday evening. Pulling into a town we would park near the public market. One would stay with the vehicle and sell Scriptures while the other two would canvass from house to house. In Las Pinas, just south of Manila, there is a famous pipe organ made of bamboo by a Spanish priest early in the 19th century. As we were canvassing there, and I was walking among the houses, there was some excitement with men running in every direction. A gambling game had hastily broken up because they thought I was a police official. When they learned my mission they came back sheepishly and I had a crowd for a brief witness. In another town I stumbled on a gambling session. One man made the excuse that he had no money to buy a Bible. As I talked with others he won a bet, but still he wasn't ready to part with his money for the Scriptures.

In this way we could cover two or three towns a day. In late afternoon we would look for a place to spend the night under the canvas we had with us. It was usually easy to get the mayor

Back to Manila

or chief of police to give us a permit for an open-air meeting. In most towns there is a plaza or square in the center of the town, sometimes with a bandstand. These were good spots for meetings, except that in many places the town church also faces on the plaza. We stopped in Cabuyao, Laguna, on our way home one Friday evening. The chief of police granted us a permit. As we started our service we noticed the priest promenading in front of his church. Shortly after a policeman came and informed us we had to stop by the mayor's orders. We showed our permit from the chief of police. The policeman knew who was boss in the town, but I suggested that Jim go with him to talk to the mayor while Fred and I carried on. We preached for a long time and then offered Scriptures for sale. The crowd gradually faded away but still no sight of Jim. He kept on talking until he was sure we had plenty of time to have our meeting!

In this way we covered all the Tagalog-speaking provinces. It wasn't always easy to find a place to camp for the night. On a couple of occasions we got permission to spend the night in the municipal building. One of our trips lasted two weeks when we crossed over to the east coast of Luzon, visiting Infanta by one road and Atimonan by another. This latter road took us over a steep zig-zag road crossing the hills which are the backbone of the Island. At first the authorities were not going to allow us to go because the grade is so steep at one point that with gravity feed the gas wouldn't flow into the motor. We filled the tank and signed a release and they let us through. The old Ford made the grade without difficulty but going down the other side was a different story. The brake bands were all worn out; even the reverse band was gone by the time we finally reached level road again. So we had a repair job and had to be towed back by a truck.

In Lucena we came upon an elderly man who had a Tagalog Bible which was apparently well used. He maintained he was a Roman Catholic and was friendly when assured we were not Seventh-Day Adventists. He was evidently a believer, and before we left he gave us a little message on the three uses of "Abba, Father" in the New Testament. This showed he was conversant with the Scriptures and also his spiritual discernment. However, he couldn't justify some of the Roman practices from the Bible.

On five such trips we visited 63 towns (only one of them

twice) and held 35 meetings. About 7,000 Bibles, Testaments, and Gospels were sold and more than 20,000 tracts distributed. Many homes were visited and personal contacts made. The good seed of the Word was sown. How much of it fell on good ground, only eternity will reveal.

Each year a large fair and carnival was held on what is now Rizal Park in downtown Manila. In 1921 Brother Wightman rented a space on the temporary walls used for advertising. He had John 3:16 painted on it in large letters. That year a fire destroyed the carnival while it was in progress. Mr. Wightman went to see if he could get a rebate since the text was not there for the full time of the contract. (It must have been his Scottish thrift.) He didn't really expect it and didn't get any rebate. They told him his text was prominently displayed in news photographs of the fire so it had a wider audience.

The following year on the opening night I went with an armful of tracts and began handing them out at the entrance. I didn't have to hand them out, people just took them from me. Some took a handful and stood beside me helping. In half an hour my armful was gone. I went around to see how many had been thrown away and there were hardly any. Another year we were stopped by the police on the second night; if people threw them away we were contributing to littering. A commercial firm had hired a plane to broadcast advertising leaflets from the air. Instead of doing it in the late afternoon when the crowds were there to pick them up, they scattered them Sunday morning. It was a case of massive littering.

In later years we rented a booth among the exhibits and sold Scriptures and distributed literature. With posters and slides and with personal conversations there were many opportunities to make known the way of salvation. One evening a group of Roman Catholic seminarians came by primed for a discussion. I didn't want this, but with a crowd around I dared not back down. I tried to use the discussion and answering of questions as an opportunity to proclaim the Gospel. At one point they referred to the Pope as Head of the Church. I asked, "Do you believe the Bible?" Since they did, I referred to Colossians 1:18, reading it out to the interested crowd. Their reply was that the Church had two heads, one in heaven and one on earth. I retorted, "Now I can understand the defect in your church.

Back to Manila

Any body that has two heads is abnormal and would be exhibited among the freaks here at the carnival." It wasn't the kindest thing to say, but it pleased the crowd and discomfited them as well as bringing the discussion to an end.

For five years we had carried on under what were often discouraging difficulties. A vacation in the mountains was more than we could afford, and we were getting weary. However, in January, 1928, the Lord made it possible for us to spend some time in Baguio. We traveled third class by train to Damortis, Anna, Len, Ken, and I. Then by bus we climbed 5000 feet to Baguio by the Kennon Road. This was wide enough then for only one vehicle so the traffic was controlled by a system of gates. There were no sides on the bus and as I sat on the outside seat at the front it seemed as if my feet were often dangling over a deep ravine beside the road. The driver was careful but fast because he knew the road and knew he would meet no oncoming traffic. The view from the top of the final zig-zag was really impressive.

The house we rented belonged to the Methodists, beside Easter School, an Anglican school for mountain children. Behind the cottage was a high hill from the top of which we could see Baguio on one side and the Trinidad Valley on the other. This fertile valley is famous for growing vegetables and strawberries. Fred Pucknell joined us for part of the time. One morning we took a taxi to the foot of Mt. Sto. Tomas, seven kilometers out of Baguio. From that point, Fred and I followed an eight kilometer trail to the top where there was a rest house. We were tired and hungry when we arrived, so we went inside to get warm and eat our lunch. It was a mistake—while we ate the clouds rolled in. We really never had a glimpse of the view over the surrounding mountains or the Lingayen Gulf below. We met some survey men there, and they offered to lead us to an Igorot burial cave on the way down. The entrance was quite low, but inside we could stand up amid the skulls and skeletons. Chiefs had apparently been buried in a crude coffin made from a hollowed-out pine tree. Fred remarked that if he would have such a skull in his room in China he would never have had to worry about thieves! The mountain people were formerly headhunters. So to make sure we retained that essential part of our anatomy, we did not disturb anything. In later years we climbed

Sto. Tomas on a bright moonlight night to see the gorgeous sunrise over the mountains. Then after breakfast at the rest house we would return home by early afternoon.

On the way home from Baguio the train was very crowded. Anna went to the restroom. Almost immediately a woman began knocking on the door. Naturally Anna thought it was someone who was impatient so didn't respond. Then they called me to intervene. The woman was quite plump and because the train was crowded she was standing. When Anna closed the door it caught a part of her fleshy arm and she couldn't get free. Above the noise of the train and the crowd, I at last got Anna's attention by shouting. When the woman was released there was a long ridge of flesh on her upper arm. It really was her own fault for leaning on the door jamb.

A year previous to that we had begun to buy a house five miles from downtown Manila in the suburb of San Juan. It was a newly developed area where the Wightmans had purchased a home. A gift from a good friend provided the down payment and the monthly installments were less than we had been paying in rent. One reason for the move was that Leonard had developed rickets and we needed a place where he could get out in the sunshine more. With our own place I could improve it myself as we were able.

After our trip to Baguio we began to plan for furlough. In those days missionaries were expected to stay for a term of seven years. Some brethren in Britain expressed their concern that we were only in our sixth year. In January Fred Pucknell decided to return to China as things seemed quieter there. In the meantime Jim Buckley had been married to Margaret Dryden from Seattle. Our family had been friends for some years with the Dryden family. They were planning to stay on for the present in Manila, so we thought it would be a good time to get away.

10

OUR FIRST FURLOUGH

"He said to them, 'Come with me by yourselves to a quiet place and get some rest." (Mark 6:31)

In faith we made booking to go on furlough in April, 1928, sailing on a Japanese ship from Hongkong to San Francisco; but it was not until the day we left Manila that we had all the money for our fare. We had packed and prepared, trusting the Lord to supply this need. With the money on hand in the morning we booked on a freighter leaving that afternoon for Hongkong. We faced two nights lay-over in Hongkong with no money to spare for hotel accommodation. Arriving late one afternoon we were able to stay on board until the next morning. At that time Leonard was three and Kenneth a year and a half. We picked up our tickets from the Japanese shipping company. They were not inclined to let us on board that day as no meals and no service would be provided until noon the following day. Our combination of prayer to God and pleas to the agent won his consent. We learned later that other passengers were refused such an arrangement.

Before the days of air travel and jet lag, the three weeks on board ship were the opportunity to rest. Furlough time is a wonderful change but hardly a rest. Folks say, "Oh, you must get a rest while you are home—would you be able to speak to our women's group tomorrow afternoon?" Considerable travelling, sleeping in strange beds, eating too much, holding meetings, and giving reports make for a very busy time. Yet it is worthwhile! Interest is aroused and prayer stimulated and the Lord's people blessed, we hope. It is good for the missionary to get away from the immediate contact of the work for it affords an opportunity to look at the work from a distance. This provides a different perspective and gives new ideas for the future.

Len and Ken were favorites on that trip. The children had their lunch before the adults so we had to lock them in the cabin while we ate. One noon Ken was missing. Two passengers, single ladies, joined us in the search. He was found on the upper boat deck with a Japanese passenger. One of the girls scolded him for taking "our" baby without telling us! It was a wonderfully calm voyage. Some days the Pacific lived up to its name, hardly a ripple on the water. Strolling on deck one day, Ken slipped away from us for a moment. To our consternation he was kneeling on a place for the ropes, looking down at the water. As I jumped to grab him I realized I needed to get a good hold lest in my rush I should cause him to fall. Later on we got a harness so Anna could hold both boys on a leash.

Usually on such trips there were other missionaries, so we had opportunities for fellowship and Bible study together. A Sunday service was arranged for all who cared to attend. That was when second-class passengers were allowed to mingle with the first-class. On later trips we traveled by freighters with less than a dozen passengers and less opportunity for fellowship. On one ship Anna and I were the only passengers, and Anna the only woman apart from some Chinese steerage passengers.

We landed in San Francisco and spent a few days staying with friends in Oakland. Ken was fascinated with the pull-down blinds which would, to his delight, roll up when released. The summer was spent in Victoria with my sisters, staying in the home I had built. This afforded time to visit assemblies on Vancouver Island as one of my old friends loaned me his car for most of the time. After Labor Day Anna crossed the country with the boys going directly to Buffalo, while I stopped to visit various cities on the way across. Crossing the Canadian prairies the boys saw snow for the first time. They decided it looked like sugar. When the train was due to stop for an engine and crew change, Anna took them for a little walk. "May we walk on it?"

Our First Furlough

Although accustomed to brown-skinned Filipinos, they had not seen blacks before. With a loud voice, Ken asked, "Is that dirty man going to make our beds?"

It had taken all the money we had to pay our fares home, so there was nothing extra for new outfits. We didn't want to look shabby as we travelled around. We remembered that a missionary from China arrived home and when she was in Victoria she looked so dowdy that the sisters bought her an entirely new outfit. She arrived at the school in Brooklyn when we were there, wearing the old dowdy dress. Whether she did this intentionally to call attention to herself, or whether she just liked that old dress, we don't know. In our case, we just left this matter with the Lord. In Portland, a brother took me to a clothing store and bought me a new suit, which was greatly appreciated. In Los Angeles just as we were leaving to speak at Avenue 54 Gospel Hall, John Murset stepped in from next door with an almost new Stetson hat. He had picked it up on the highway where it had probably blown out of a passing car. He said, "This doesn't fit me, perhaps it will fit you." I replied, "If the Lord intended it for me, it will fit me." And it did! But I almost lost it that same evening. After the service I went to the cloakroom to get my new hat. Since almost everyone had already left there was only one hat left—and it definitely wasn't mine! It evidently had been used for some time. Explaining my dilemma to one of the brethren, he said, "I can guess who has your hat!" Going outside some of the men were standing on the sidewalk talking. Going to one old gentleman, my friend said, "Brother, are you sure you have your own hat?" "Of course," was the reply. "Would you mind looking?" The old gent removed "my" hat, looked at it incredulously and said, "Well, I never! This isn't my hat!" Right away I put my name in my hat in case there should be another such incident.

It was Thanksgiving before I reached Buffalo, in time for the conference there. Much of the winter and spring was given to travelling and having meetings. Most of the time I was alone as it was too hard to travel with children. We did go together once to the New Jersey area to stay with the Will McKellin's who had been at Brooklyn with us. After a day or two their boy was sick and since it might be measles we moved over to New York City. Next day we learned the McKellin boy had measles and chicken pox, so Anna hurried back to Buffalo. There they both had both sicknesses, not very severe but bad enough to keep them in.

That spring I was privileged to spend a weekend in Baltimore with Major and Mrs. Barlow and their son Erle. It was a thrill to hear from them the story of the early days of the work in the Philippines. They continued to be faithful prayer partners in the work. Major Barlow and later his son Erle were a great help in the assemblies in the Baltimore area until the Lord took them home to Himself. Major Moses Barlow passed away March 14, 1934, and was buried in Arlington National Cemetery. On our visit to Baltimore in early 1977, it was a great joy to me that Erle's son opened the meeting for me in one of the chapels. (Major Moses Barlow has often been confused with Capt. John Barlow, a marine captain who was vitally interested in missionary work in New York and later in Toronto and whose son, Dr. John Barlow was editor of MISSIONS magazine. These men were not related, except in the bonds of a common faith.)

In May, 1929, on our cross-country trip we arranged to stop over in Chicago for the annual meeting of the Chicago Missionary Service Committee. In the evening meeting another missionary (who shall remain unnamed) and I were to give reports and be followed by a devotional challenge by T. B. Gilbert. That would allow us 25 minutes each. The first speaker would have been wise to stop when his time was up but he rambled on like a car that has lost its brakes. T. B. Gilbert suggested I take what was left after the first speaker had taken 45 minutes. However, I thought the devotional challenge was important. Also, I counted on the psychological effect I would gain by taking only five minutes to relate one story. I felt sorry for the other missionary as he had only harmed himself.

After a return visit to Victoria, we sailed from San Francisco by Japanese liner to Hongkong, with stops at Yokohama, Kobe, Nagasaki, and Shanghai. From Hongkong we came by a President liner to Manila and one of our fellow passengers was Dr. Frank Laubach who later became well known through his literacy movement.

Getting settled back into our home was a bit of a chore as it required a lot of cleaning and building of cupboards. We were able to get a Ford sedan for P350.00. At the same time we were

Our First Furlough

praying about our next sphere of service. There was no need for us in the Walled City work since the Shepherds were helping the Wightman's there. Both of them were also involved in the huge task of reprinting Bibles in the Philippine languages for the American Bible Society. Perhaps I can digress at this point to write something about the work of Bible Societies here.

During the Spanish times, no Protestant missionary work was allowed. Some Filipino revolutionists had been exiled to Spain. Through them the British and Foreign Bible Society began preliminary work on Philippine translations. One of those involved in this was a Spanish priest, Padre Lallave, who had been some years in Pangasinan. There he had acquired a Spanish Bible and had begun preaching some of the truth he learned there. He was charged with heresy and forced to return to Spain. Remembering his friends in Pangasinan he translated most of the New Testament into that language, encouraged by the Bible Society.

Meanwhile, God was preparing another man to carry the Word to the Islands. A young Spaniard named Castells had been brought to a knowledge of the truth through Dr. Eric Lund (later a missionary to the Philippines), in Barcelona. In 1888, Lallave and Castells went together to Manila with a supply of Scriptures. They were warned of the risk they were running, once the reason for their visit should become known. Leaving their boxes in customs they booked into the Oriente Hotel in Intramuros. Within a week they both became violently ill. It was said to be typhoid but poisoning was suspected. Lallave, because of his age, died and for days his body lay unburied because of the hatred of the friars. Finally the British consul intervened and gained permission for him to be buried in the small Protestant cemetery in Makati. Castells recovered and sold a few Bibles he had in his baggage but then was arrested as a spy. He was banished and told never to return. The boxes of Scriptures were returned to Singapore where they spent a decade gathering dust.

Three weeks after the U.S. Forces captured Manila from the Spanish, the agent of the British and Foreign Bible Society in Singapore landed in Manila with those Scriptures. For the first time, free entry of Scriptures was allowed and also the sale of God's Word. When the agent went north to Pangasinan the demand was so great that the agent had to take refuge in a house and sell through a barred window.

The American Bible Society established an agency in November, 1899, and the two societies divided the task of translation and publishing. Soon there were seven complete Bibles and smaller portions in various Philippine languages. By mutual agreement the British Society withdrew in 1919 to avoid overlapping while the American Society withdrew from Korea. Translation was not only difficult but sometimes dangerous. A teacher who was assisting in the Panayan translation was warned to break off relations with the Protestants. Because he refused he was brutally murdered. On one of the Islands two colporters set off across the Island by a lonely trail and were never heard from again.

Some languages do not have very precise words for colors. When translating Matthew's Gospel, the translators were not sure about the best way to translate "purple robe." Taking a piece of purple cloth they went around asking people what color it was. Most replied, "kulay ng ube." Ube is a root crop with a deep purple color. This was what the translators adopted, though the modern version uses an expression meaning "deep red."

For several years the Scriptures in Philippine languages were being printed on a Christian press in Yokohama. In the great earthquake and fire there in 1923 that press was destroyed. The charred remains of the proprietor were identified only by a bunch of keys beside them. The vault in which the lead plates were stored contained only a few inches of molten lead on the floor. This threw a heavy burden upon the Secretary in Manila, Bruce Cameron, a good friend of ours. Some mats for making plates were available in Manila or New York for temporary needs. However, it was decided to make some badly needed revisions in most languages.

Early in our second term I was preparing translations of booklets for the Scripture Gift Mission in London. When we first came to the Philippines, a friend in Victoria wrote asking them to send us a grant of free booklets. That was the beginning of our fellowship with SGM which still continues. In 1927 Mr. Francis Brading of SGM visited us, and in more recent years we have had visits by Mr. Ronald A. Young. We have had a part in

Our First Furlough

the preparation of most of the Tagalog booklets they have published. Just before the new translation was ready for printing in 1933, I asked Mr. Cameron if I could have access to the galley proofs so that a new booklet would be up-to-date. I soon noticed a number of errors, not only typographical, but some that were more serious. I drew the attention of Mr. Cameron to these and it was discovered that one pastor who was supposed to have gone over the proofs had failed to do so, even though he had given his OK. It is difficult to understand how anyone who claims to be in God's service could be so negligent in dealing with the holy Scriptures.

At that time, I was slowly recuperating from a time of sickness. Mr. Cameron suggested that we go to Baguio for three months. The Bible Society would pay the rent of a house and I would devote that time to reading over the Tagalog manuscript. This arrangement had advantages for both of us. It was not only typographical mistakes that I corrected, but notes were made of anything that seemed to me to be dubious and these were referred to Dr. McGill, a Presbyterian missionary who had a foremost part in the translation. In later years, Dr. and Mrs. McGill were interned by the Japanese at Los Banos Concentration Camp as we were. Dr. McGill passed away there on account of malnutrition, and I was one of the pallbearers.

One incident of how God uses His Word is worth repeating. On the island of Bohol there was a godly doctor, Dr. James Graham. He built a hospital there and every patient when he or she left for home was given a New Testament. A man from up in the mountains brought his daughter for treatment and heard the Gospel and received a New Testament. Nothing more was heard from that family. Six years later a colporter was visiting a village, but the people were not interested. They averred that "that book makes men crazy." The astonished colporter asked what they meant. They told him that up the mountain was a barrio where they had such a book. Now they have no cockpit, they don't drink "tuba" (a wine made from coconuts), and they even go to town to pay their taxes. Such "insanity" deserved a closer investigation. The colporter found a congregation of believers in that barrio with a tattered New Testament. They were delighted at the opportunity to purchase the entire Bible.

In the 1950's when the Philippine Bible Society decided to

prepare a version of the New Testament in up-to-date Tagalog, I was asked to join the committee. My knowledge of Greek is very meager, and I am not a linguist. However, through the years I have devoted much time to the study of the Scriptures, and with the help of many writings endeavored to probe the real meaning of the words used. Later on when work was proceeding on the Old Testament I was asked to read through the new translation. It was also my privilege to attend a translators' seminar for a month in Baguio and to get to know such experts as Dr. Eugene Nida and others.

This was at the time when Roman Catholics were cooperating in translating the Bible. Some brethren in other lands were very fearful about this cooperation. Personally, it seemed that the priests had a scholastic advantage over their Protestant co-laborers, some of whom had a liberal background. The new version of the Tagalog Bible is now published, both with and without the Apocrypha. For the most part it is considerably more readable than the old version. Old grammatical forms which are seldom used have been eliminated.

My concern has not been so much with the Roman Catholic participation in translation. It is a welcome change to know that the Bible is no longer a forbidden book to the rank and file, but is being read and studied by Roman Catholics. My concern has been in regard to the modern theories of translation. The theory of dynamic equivalence means that we endeavor to ascertain what the Biblical writers meant and then transfer this into acceptable and understandable equivalents in the receptor language. This is certainly a vast improvement over the older way of an almost literal translation, word for word. Yet though these theories certainly do have merit, what perturbs me is the tendency to ignore verbal inspiration. For many, of course, verbal inspiration is "old hat." But the precision of Scripture is often a delight to reverent students of God's Word. Thus, in new translations many of the repetitions which indicated divine emphasis have been regarded as superfluous. In the poetical books some rich meaning has been sacrificed, it seems, for the sake of a poetic style in Tagalog. Well, it is impossible to come up with a translation that will satisfy everybody. In the multiplicity of modern English versions there are none which are sure to satisfy everyone.

Our First Furlough

Through all of our missionary service we have been convinced of the value and importance of the Scriptures. The truth of Psalm 119:130 has been proven again and again, "The entrance of your words gives light; it gives understanding to the simple."

In our visits to the Santol Sanitarium, I once talked with a man who said that he believed in Christ. Yet there was no indication that he had experienced salvation. I decided to probe a little and asked him, "Are your sins forgiven?" He was not at all sure about that. So I showed him Acts 10:43, "All the prophets testify about him that everyone who believes in him receives forgiveness of sins through his name." I explained what it means to believe in Christ and pointed out that our part is to believe and God's part is to forgive. He was keenly interested, so again I asked him, "Do you believe in Christ, that He died on the Cross to bear the punishment you deserve for your sins?" He said he believed, so again I asked "Are your sins forgiven?" He was not sure. I had him read the verse several times, each time asking him if his sins were forgiven. Then I saw his face light up; it was almost as if someone had turned on a light. "If this is true, then my sins are forgiven." He was assured that it was true because it was the word of God. When I returned the following week he greeted me with a smile. "Are your sins still forgiven," I asked. "Oh, yes," he replied, "and please go to that man over in that bed. He too wants to know about forgiveness of sins." So I knew the work of grace was real for he had already been witnessing about his newfound joy.

In that same hospital, Fred Pucknell and I walked into a room of a patient who we learned had been on the editorial staff of a popular Manila Weekly. As we handed him some literature, he recognized that we were missionaries. Picking up a magazine he said, "Perhaps you can answer my questions. I have many doubts about immortality and the hereafter." The magazine articles had not helped him. It is no wonder he was thinking along those lines because it was evident he had little hope of recovery from tuberculosis. Fred said, "Before we discuss those questions, you need first to settle your relationship with God through Christ." After a few further visits, he accepted Christ as his Savior. So on another visit we said to him, "Now that you trusted Christ as your Savior we are now in a position to discuss those doubts that you had before." His unforgettable reply was, "Since I trusted in Christ I have had no more doubts." Not that he knew much more about immortality or the hereafter, but he knew Christ. The entrance of God's Word had given him light.

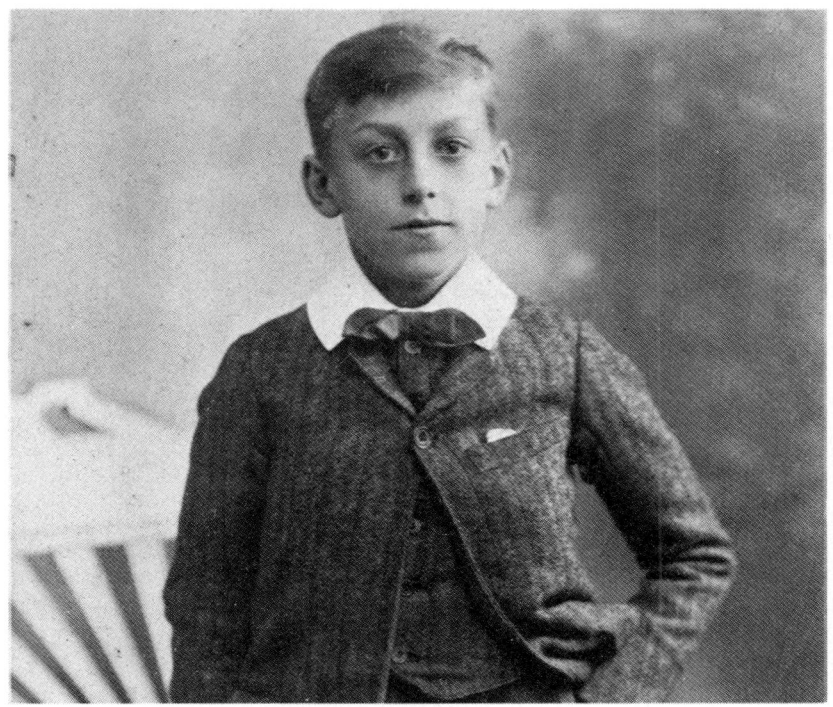
Cyril Brooks as a boy in England, at about the age of 10.

Cyril and Anna Brooks on their wedding day, September 20, 1922.

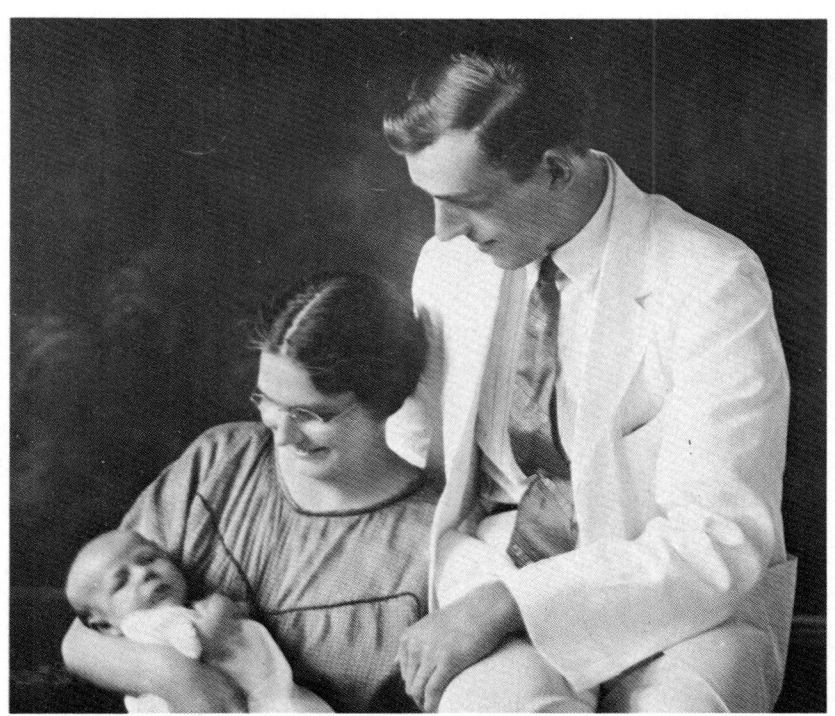
With their first son, Leonard, in 1924.

Family photo, about 1935. Children: Kenneth, Rose and Leonard.

Brooks family with U.S. servicemen on a picnic in 1940.

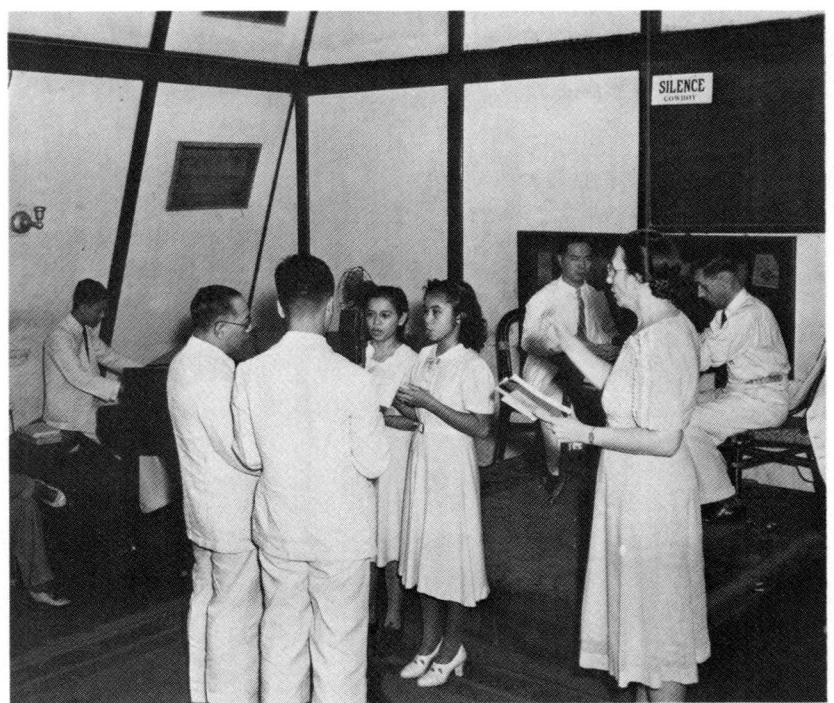

Broadcasting from the studio of KZRM Manila in 1940. Cyril Brooks is seated at the right.

Brooks family in the USA after the Japanese internment camp experience. (1945)

Sulpicio Guillen the first convert in assembly work in 1913. He died in 1978 and his wife Irene died in 1984. This picture of the Guillen family was taken in August of 1965.

The San Juan Gospel Hall, around 1952.

A group of young people, from the San Juan Gospel Hall, prepared to distribute literature.

The San Juan Gospel Chapel in 1977, formerly the Gospel Hall.

San Juan ladies with Anna Brooks.

Bible School of the Air broadcast with Ken Brooks, Ken Engle and Cyril Brooks. (DZAS, Manila)

Anna and Cyril Brooks at their desks in the Bible School of the Air office in 1955.

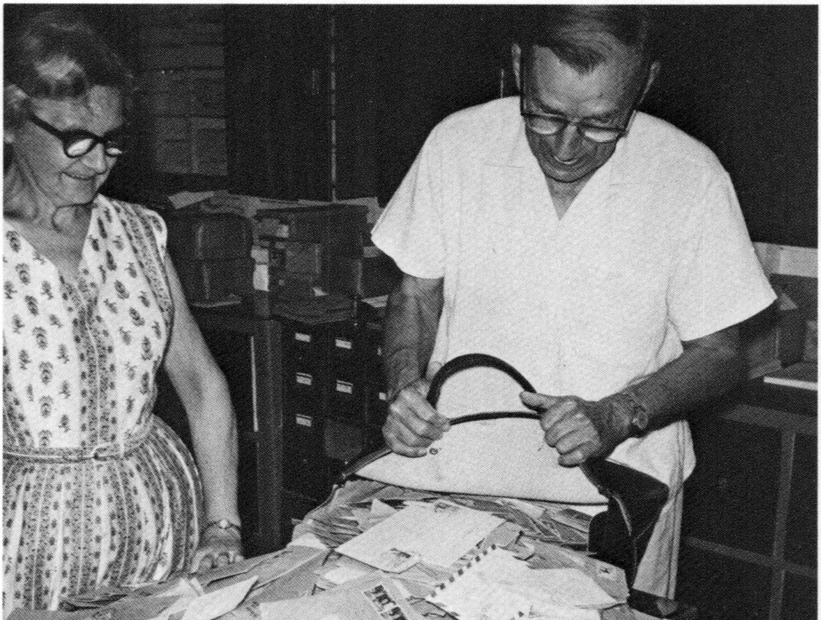

Anna and Cyril Brooks as they view the Bible School of the Air mail.

Cyril with a display of the correspondence courses.

A group of believers in Nahapay, Iloilo. Elino Aragon, director of the Bible School of the Air, is on the left. These believers are meeting as a result of taking courses from the Bible School of the Air. Iloilo is in the Visayas, and is quite a distance from Manila.

Faith Academy, the school for missionaries' children near Manila. Cyril Brooks served for many years on the board. Several of the missionaries of Christian Missions In Many Lands have served on the faculty and as houseparents over the years.

Cyril and Anna Brooks on their 40th wedding anniversary in 1962.

CMML missionaries in Manila in 1962. Ken and Mary Lou Engle, Charles and Gladys Cox, Len and Esther Brooks, Cyril and Anna, Glynn and Lela Dean & Milton and Marjorie Haack.

A group of CMML missionaries in 1982.

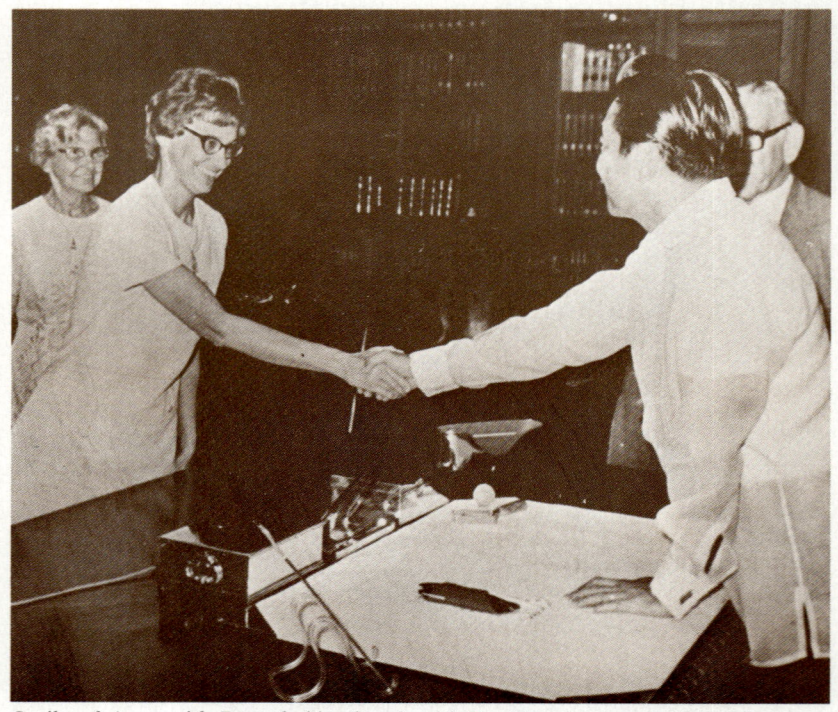
Cyril and Anna with Rose shaking hands with President Marcos in September of 1972. Cyril and Anna were honored for their 50th wedding anniversary and 50 years in the Philippines.

Bible School graduates at the Emmaus Bible Camp in 1983. This is a short term Bible school held each year at the Bible camp.

Rudy and Guadalupe Ponce de Leon. Rudy has taught at the Bible School and also directed it. Guadalupe is a medical doctor. They have been active in the youth work over the years.

Cyril and Anna's 60th wedding anniversary celebrated in Manila in 1982. David (grandson) and Lois, Len and Esther, Elaine and Ken, Ruth Shannon (niece) and Rose.

Anna and Cyril in Baguio City.

11

THE BEGINNING OF WORK IN SAN JUAN

"Therefore, my dear brothers, stand firm. Let nothing move you. Always give yourselves fully to the work of the Lord, because you know that your labor in the Lord is not in vain." (1 Cor. 15:58)

Now after that lengthy detour through "Bibleland," let us get back to our search for the next sphere of service. Our home was in San Juan, a suburb of Manila, but only a block or two from the boundary of another suburb, Mandaluyong. It seemed logical that we should be working near where we lived. Along with prayer for the Lord's guidance, I set out first to survey Mandaluyong (formerly known as San Felipe Neri). This was done by going around from house to house with Gospel literature. While we were noting what response there was to this, we could also look for evidence of Christian work. Beside the large Roman Catholic church and an Aglipayan church (a split-off from the Roman Catholics at the turn of the century), there was a Methodist church. Also we heard about others possibly working there.

So we turned our attention to San Juan where there was apparently then no Protestant work. There was a Methodist chapel in Sta. Mesa, a mile or more from San Juan. After waiting upon the Lord in prayer, we believed we should make an effort to evangelize this town. In November 1929 we rented the ground floor of a house on J. Basa Street. This was right beside the public market and faced on a vacant lot which was opposite the San Juan Elementary School. The Agora building now occupies the vacant lot. Thursday afternoons when school was dismissed we had children's meetings and once the attendance went up to 200, which was a bit more than we could properly handle. Sunday mornings I would go through the market with tracts and mimeographed invitations to a Sunday evening meeting. Some of the brethren from Intramuros Chapel came out to help us but the response was quite small.

However, one evening we were heartened by the influx of a group of about thirty who came together and seemed quite interested. We learned that they were members of the Methodist church but were disgruntled with the pastor because he so seldom visited them in San Juan. This group was led by a woman of uncertain age—she didn't know herself! Timotea Carreon, Tea for short (pronounced Tay-a), was certainly a believer in Christ, and she had rounded up a number of relatives and neighbors to visit our service. Soon she was praising the Lord that someone had come to her town to preach the Gospel. The Methodist pastor, of course, was not happy with this turn of events and he remonstrated with me for stealing his sheep. I assured him they came of their own accord, not from any specific invitation from me. I suggested that if he fed his flock good spiritual food, his sheep would stay with him. I doubt whether he knew how to feed himself, let alone others.

Tea informed me that at her expense a small bamboo and thatch chapel had been erected in the Salapan district (located where the elementary school is now). "Would we go and have children's classes there some afternoon?" So each Friday afternoon we taught the children choruses, verses, and a Bible story. Tea rounded up the children, literally running around the area to do so in spite of her age. Then she stood back and beamed with delight that her chapel was being used. Almost every week we would find a little gift on the seat of the car, a few eggs, ears of corn, a bunch of bananas.

We relocated in another storefront on N. Domingo, the main street, where it would be easier to get passersby to come in. Mr. Taylor, secretary of the Army and Navy YMCA at Fort McKinley, had given us a surplus army movie screen. It was of heavy

The Beginning of Work in San Juan

canvas, silvered on one side and quite large so that we had used it sometimes as a tent. I got some sailmakers to shape it into a tank and put eyelets around the top edge. With a carpenter we made four wooden sides which could be bolted together. Thus we had a portable baptistry. Among the first to be baptized in it was Gregorio, the carpenter—he had been making his own burial place! Tea and some of her family were also baptized there. We used it for the first time on August 31, 1931. As I had coated the outside with tar, it was quite waterproof.

Another who was baptized there was Trinidad Dayton, a Filipino married to an American. Though he had a responsible position on a sugar estate in Canlubang, Laguna, he maintained a home in San Juan. Trining (as we know her) was friendly with Pelagia Alfonso, daughter of Tea. One day Stevie, the son of Trining was sick with a fever so Pelagia suggested they have prayer for him. It was a common practice then to call some Christians together to pray for a sick person. Trining didn't object though she was not accustomed to this practice. The next day Stevie was better. But it was not so much the answer to prayer that aroused the interest of Trining, it was the way they prayed. "You talk to God as if you know Him and as if He is right here." They assured her they did have a personal knowledge of God. Trining decided to attend the services with them, and one Sunday during the singing of a hymn she accepted Christ. Some years later a visiting friend of ours asked her, "How did you find Christ?" Trining's reply was, "Oh! I didn't find Him, He found me!"

Gregorio, whom I have mentioned, had a bad habit of nearly always being late in getting to the services. One year some of his children were to have a part in the Christmas program but they never showed up. After the program was over and most of the people had left and we were just about to lock the door, Gregorio arrived with his children! He was not a very stable Christian and after a time he left us to go to the Iglesia ni Cristo, a sect started by Felix Manalo. Talking with Gregorio one day, I asked him why he was going there since they deny the Deity of Christ. He said they had more discipline than we did. Asked about this, he said that every Saturday their preachers went to the home of Mr. Manalo and were given their sermon material for Sunday. So it was the same sermon in every church. I replied that in the penitentiary the discipline of the government was most evident, but they had no freedom. We preferred the liberty of the Holy Spirit to prevail in our services.

For some years we carried on classes for children in different barrios each week. A favorite chorus then was "Joy, joy, joy, with joy my heart is ringing." So I got a new name; "Mr. Joy, joy." Many years later sitting in my car near the market, two women passed and I heard one say, "That's Mr. Joy, joy!" For a time an old lady who had been discharged from the Culion Leper Colony helped in this work and later on we were able to enlist the help of some of the young women in San Juan. One day one of these was trying to list the names of the children and was having difficulty getting the surname of one child. She asked the girl whose daughter she was, to which the child replied, "I am the daughter of my mother!"

During a typhoon in 1932 the little chapel that Tea had built was blown down. There was a lot of damage but Tea and her husband's ramshackle home just out of town stood amid more substantial houses which blew down. Said Tea to her neighbors, "You prayed to the saints, but we prayed to the Lord and He protected us." She was practically illiterate though she could read, but I doubt that she ever read anything much more than her Bible. She went to visit Trining's mother who had recently been saved and found her chewing beetlenut. There were chairs to sit on but the old ladies preferred squatting on the floor. Said Tea to Antonina, "Your body is the temple of the Holy Spirit, you should keep it clean for Him." That was the end of that dirty habit.

Tea had been saving from her very meager income. When she had money she would buy some GI roofing or some hardwood posts. So in early 1933 she had some men erect the frame of a chapel on a small lot on H. Lozada Street. Then she said to me, "Instead of paying rent for a chapel, why don't you finish up what I have started." So we were able to buy some materials and on July 4th we had a working bee, a cooperative effort which the Tagalogs call "bayanihan" (a famous Filipino dance troupe adopted this as their name). The lower parts of the walls were adobe stone and the upper part wooden siding. The men and women worked with a will all day. The women prepared a delicious dinner as well as snacks. There was a happy spirit of

The Beginning of Work in San Juan

fellowship and by nightfall the walls were up. Later a cement floor, windows, and doors were added. It was only a hundred yards or so from Trining Dayton's house and she gave permission to have some of the Sunday school classes at her place.

At this time our home was about two kilometers from the main part of San Juan. It was in a new housing area with plenty of empty lots around, an ideal place for our boys to play and roam. We could not afford to build a fence or a wall around our property, so growing a garden was largely an exercise in futility. One of our neighbors had goats which roamed the neighborhood, and they devoured anything we attempted to grow. I got hold of some cactus full of thorns which could only be handled with gloves. I thought the goats wouldn't eat those! How wrong I was! They found them to be a luscious meal! One of the goats was a big billy goat to which our house-boy, Vicente at the time, had a special aversion. One day Vicente spotted "billy" enter our neighbor's yard as the gate had been left open. The neighbor's dogs were sleeping and Vicente sneaked up and shut the gate (unknown to us). When the dog awoke, "billy" trotted towards where he had come in but found he couldn't get out there. Vicente's glee was great—until I made him go and open the gate and apologize to our neighbor.

Missionary work isn't all preaching and teaching. One night, some years later, I heard a commotion in the yard. A bull had entered our yard and Gregorio who was then our helper was trying to get him out. In the chase the bull ran over the septic tank. The collapse of the cover under the weight of the bull left him and us in a predicament. Gregorio got a rope around the bull's horns but our efforts to pull him out were ineffectual. Jumping in the car I went to the "municipio" to enlist the aid of some policemen. The only one there couldn't leave, but he told me where I could probably find two men on their beat. I found them in a primitive barber shop sound asleep on benches. Having aroused them from their slumbers, we drove home and with their help extricated the bull from his messy environment. He showed no appreciation for all our efforts! He was very indignant and with difficulty we tethered him to a house post until morning. The policemen said to take him to the municipio then. Gregorio went ahead and I followed in my car. Alternately the bull would refuse to budge and then dash after Gregorio. Delivered to the police, I asked them not to release him until the owner made some compensation. When I returned the bull was gone and the owner refused to do anything.

During our first term I was asked to conduct services for Filipino veterans who were patients at the Santol Tuberculosis Infirmary (later Quezon Institute). This was an extension work of the Army and Navy YMCA which was turned over to me. Later this led to a program of visitation through the whole place. Anna and I went every Tuesday afternoon to distribute reading material and to talk to the patients who showed any interest. Sometimes we were able to take small bouquets of flowers too. Patients were mostly long term and in addition to the occasional believer we had the joy of leading others to Christ. A man who was dying of T.B. had a bright testimony and when I prayed with him he would, with great effort, say, "When I am weak, then am I strong." Some, of course, were unresponsive, like the man who would not believe in God's love because he too was dying and leaving behind a family. An American confided that his case was hopeless; he had sinned the unpardonable sin, he thought. His sin was great but I assured him not beyond the reach of God's grace. He did not accept Christ, and when I returned the next week he had passed into eternity. Should I have been more persistent in my appeal?

One of those saved there was Mr. Candido Aguilar who had been a sales manager for Singer Sewing Machine. He made a partial recovery but suffered a great deal at the hands of the Japanese police during the war because of his contacts with the guerillas. After the war he was a great help in the work at Binangonan and Tanay.

We often had open-air meetings in different parts of San Juan as we endeavored to reach the townspeople with the Gospel. At one time we had two weeks of nightly evangelistic meetings in the little chapel. For the first week there was no response. We had invited a preacher friend, Mr. Gebala, to preach the Word. After one week he came to me and was frustrated because he felt he had no liberty in preaching. Something was wrong so he thought he should not continue. I urged him to continue because I felt sure that the problem was not with him but with the believers. There was some disagreement among them and there seemed to be two factions. So after the Sunday evening meeting

The Beginning of Work in San Juan

I asked them to all go with me to the basement of Mrs. Dayton's house where we would try to unravel this problem among ourselves.

After some discussion and even some argument, one of the young women replied to accusations some were making regarding her. While she spoke, she had what seemed to be an epileptic attack. Now that I have had more experience I am inclined to think it was a demonic attack. There never has been any recurrence. We took her to a doctor and then to our home where she recovered after a few days. The shock of this experience seemed to awaken the believers to a sense of their own failure and a better spirit prevailed.

As a result, in the second week we saw some blessing. One of those saved was the sister of Trining Dayton. Dominga Capati was a good golf player and went on to become ladies' champion which she held for several years here in the Philippines. Unfortunately, she did not take a stand on playing on Sunday and golf took a larger place in her life than the Lord. She had represented the Canlubang Sugar Estate in playing golf. When she passed away a few years ago the Estate took care of the funeral arrangements, with a priest to officiate at the graveside. The family wanted a Protestant service so the owner of the Estate compromised, "Let both take part." The only service was at the grave side, so I asked the Filipino priest if he had any preference who should go first. He suggested that I should. There was a large crowd, people from the Estate and sports writers. I took the opportunity to preach the Gospel and spoke in Tagalog which aroused more attention. The priest followed and all his service was in Latin. Later on we heard that the son of the owner of the Estate was disgusted with the priest's performance. "The American spoke in our language but our Filipino priest spoke a foreign language."

On the last afternoon of our evangelistic campaign, Brother Gebala gave an invitation for anyone who was willing to trust Christ to stand. Almost right away a woman, Felisa Mallari, sitting near the front, stood up. Her husband had not been as interested as she, but that afternoon he wanted to see what was going on. So he slipped into a seat in the corner on the back row. Nicolas was like Zaccheus in that he was a short man and also curious. When the preacher remarked that one had stood up,

Nicolas wondered who it could be. His curiosity led him to stand up and to his surprise it was his wife who was standing. The preacher, not knowing he stood out of curiosity, expressed his thanks that a man in the back row had also stood up. He was not saved that day but it was not long before he was. Soon after his conversion, working on a job as a carpenter, he was being teased by his workmates about becoming a Protestant. "Don't you know," they said, "the Protestants are divided into many different branches. The Roman Catholic church is one; it must be the right one." Being a young Christian, Nicolas didn't know how to answer but asked the Lord for help. They were sitting in the shade of a large mango tree as they ate their lunch. Pointing to a telephone pole nearby, he said, "Look at that pole! It is all one—no branches! But it is dead! Where do we come for shade and fruit? To this mango tree with its many branches, for it is alive."

In those early years of the work in San Juan we were often distressed and discouraged because of the immaturity of many of the believers. They were so often like the Corinthians. "Brothers, I could not address you as spiritual but as worldly—mere infants in Christ. I gave you milk, not solid food, for you were not yet ready for it. Indeed, you are still not ready. You are still worldly. For since there is jealousy and quarreling among you, are you not worldly? Are you not acting like mere men?" (1 Cor. 3:1-3). So often the things they were quarreling about seemed so trivial and childish.

One evening on our way home from prayer meeting, we gave a lift to one of the men. He was telling us about some of these difficulties and problems. After he got out of the car and we drove on, I was feeling very sorry for myself and very much discouraged. What was the use of going on! I thought, "If they want to squabble over such childish matters, I think I'll leave them to do it on their own. I'll leave them and start up a new work somewhere else. I just can't put up with them." Then as I drove on it seemed I heard the Lord speaking, not audibly but very clearly. "They are my children and I put up with them." Still feeling very sorry for myself, I thought, "Well, Lord, if you can endure them, then I guess I'll have to as well." But the Lord wasn't through with me yet, for again I heard his voice, "Yes, and I put up with you too." That blow hit me where it hurts,

The Beginning of Work in San Juan

right on target. I got a fresh look at myself, my miserable self-pity and pride. How much had I been showing the Spirit of Christ to those young believers? Also I realized afresh the patient mercy and longsuffering grace of our Lord to one so unworthy.

It was during that second term, in the early 1930's, that we passed through times of severe testing financially. It was the time of the depression in the United States and many banks in the U.S. were failing. Early in 1934, I had several checks on U.S. Banks but the local bank would not accept them, even for collection. For all they knew the bank might have closed since the check was written a month earlier. Our good friend, Bruce Cameron of the American Bible Society, kindly came to our assistance. The Bible Society had received its annual subsidy before the bank failure, so they had substantial peso funds on hand here. He kindly accepted my checks and gave me the local currency. None of the checks were returned.

As a result of these critical times we were falling behind on our monthly installments on our home. We expected that the real estate company would foreclose on the mortgage. One day I called on the manager, P. D. Carman, and frankly told him our predicament and that I thought he would be warranted in foreclosing. He was very considerate. He said, "I don't consider myself a Christian, but I do have a heart for those in difficulty and I know you have been trying." Instead of foreclosing he arranged for the mortgage to be transferred and renegotiated by a Filipino bank. Since we were then British we could not have done this ourselves.

Later on we saw how the Lord was working in all these things. During the Japanese occupation all alien property was taken over by the Japanese. Even if the owners were allowed to stay in their own homes they had to pay rent to the Japanese. Whenever they questioned me as to who owned the property I always told them it was mortgaged to a Filipino bank. They never pursued the matter any further. However, the bank notified me that they needed to renew the mortgage as its time had expired. When I explained the situation, they told me to go home and they would notify me in due course, because the renewal of a mortgage had to be approved by the Japanese. They just let it ride because they didn't want to lose their claim on the property.

So we lived in the house rent free and no payments until we were interned. So even in those financial trials years before the Lord was providing for the future.

One evening chance visitors stopped by just at supper time. All we had to offer them was bread and butter and fried bananas. From my diary on August 12, 1936, I cull this, "No gifts. Stocks of food very low. Wonder what the Lord is trying to fit us for. Praise is indeed a sacrifice. He is able! Outlook couldn't be blacker." Then four days later on the 16th was this entry, "Received several gifts. Prayer heard." The Lord has graciously showed his great faithfulness to us through all the years. Praise his name!

On November 16, 1931, our daughter, Rose Ellen was born and named after her two grandmothers. At that time, Miss Jeannette Lape, a fellow missionary from Glendale, California, was living with us. Kenneth had expressed one day his desire to have a baby sister. Jeannette told him that babies come from God so he should ask God for a baby sister. This he did but for some time after there was no more mention of this desire. Jeannette said, "Ken, I don't hear you praying any more for a sister." He looked at her with wide-eyed surprise, "God doesn't forget! I asked Him once and that was enough; I don't want a dozen." As the time drew near, Anna wanted to prepare his mind to the possibility that the baby might be a boy, so she said, "Ken, if the Lord sends us another boy, we'll love him just the same, won't we?" To this she got the reply, "Indeed we won't, we'll send him back!" God honored a little child's faith—the new arrival was a girl.

12

A DECADE OF ACTIVITY

"God is able to make all grace abound to you, so that in all things at all times, having all that you need, you will abound in every good work." (2 Cor. 9:8)

The 1930's was a busy time, a decade of activity in the work of the Lord. As it commenced we were just getting started in the work in San Juan. Though we were away for furlough from 1937 to 1938, the work continued. It was during that furlough that Lutgardo Ramos went home to be with the Lord. We greatly missed this dear man of God just as we had earlier missed Brother Simeon Endaya. From the first we wanted to see the assembly truly indigenous, particularly with its own elders. In a pioneer work the missionary faces a dilemma. Should he continue to do almost everything himself? With his superior knowledge of the Word, he can probably do things better himself. However, there is danger of just bringing into another culture what he has been accustomed to in his own land. That is an area where he needs to be sure of the teaching of God's Word and not follow his own traditions. Or should he turn things over to the nationals, even though things may not go as smoothly or correctly, until they are better taught in the Word? We had no doubt the latter was the only way to build up an indigenous assembly.

As is so often the case, the women outnumbered the men and

were usually more active and more spiritual. Sometimes I wished some of the women were men! Why couldn't they pray in the prayer meeting? That question was solved by dividing into groups for prayer. After a time of Bible study, the prayer requests are presented. Then we break into groups of three or four, young and old, some in English and some in Tagalog. In this way all are involved and are able to take part. The whole group comes together for a final prayer.

Early in the work we started a custom which still continues. That is for the first week of the year there are prayer meetings every evening. In this way they try to establish a spiritual tone for the whole year and pray about the projected plans for the coming year. At the present time, they have national workers come in to give reports each evening so they can pray for the outreach in other areas. In one of those early series, I heard someone moving about during prayer time. This was not uncommon for people go out and come in or go to the window to spit. However, I did notice that three men who had never prayed before, prayed that evening. After the meeting old Tea informed me that she had gone to her husband (they rarely sat together) and nudged him to get up and pray. Then she went to the husband of her granddaughter and to some other relative. It may not have been the prompting of the Spirit but at least it was effectual.

That dear sister, Timotea, was unusual in her ways. She rarely missed a meeting. Sometimes she swam or waded across the stream when the bamboo footbridge had been washed out. She would go to her daughter's house to get dry clothes. On one occasion we were away for a little while. When we returned, Tea told us about a neighbor woman that she had led to the Lord. This woman was moving away and Tea thought she should be baptized. So Tea baptized her in the river! At every service she would say "Salamat sa Panginoon" (thank the Lord). At her husband's funeral I thought to myself "She won't say that today." I should have known better. After the committal service at the graveside, Tea took my hand, "Salamat sa Panginoon—he is with the Lord now." When she heard we were going on furlough, however, she was not so thankful until we assured her we would return. Perhaps the smallest gift but also the most precious was the one peso she gave us toward our fare. She

A Decade of Activity

wanted to bring chickens and other things to the ship until her family assured her we would be well fed on the ship. Once she did give us a kid of the goats which our houseboy killed and skinned.

In 1940, Morales Street near the chapel was being widened to become what is now Aurora Blvd. The widening would not involve the lot on which the chapel was built but would make it a corner lot which the owner wanted for his own use. The assembly decided to look for land to buy and found the present property on A. Lake Street. The first intention was to buy only the front half, but through the negligence of the agent we had to take the whole lot. In this God overruled because now even that is too small.

One afternoon we all banded together to help move a house on the property to another location. Long bamboo poles were tied under the house and scores of men lifted the house on those bamboos. Since I was a bit taller than the average Filipino it felt to me that the whole weight was on my shoulder! The old chapel was dismantled so as to use as much of the material as possible in rebuilding. In 1941 it was all enclosed but still had a dirt floor.

During the 1930's, in addition to the work at the chapel and the open-air meetings, there were children's classes as I have already mentioned. The weekly visits to the Santol Sanitarium have also been referred to earlier. Anna had a Bible class one evening a week in Abiertas' Home, a home for unwed mothers. Usually she took some girls from San Juan to help her. When we returned from furlough in 1929 we bought a second-hand Essex (only old-timers will remember those cars). It served us well but needed a lot of care. Once we were going to Baguio when suddenly there was a clatter under the hood and a terrible vibration. When we stopped to investigate we discovered that one of the four fan blades had broken off. Being a long way from any repair shop, I decided the only way to restore balance was to break off the opposite blade. By stopping at the bottom of the zig-zag on the Kennon Road and by draining our radiator and putting in cold water, we made it up the mountain without any difficulty.

Coming down on that trip, as we got to the lowlands, the differential gear was stripped. We were towed into a garage in a nearby town where the trouble was diagnosed. No parts were available there, so we left the car and travelled home by bus and train. My mechanic advised that a new part, even if we could find such, wouldn't mesh with the old gears. With his help we were able to find a complete unit for that old model in a junk shop. I carried it up north and had it installed, and it worked perfectly.

So when Anna went out alone at night, the boys would say, "Let's pray that Mom doesn't have any car trouble." I *wasn't* the man who said to his wife, "I've had this car all these years and never had a wreck," and she replied, "You've had this wreck all these years and never had a car!" I hit a carabao on the rump once. Fortunately I was going slowly so the carabao walked off as if nothing had happened, but I had a bump in the fender and a smashed headlight. Before leaving on furlough someone gave me P37.00 for it! Registration which was due would have cost P35.00!

In 1931, the Manila Evangelistic Institute was commenced by Dr. Paul Culley of the Association of Baptists for World Evangelism. A year or two later when they had no male missionaries in Manila, Miss Ellen Martien asked if I would teach doctrine there. I pointed out that possibly my view of doctrine would not be acceptable. Holding up a Bible, Miss Martien said, "Stay within the covers of this Book and it will be acceptable." Under that arrangement, I agreed and in addition to teaching doctrine, I also taught Romans. Later on Dr. Russell Bradley Jones took over direction of the Institute, and I offered my resignation because of my lack of scholastic qualifications. He kindly refused my resignation. We enjoyed some happy fellowship with these men. One year I was asked to teach Revelation and Dr. Jones was teaching Daniel. As some of his views on prophecy differed from mine, the students used to try to play one off against the other.

In December, 1931, I first met Sandy Sutherland. He was from an assembly in Scotland and had gone to the U.S. for further studies. From there he came to the Philippines in connection with ABWE and pioneered work in Palawan. He was not happy with their financial policies so severed connection with them and continued to serve the Lord independently in southern Palawan. He located at Brookes Point and reached out from there. Later on some of us in Manila, along with some

A Decade of Activity

Filipino believers, contacted some of the assemblies in Scotland about commending Sandy to the work of the Lord here. In October, 1936, Sandy and Maisie were married at the Chinese Gospel Chapel, then on Gandara St. in Manila. As I was driving Sandy down to the wedding in our dirty, dilapidated old car, he insisted that he and his bride would ride with us from the chapel to the reception at Dr. and Mrs. Culley's home. I didn't have time to even get it washed! True to its cantankerous style, the old car would not start when the bridal pair got in, so we had to get a push to start it. Anyway, we said, their married life started out with a good push!

It was in October, 1932, that the first issue of a monthly magazine, The Philippine Evangelist, came off the press with Dr. Culley as editor and Mr. Wightman as publisher and printer. For seven years I wrote the Sunday school lesson notes for each week in that magazine. For part of the time I was assistant editor, taking over for Dr. Culley whenever he was out of town. This magazine had a useful ministry through many parts of the Philippines in those years but perforce came to an end when the war in the Pacific brought the Japanese to these shores. For some years the English Sunday school notes were translated into Tagalog and printed as a supplement.

Dr. and Mrs. Culley were also instrumental in starting the Philippine Keswick Conference. It was intended mainly for students when they were free from classes between Christmas and New Year. The first conference was held at Montalban below the gorge in December, 1931. Sandy and I were invited as speakers. They had borrowed one large canvas to shelter the ladies. For the fellows there were shelters of cogon grass. Early one morning it began to rain and the grass didn't shed much rain. Sandy and I put our campcots over our baggage and sat in the river where it was not quite so chilly as in the driving rain. It was a precious time of fellowship though somewhat wet!

Some time later a committee was formed and I was asked to serve as chairman. With the help of students, we would prepare the grounds. Branches of acacia were pounded into the ground as frames for seats in an open-door auditorium on the side of the hill. Many of them would be sprouting leaves by conference time. We rented two "bankas" (canoes) to make a raft to cross the river and had tents and other supplies.

Those were times of much blessing in the lives of many. The testimonies at the camp fire on the last night were thrilling. One young woman, a very attractive girl, said one evening, "I came here with my own ideas for my life. Now I only want God's will to be done." For her, how true was the hymn, "I know not what awaits me, God kindly veils my eyes." She married a very fine pastor in the Visayan Islands. During the final days of Japanese occupation, some of their troops went on a rampage. That fine young woman, with her two children, were brutally murdered by the Japanese in front of the pastor whose life was spared.

Montalban was a picturesque spot with high and steep hills lining the gorge. Each evening it was a fascinating sight to see thousands of bats swarm out of their caves and fly down the valley at sundown. One day a group of fellows climbed the mountain. Darkness overtook them and they were stranded on a ledge up there all night. They could see the camp so we kept a bonfire burning for we had been able to contact them by voice but not reach them. In 1938, that site was washed out by floods so a location was found on a hacienda in the hills below Antipolo. This included the partial use of a large farmhouse. Today the Valley Golf and Country Club occupies that place and Faith Academy is nearby. In 1941, we were preparing for another conference there. At noon resting on the hillside I looked down across the valley to Manila and wondered what would happen if war came. It did come before we could have that conference. The work party for December 8th was cancelled by news of the bombing of Pearl Harbor.

Another activity in that decade of the 1930's was a radio ministry. On January 7, 1934, Dr. Paul Culley began a 15 minute program called the "Gospel Singers." It was, I believe, the first evangelistic program on the radio here in the Philippines. At first the radio company would not allow any preaching as they were afraid of adverse Roman Catholic reaction. However, Dr. Culley got around that by introducing each hymn and telling what it was about. At the end of that year Dr. Culley was leaving for furlough and asked Dr. Jones to take it over. But the latter was not a singer like Dr. Culley so he made it plain that he would give a short message.

Dr. Jones invited me to bring the message on February 24, 1935. Obviously I had no experience of speaking into a micro-

A Decade of Activity

phone—we didn't even have public address systems then. We didn't own a radio to listen to others, so I was quite nervous and it was probably that which induced a sore throat and husky voice. But Dr. Jones wouldn't let me back out, so I brought the message I had prepared on "True Satisfaction."

A year later, in March, 1936, when Dr. Jones was leaving the Islands he asked me to take over the responsibility for the program. By then we called it "The Gospel Messengers." Our team was cosmopolitan: Mrs. Edward Bomm, an American, was soprano, Miss Josefina Orteza, a Filipino, was alto; Dr. Ho Seng Huang, a Chinese, the bass. I forget now who the tenor was but for a time Henkey Pouw, an Indonesian, was the pianist. That was before wire or tape recordings were discovered so every program was live. No opportunity to replay it and correct any mistakes. One Sunday evening our program was moved up 15 minutes, and we had not been notified. Fortunately, we were usually there in good time but that evening I was almost in a panic when the quartet strolled in casually just a minute before going on the air.

Free booklets were offered on this program, and there was an encouraging response. One lady wrote that she was so tired of her life she contemplated suicide. Hearing the quartet singing, "All this I have done for thee, What has thou done for me?," she was awakened to the goodness of God and the grace of Christ.

Another lady wrote about her difficulties with her family so we asked if we could visit her. When we did, she poured out her story and we tried to extend to her the comfort of the Scriptures. Before Anna and I left, I asked if we might pray for her. She seemed a little surprised, possibly thinking we would need a shrine or something. In simple words I prayed for her and told the Lord about her sad situation and asked Him to make Himself real to her. As I prayed I heard her crying. After the prayer, she looked at me with tears on her cheeks and said, "Never in my life have I heard a prayer like that!" It made me realize afresh the privilege of talking to God in prayer. So often we are prone to take that privilege for granted. The war intervened and we lost contact. Some twenty years later one of the teachers at Faith Academy brought to the evening service in San Juan a neighbor who was a believer. This lady said, "Don't you remember me?" It was embarrassing to admit that I did not, but it turned out she was the lady with whom I had prayed. She was now a believer in Christ.

The radio ministry was carried on by others during our furlough from 1937 to 1938 but upon our return I resumed it until December 7, 1941. On that program I spoke on the Four Freedoms which President Roosevelt had declared, but I applied them in a spiritual way. At the close I saw I had about a minute left so picked up a card which a missionary had sent me on which were listed some of the "Fear Nots" of Scripture. Even as I spoke, the Japanese were on their way to Pearl Harbor and next morning bombed places in the Philippines. We lost some of our freedom but learned too that we need not fear.

It was that radio ministry that led us into another sphere of activity as we entered the 1940's. It was the custom of the U.S. Fleet in the Far East to spend the summer at Tsingtao in China and the winter in Manila Bay. On a submarine tender, the USS Canopus, was a Christian sailor, Virgil Wemmer. He was discouraged because he had not found a Gospel preaching church and could not locate a Christian program on his radio. He chanced on our program and wrote that he was hungry for Christian fellowship, even though a few fellows used to meet in the apartment that one Chief and his wife rented in Manila.

We had often been concerned about U.S. servicemen in Manila. Quite a number were stationed in Manila or out at Fort McKinley. It seemed that nothing was being done in a spiritual way for them. In earlier years, the secretary of the YMCA at Fort McKinley was a fine Christian. But our hands were so full of other work and we felt our first responsibility was to the Filipinos. Occasionally we had contacted some fellows. During our first term we were able to help a Navy man. In a watchnight service he testified, "Once I thought Christianity was a matter of right creeds, but now I know it is centered in a person, the Lord Jesus Christ." He seemed to be getting cold spiritually just before he returned to the U.S. We had not seen him for some time, but I learned when he was leaving. Wrapping a New Testament with his name I left it at the ship by which he was leaving. While on furlough I learned he was at Moody though I had not heard from him. When I called on him there, he told me that it was the New Testament that brought him back into fellowship with the Lord and led into his going into the Lord's service as a teacher.

A Decade of Activity

We met with Virgil Wemmer and some of the fellows at the apartment of CPO King. Soon after it was decided to look for another place to meet with more room. Many of the fellows would congregate at the Army and Navy YMCA in the Walled City, so we asked Mr. Wightman for permission to use the Gospel Hall in that district on Saturday evenings. Yet even this was not exactly suitable; what they needed was a home atmosphere. I thought our home was too far out and too difficult to find, but the fellows didn't think so. So a regular Saturday evening meeting was begun there. Some would come out in the afternoon and stay until Sunday afternoon. We got permission to use a vacant lot at the back where they put up lights and a volleyball court.

One fellow said, "Since I left my home in the States, this is the first time I have been in a home." One of the regulars, Archuletta, or Archie, was a great pal with our boys. He asked if he could bring another fellow who was not a Christian. A good bit of Saturday afternoon was spent with that fellow, and he seemed very close to a decision for Christ. Finally he said, "I don't know whether I could hold out! It is tough being on a submarine. If I could try it out for a week or two and see how it goes." I assured him he couldn't take Christ "on approval" to see if it works. I assured him that when he received Christ the needed strength would be given him. Whether or not he subsequently trusted Christ, we don't know.

One of the fellows who came to our home was John Tinkle, a really keen Christian. He had come to know the Lord at Long Beach, California, through the ministry of Dawson Trotman in the early days of the Navigator work. He was an enthusiastic memorizer of Scripture who had memorized some 600 verses. He was keen on getting others to do the same. As they washed and wiped dishes in the kitchen they would drill on their verses. Later John's ship was sunk by the Japanese in the battle of the Java Sea. Some would say he went down with his ship; his body did, but his spirit went home to be with the Lord.

Two young fellows in the army Air Corps (before the days of USAF) stationed at Nichols Air Base were nominal Christians. John Bristow and Jesse Miller were only 18, lonely and homesick. One Saturday evening they went to the YMCA thinking they might as well take in a show, though they weren't happy about doing that. A sailor invited them to go out to our home which proved a turning point in their lives. However, John's war experiences seemed to have adversely affected his spiritual life and we lost touch with him. Up to that time Jesse had thought of the Bible as a book to be carried to church. Then he learned it was to have a vital part in his life. Through the blessings he received in our home, Jesse made up his mind that if ever he had a home of his own it would be open to servicemen. The story of how that determination came true must be left to a later chapter. We thank God for the contacts that were made at that time and also for the influence that those Christian fellows had upon our two teenage sons. Sometimes it seemed our time and strength was being stretched to the limit. How much longer could we keep it up. Sandy and Maisie Sutherland were with us for a while around Thanksgiving, 1941. Sandy said, "Cyril, you can't keep up this pace. You will have to give up something." Only a few days later, after the Sutherlands had returned to Palawan, the Lord took care of that situation with the outbreak of war in the Pacific.

13

WAR CLOUDS GATHER

"Though an army besiege me, my heart will not fear; Though war break out against me, even then will I be confident." (Psa. 27:3)

As mentioned in the last chapter, our second furlough was 1937 to 1938. During this furlough we tried to manage that Leonard and Kenneth would have a year in public school. In the Philippines we had been teaching them ourselves using the Calvert course. Though this demanded a good bit of our time, we felt it was the best approach to their education at that time. When we returned here they were able to enter Bordner High School as some previous regulations were relaxed. That also made it possible for Rose to attend primary school. One of the highlights of that furlough was witnessing Leonard and Kenneth being baptized at Elmwood Chapel in Buffalo, New York, on January 30, 1938.

Prior to our furlough, we had been joined in the work by Miss Jeannette Lape from Glendale, California. She had had some health and temperamental problems and these were probably aggravated by our absence. Early one Saturday morning we received a cable from a good friend in Manila, Miss Edna Hotchkiss of ABWE, that Jeannette had a nervous breakdown and should be accompanied home as soon as possible. Miss Hotchkiss offered to accompany her but that would mean a return ticket for her. The total cost would be around $1200.00. I immediately phoned Mr. Richard MacLachlan, editor of "Voices From the Vineyard" in New York, and also Tom Millham of her commending assembly, suggesting that any available funds should be sent to the latter for transmittal to Manila. Both of these brethren got in touch with others over that weekend. In the goodness and grace of our Lord, and through the generosity of the Lord's people, the needed funds were cabled to Manila on Monday. It was a real boost to our faith to see how quickly God answered our prayers. After she recuperated, Miss Lape was very anxious to return to the Philippines but the brethren in Los Angeles did not feel it was wise to commend her. She did return with another missionary group but after a few years had again to be invalided home.

On one of my itineraries on that furlough I arranged to visit Fort Dodge, Iowa. My purpose was to talk with Brother Lloyd Walterick who was then publishing "Light and Liberty." Along with others I was concerned that Voices was appearing infrequently and irregularly. It was feared this would mean a lessening of missionary interest. To my delight I learned that Brother Walterick had just returned from a visit to New York where he met with several brethren who had a similar concern. Among them were Harold Harper, a good friend and a frequent giver to missionaries, and also Charles Bellinger who had been one of our teachers in the missionary school in Brooklyn. Although Brother Bellinger was a busy businessman on Wall Street, for several years he headed up this new ministry of serving as a liaison between missionaries and the home assemblies. In later years, after the homecall of Brother Bellinger, Christian Missions in Many Lands came into being and later on amalgamated with the group from the "Voices From the Vineyard" and the "Missionary Fund." Missionaries all over the world owe a deep debt of gratitude to the many brethren who have given of their time and energy in helping the Lord's work in other lands.

War clouds were gathering in Europe, and Hitler's ruthless tactics were becoming evident as we returned from furlough in 1938. On the cross-Pacific voyage one war rumor made us wonder whether we would reach our destinations. My nephew, Cyril Weller, had been accepted by the China Inland Mission for service in China. However, he could not travel with us to Shang-

War Clouds Gather

hai because a party of single ladies was booked on that ship. CIM policy did not allow single men to be on the same ship with single ladies of their mission. An older CIM missionary was booked, Mr. Henry Ford. He once wrote, whimsically, to Henry Ford of motor fame, asking if it was true that Ford Company would provide a vehicle to a namesake of its founder. He was told that rumor was not true. Mr. Ford, who was of short stature, had been informed that two small boys would also occupy his cabin. The two boys (Len and Ken) were both taller than he!

We were soon involved again in the work when in 1939 war broke out in Europe. We were vacationing in Baguio in 1940 when the German armies overran Holland, Belgium, and France. Henry de Vries, who had spent several years in missionary work in Mindanao, was in the opposite side of the duplex. He came in to listen to the news broadcasts and was quite excited because, being from Holland, he knew many of the places mentioned and had relatives in some of them.

Just after the evacuation of the British from Dunkirk, in my visits to Santol Sanitarium, I was conversing with an American priest who was a patient there. He expressed the opinion that Britain was doomed and that Hitler would be victorious. I suggested that if he would consider the Bible and history he would find he was mistaken. Even though in this present age Israel as a nation has been set aside by God, yet still they are his people, "For whoever touches you touches the apple of his eye" (Zech. 2:8). Any ruler or nation that has persecuted the Jews has eventually suffered for it. Maybe if Hitler had been a better student of history, not to say the Bible, he would not have gone down in such an ignominious defeat.

In the second half of 1941 good numbers of servicemen were coming to our home. Frequently there were fellows off cruisers which stopped in Manila for the weekend. We learned that American ships crossing the Pacific were being convoyed because of the growing anti-American feeling in Japan. Early in December, 1941, we knew that it was becoming more difficult for the servicemen to get overnight passes. There were three fine Christians on the USS Astoria which called here. This cruiser was later sunk in the battle of Coral Sea and two of those men went down with the ship. We didn't realize then how poorly prepared for war in the Pacific America was at that time.

The surprises the Japanese gained at Pearl Harbor and here in the Philippines were really inexcusable on the part of our military authorities.

Tighter restrictions had hindered some men from coming to our house on the weekend of December 6 and 7. One of the fellows, Ray Harper, worked at Cavite Navy Yard encoding messages. He owned a car which he sometimes left with us. That Sunday as he was leaving, he said, "I am taking the car to get it greased. I'll bring it back Monday. If anything happens it will be better here." Then realizing he had perhaps said too much, he dashed off without answering our questions. He never was able to return.

At breakfast Monday morning, December 8, we heard that the Japanese had bombed Pearl Harbor earlier that morning (Manila time). That meant war—how soon would it affect us? Taking the children to school, I warned the boys that school would probably be dismissed and that they should get Rose at her school and come right home. My schedule was to go to Taytay to work with some of the students on the grounds for the Philippine Keswick Conference. With the outbreak of war, there would be no conference and so the work party was called off. Soon we heard bombs had fallen on Baguio. Just before noon flights of planes attacked Clark Field, just at a time when planes had returned from reconnaissance. Planes were refueling and pilots eating lunch. Few got off the ground before they were destroyed. Bombers were still waiting orders to attack bases on Formosa. We wondered what had happened to Jesse Miller who was then at Clark. That night the Japanese bombed Nichols Field, and from our bedroom window we could see the explosions.

Having knocked out most of the U.S planes, the Japanese would come in tight formations, usually about noon. Coming in from the north they would turn west above our area and drop down to bomb shipping in Manila Bay and on across the Bay to Cavite Navy Yard. Our anti-aircraft fire was quite ineffectual as it didn't have sufficient power or range. As we watched one day we heard the whistle of a falling shell and flattened ourselves to the ground. It apparently was an anti-aircraft dud which fell in an adjacent lot. Every night there was a complete blackout. Nobody seemed very sure what should be done, but American

War Clouds Gather

propaganda was that help was on the way. So we foolishly thought that soon the tide of battle would turn against the enemy.

Towards the end of December I received a call from a former ABWE missionary, Capt. Skolfield. He had gone back into the U.S. Navy and had been stationed at Cavite when it was bombed. He had salvaged some of the supplies and taken them to an apartment in Manila. He told me to take some of them and had given other supplies to ABWE missionaries. Filling the car two or three times we transferred some of these to our home. One item was supposedly a 100 pound bag of sugar but when we opened it, it proved to be salt.

These supplies were very welcome because we had opened our home to several missionaries stranded in Manila. Some were on their way out of China and only got this far. Others were on ships going on to India but were caught here. They were told to disembark as the ships would proceed to an unknown destination. They offered to sign releases if only they could stay aboard at their own risk. They were refused and the ships sailed with their hold baggage. After the war was over they learned their baggage arrived safely in Australia and was in storage there. For a time there were 13 of us in our home; so in the place of servicemen there were these missionaries.

After Christmas the Filipino-American forces retreated to the Bataan peninsula. Avoiding main streets around Manila, some busloads passed near us. Oil storage tanks in Pandacan were set afire to prevent the Japanese getting them. U.S. military supplies that couldn't be taken to Bataan were thrown open to the Filipinos. We heard that some men took a large crate thinking it must be something valuable, only to discover that it contained the remains of an American waiting to be shipped. President Quezon and some leading Philippine government personnel, along with Gen. MacArthur and his staff, went over to Corregidor Island at the entrance to Manila Bay. This fortress was built to resist and repel invaders from the China Sea but offered little resistance from the rear.

Manila was declared an open city on January 1, 1942, in order to spare the city from fighting and loss of civilian lives. The Japanese bombing had largely been of military targets. However, in bombing shipping on the Pasig River they had struck a large Roman Catholic church. This was put to good propaganda use—pagan Japan with no regard for Christian Filipinos! This propaganda may have had a bearing later on release of missionaries in Manila from internment. With the Japanese landings at Lingayen Bay, north of Manila, and Atimonan, south of Manila, some foreigners headed for what were supposed to be evacuation points. Some of the missionaries went to Baguio but we decided it was better to remain in our homes and leave the outcome with the Lord.

On January 2 we saw a truckload of Japanese troops pass on a nearby corner. We decided to sit tight and await developments. A former houseboy came with a sack of flour from a warehouse that the owner threw open to the Filipinos. Much time was spent in prayer together as a group these days. Psalm 46 was a source of comfort as we realized that "God is our refuge and strength, an ever present help in trouble." One afternoon we saw a truckload of Japanese coming up our street. As it approached I started towards the door, thinking that as head of the house I should be the first to approach them. The truck drove on without stopping. One evening our Filipino neighbor from across the street came with the information that he had that day seen the Japanese who had been living next door and they told him they would be around to pick us up. He suggested I hide out with him or go to the provinces but these suggestions were impracticable. In my reading Jeremiah 15:21 proved to be a real cheer, "I will save you from the hands of the wicked and redeem you from the grasp of the cruel."

The house next door had previously been occupied by a Japanese married to a Filipino. They moved there when we did in 1937 and were very friendly. Later they moved to another home, and their place was taken by a group of young Japanese men who worked in Japanese bazaars in town. Every morning they did their calisthenics before going to work. Across from the San Juan Chapel a Japanese had rented a home. He spent a lot of time going around, ostensibly going to play golf. These were only two examples of how the Japanese had infiltrated military men and spies in strategic places.

Our former neighbor, Mr. Imamura, was appointed to act as liaison between the Filipino police and the Japanese military authorities. At a later time during the occupation I went to see

War Clouds Gather

him to request his help in regard to Mrs. Bomm who had been picked up one night and taken to Fort Santiago. As I waited in his outer office, I heard him giving a typical Japanese propaganda line and my heart sank. Out came a number of Filipino police sergeants and the receptionist ushered me into his office. He was most cordial, saying, "Our countries are at war but you and I are friends." I had occasion to seek his help at other times but went to his home. I would go after dark to the back door. He came out to the kitchen to speak to me one evening while in his sala; he was entertaining the top Japanese general!

Santo Tomas University has a longer history than either Yale or Harvard. The grounds of this Roman Catholic university were taken over as an internment camp. All enemy aliens were to report there by January 15, so we delayed to the last day. We loaded up two or three "carretelas" (the typical Filipino horse rig) and set off, leaving behind a group of tearful believers. In Santo Tomas, American committees had been set up to operate the camp under the supervision of the Japanese. We lined up to fill in forms providing information about our homes, cars, and finances. Learning that we were missionaries, the American in charge said, "You missionaries are going to be moved somewhere else today—you may as well fill in the forms there." Actually we were about to be released as house prisoners so no forms were filled in. In this way our car was one of the few that was not confiscated. Later on, since we could not use it, we sold the battery and tires. Then someone wanted to buy the car. They brought tires and one evening we pushed it a couple of blocks to a neighboring house. Just after we had it in the other garage a Japanese patrol car went by!

While waiting at Santo Tomas that day, I was called into an office where they asked me about some who had not yet surrendered. It was a relief *not* to know their whereabouts. It gave me an opportunity to glance over the listing of missionaries compiled by the Japanese. It seemed to be quite complete and I was surprised that we were listed as "Plymouth Brethren," since we don't use that term ourselves. I thought that it was rather strange that not once during the occupation did the Japanese ask to even see our passports.

The same afternoon all the missionaries, Roman Catholic and Protestants, were called together to listen to a propaganda speech. We were told about the magnanimity of the Japanese, that they came to the Philippines with the same purpose as ours, to help the Filipino people. We were to be released to go to our homes or institutions and would be given instructions. We would only be allowed to go out for religious services, for medical attention, and necessary shopping. We would have to report to the "Religious Section" of the Japanese Army who would accept responsibility for us. Later on we were given one red armband with a Japanese character indicating we were enemy aliens. One to a family, to be worn when we went outside our homes. Soon these proved to be a boon. Filipinos now knew we were not Germans. So there was no need to bargain in the market for we got the best price right away. Extra things were put in our basket and on one occasion at least, money was quietly slipped into my hand by an unknown donor.

So that same evening we were back home again. The believers at San Juan rejoiced at our immediate release. They compared it to Peter's release from prison! We had been released without signing any statement or making any promises. Some were not so fortunate. Some denominational leaders were called in by the Religious Section and ordered to sign a prepared statement. Some leaders, mostly of liberal theological views, did sign. However, a few, such as Mr. Fonger of the American Bible Society, Mr. Ed. Bomm, and Dr. Santiago Cruspero (a Filipino) of ABWE refused to compromise their Christian witness. Those Americans were imprisoned in Fort Santiago which had a reputation for privation and torture. Officials from the Religious Section visited some of the churches to listen to the sermons on Sundays. Being a smaller group and also being out in the suburb in San Juan, we were spared such visits.

One of the Baptist missionaries died of illness in the Baguio Camp so the church of which he was pastor in Manila held a memorial service. Up to the last minute they hoped Mr. Bomm would be released for that. So when it was obvious that he would not be there, they asked me to substitute. The Lord wonderfully helped in giving a suitable message at such short notice. On another occasion there just as I stood up to preach some Japanese officers came in. Shortly after I was called to the Religious Section and the chief there asked if I would like to be repatriated. I presumed it would have included the family but

War Clouds Gather

no mention was made of them. This offer I declined on the grounds that there were others who had been stranded here on account of the war. They should have the preference, and a few did manage to get away to Shanghai to sail on the evacuation vessel, S. S. Gripsholm. Learning that I was from British Columbia, the chief told me he was raised in the Fraser River valley of that province.

Each week we had to send in a report of our activities—what services we attended and so forth. If we had taught a class or had preached we had to give the topic of our message. One week they sent me a letter, noting that I had preached on such a Sunday and asked for a copy of my sermon. It is not my custom to write my sermons, simply an outline. Since I had preached in Tagalog I typed out my message in Tagalog, being fairly sure they would not be able to understand it! Shortly there was another request for a copy of my sermon and "if I had preached in Tagalog, please submit an English translation." Since they wanted so much to read my message, I decided they would have the way of salvation clearly presented.

They were at that time inviting various Filipino preachers to give a short message on the radio on Sunday mornings. Of course, they demanded that the message be approved by them before it was aired. They asked Dr. Cruspero to give a message but rejected his first manuscript. It rather amused me that Dr. Cruspero should ask my advice, an enemy alien. He wanted to use the opportunity and yet not compromise his stand for Christ. We went over the manuscript and made some changes. In one place he had mentioned the Empire State Building in an illustration. Instead we substituted a tall building in Manila. His revised message was accepted.

Services continued in the San Juan Chapel on a regular basis, except that there were no evening services. Of course, such things as open-air meetings or children's classes outside were not allowed, nor any literature distribution. There was a supply of literature on hand. As there was a shortage of paper or any kind of supplies, we sold this as waste paper. It was no doubt used for wrapping or making bags in the markets. So with a dearth of reading material we hoped that people would even read such wrapping material.

14

THE JAPANESE OCCUPATION

"Can God spread a table in the desert?" (Psa. 78:19)
"You prepare a table before me in the presence of my enemies." (Psa. 23:5)

Just before the Japanese entered Manila, we got off a cable to the brethren in New York letting them know that we were then all right. They had no further word about us until January, 1943, when evacuees on the S.S. Gripsholm passed on word about us. It was a trying time for our loved ones, especially Anna's mother and father. One day they thought her mother had gone. The doctor (a fine Christian) from across the street thought he was too late until he noticed a slight movement. He was able to revive her but said the best medicine would be a letter from Manila. Anna's three sisters sent short notes through the Red Cross in late 1944, but these were not received until after our liberation.

For almost three and a half years we had no letters except one from Echoes of Service in Bath. For some reason letters from Britain seemed to get through, for one of our fellow workers from there received a number of letters. This meant, of course, that we were entirely cut off from our usual sources of supply as no gifts could get through to us. In the early days some of those in the internment camps were given Red Cross food packages but these were not given to us on the outside; supposedly, the local markets were available to us!

How did God supply our needs during the time we were living in our own home as house prisoners? Some of the local people gave us gifts, usually of food. The believers were themselves suffering yet they gave to us. Occasionally gifts came from some we had not known previously. We also were able to sell some things. This, of course, had to be kept from the knowledge of the Japanese, but we were able to dispose of our car and piano and some other things. Then some of the Chinese offered to lend us money without interest until after the war. This was to their advantage as it was like an investment to be repaid in good currency. They had no confidence in the Japanese currency which was referred to as "Mickey Mouse Money." Some of these declined repayment after the war.

Of course, the Japanese were also curious about the source of our income. Filipinos who helped us would be under suspicion of aiding the enemy. One afternoon a Japanese officer and soldier along with a Filipino policeman visited us. Fortunately, we were all home at the time. They evidently wanted to know who was helping us. It added to their prestige to talk through an interpreter. They started by asking questions in Tagalog which the Filipino was to ask us in English. I took the wind out of their sails by replying to the policeman in Tagalog. They exclaimed, "Oh, you speak Tagalog!" It would have been undiplomatic to point out that probably I spoke it better than they did. They asked how we made a living. I directed their attention to our garden where we had planted sweet potatoes and squash, etc. Actually it wasn't very productive, but I didn't think it was necessary to add that information. Obviously that was not enough, so they asked, "What else?" I mentioned that some of our church members helped us. Pencils and pads were at the ready—"Oh, who are they?" "Oh, I couldn't tell you all their names—there are many of them." "How much do they give you?" Time was spent in telling how different ones (no names, of course) gave a few ears of corn, a little rice, or perhaps some eggs. I omitted to tell them that our Japanese neighbor had once sent us a package of goodies! Finally it became evident that I was not about to supply them with any specific information. As they left I picked up a Japanese New Testament that had been sent to us long before. I explained to the officer that I had had it for some time, and since I couldn't read it I would be happy for

The Japanese Occupation

him to have it. He evidently recognized what it was and said something in Japanese to his companions which seemed to amuse them. Often I have wondered what became of that Testament. We just committed it to the Lord.

In many ways we had to improvise. Several navy men used to keep an extra white uniform at our house. We hid these in the air space below the roof lest the Japanese should find them. As time went on these were made over into clothes we could wear. Shorts instead of long trousers was one way of economizing.

Before long there was no wheat flour obtainable. Rice flour or cassave do not respond to yeast in the same way. We could get yeast for some breweries were still in operation. We had a corn mill which was used to make corn meal and rice flour. Len and Ken used it to make peanut butter and sell it. Each evening we grated a coconut and squeezed it to get coconut milk. What was left after squeezing was fried with sugar, and this added flavor and nourishment to cereals and puddings. Feeling it was important for Rose to get some milk, we purchased carabao (water buffalo) milk from a boy each morning. He augmented his profits by diluting the milk with water.

With a box on the back of my bicycle, marketing was done downtown in Manila. When the tires wore out, the Filipinos very ingeniously made tires from the side walls of old automobile tires.

All radios were called in for inspection and modification to eliminate any short-wave reception. Our house was surrounded by vines for shade purposes. A wire was strung all around the house among the vines. One short end protruded through a crack in the siding. Each evening this was connected with a short wire to our radio. Most evenings at 10 p.m. we could pick up an English news program from Free China. Thus, we kept in touch with the progress of the war. Japanese programs were not dependable for accuracy. We generally figured it was the opposite of what they said. The Tagalog newspaper was named "Taliba" (Sentinel). Newsboys would cry, "Taliba! Balitang baligtad" (Sentinel! News in reverse).

One of Len's customers for peanut butter was a former radioman. He had hidden a shortwave in his house. Gists of important news were typed on small sheets of onion-skin paper. When Len delivered peanut butter, he would come away with one of these news sheets secreted in the handlebars of his bicycle. One morning on his way there, a friend stopped him with the news that the Japanese had raided the radioman's house, found his shortwave, and taken him to Fort Santiago. They evidently had watched for some time and were picking up people who had visited that house. Len was on their list evidently, so for a while he kept out of sight. The military police did question an acquaintance as to the home of Len, but he pleaded ignorance.

One of the diversions of those days was a monkey that had been given to Len. It had been brought from Bataan by someone who managed to get away from there. It afforded hours of amusement except when it got loose and seemed to delight in evading recapture. It would patiently work for hours on any knot in order to get free. Boys came by to tease, carefully staying beyond the reach of the monkey's rope. One day in leaping at these tormentors the rope broke! The boys fled with an amazing dash of speed! A fruit vendor would pass an apparently somnolent monkey, but the moment his back was turned he was minus one banana. Len loaned his monkey to a friend for a few days. During its absence a neighbor called to say Len's monkey was in their yard. It wasn't Len's but one quite similar, so then we had two of a kind. Unfortunately, this second one came to an untimely end. His rope got around his neck so when he leaped it was suicidal.

Sometimes the boys would visit friends in the neighborhood in the evening. One evening Len was accosted by some Japanese and ordered to report to their office the next morning. The Japanese didn't usually venture abroad much at night, and when they did it was always in a group. It could have been too dangerous for one or two alone! I couldn't go with Len as I had to report to the Religious Section that same morning. Anna went with him and I warned them not to offer any information, just answer questions. Asked why he was wandering about at night, Len said he went out for a little exercise before turning in. Looking at his records they noted he was British but was born in the Philippines. "How many times have you been to Britain?" Len told them he had never been to Britain. They never asked about going to the U.S. or Canada, and they apparently never thought of it. They told him to go home—it was good to exercise but not to do it at night because there were many bad people about. That deliverance was surely an answer to prayer.

One of our friends who had previously been one of my Bible students, Mr. Max Atienza, told me he had contacts with the guerrillas. If I would give him a list of the servicemen we knew he would try to get information on their present whereabouts. We had no knowledge about most of them. We did hear about Virgil Wemmer. One afternoon as our laundrywoman was returning our clean clothes, two young women came to the door. When I invited them in they seemed reluctant to state their mission until after the laundrywoman left. Then they told me they worked for the Japanese in a car repair place in Manila; there were some American prisoners of war also working there. They handed me a little note from Virgil. I asked if they could smuggle in anything for him and another fellow he named. They would try some small packages. They were not allowed to talk to the POW's but a fellow they worked with would leave something in the lavatory and signal Virgil to go in when he came out.

In the meantime Max Atienza said that one of his contacts had been caught by the Kempetai (Japanese police), so he didn't know whether we would get any news or not. However, after a while the list I had typed was returned with notations about most of the fellows. Jesse Miller was then working on construction of an airfield just south of Manila. Later he was taken to Japan and worked there until release after VJ Day in August, 1945. Ray Harper was in Puerto Princesa in Palawan. There some of the prisoners were chosen to be shipped to Japan and others to remain in Palawan. Ray was among the latter but switched places with a fellow who thought it would be safer to stay in Palawan. A number of the ships carrying prisoners to Japan were torpedoed by U.S. submarines who had no idea there were Americans aboard. George Wightman, son of our fellow missionary, was among those killed in this way. Ray got safely to Japan and later was released there after VJ Day. The prisoners who remained in Palawan, when liberation was within sight, were herded into a cave and massacred by the Japanese.

We were aware of the guerrilla activity going on. This was not only against the Japanese but also against Filipinos who collaborated with them. The latter were usually warned to desist or suffer the consequences. About twenty such were killed by guerrillas just in San Juan. One of them lived a couple of blocks from us and his wife had once sent us some food. One day I saw an American ride into San Juan on horseback. There were times when a guerrilla would approach a man in downtown Manila, shoot him in broad daylight, and then disappear among the crowds. In early 1944 we saw a wellworn copy of LIFE magazine and also got hold of a small-town newspaper. We knew nothing about anyone in that little place but we read the entire paper. The prices in the ads, the announcements of births, weddings, and deaths, all gave us a little inkling of wartime life in the U.S. On most of such items brought in by U.S. submarines there was stamped the famous words of MacArthur, "I shall return." As the hopes of Filipinos were raised and sustained by this promise, so our hearts are cheered by the promise of One who is greater, "I will come again."

Yet those were days when we learned to be very suspicious and cautious. It paid to be non-committal to any but most intimate friends. So we were hesitant to share the good news about the war that came our way. We were never quite sure who we could really depend upon.

Because of the severe shortages there was a great increase in theft and other crimes. Children would feel through the muck of a gutter for such items as nails, screws, and bolts. Washed off they could be offered for sale in flea markets. People learned to watch their laundry on the line lest it disappear. A bamboo pole through a barred window was one way of lifting loose items of clothing. At night men would climb poles to cut electric wire. In our neighborhood they formed a vigilante group. Any suspicion of burglars would cause an alarm to be sounded and everyone would turn on their lights while the men sallied forth with "bolos" (machetes) and flashlights. The crime rate quickly dropped in our district. One of our China missionaries living nearby had her purse snatched one day.

All this was a contrast with conditions before the war when there was very little crime. We used to leave our home unattended, the ground floor all open, and nothing would be taken. Hold-ups and purse-snatchings were rare occurrences but war conditions changed all that.

The Sutherlands had returned to Palawan just before the outbreak of the war. No word about them reached us until after the war. They had left their home in Brookes Point and taken refuge in the hills. They couldn't surrender before the deadline because there were no Japanese around to whom they could surrender. So they were forced to move from place to place and occasionally sneak into Brookes Point when they had a need there. They suffered many attacks of malaria which was rampant in those parts. In 1944 they met some U.S. Navy men from a submarine which had been wrecked in those waters. These men were aided by the guerrillas and were able to make contact with headquarters in Australia.

It was about that time too that their little boy, Alastair, had a prayer of his own each evening. When pressed by his Dad, Alastair said he was asking God to send a submarine to take them out of there. Such a possibility had not occurred to the parents. The navy men told them that a submarine had been ordered to pick them up one night and they invited the Sutherlands to go along. What a thrill when, barefooted and in ragged clothes, they stood on the steel deck of that submarine. Alastair's prayers had been answered. At MacArthur's headquarters, even in his weakened condition, Sandy was pumped for all the information he could offer. They were allowed to write to their loved ones in Scotland but were forbidden to tell how they got to Australia. Other missionary friends from Mindanao were taken out in the same way.

On the island of Panay a group of Baptist missionaries had hidden out in the hills and forests of that island. Although Japanese soldiers were in the vicinity on different occasions it was not until December, 1943, that they finally located the hideout. Just before Christmas these missionaries and some others who had taken refuge with them were killed by Japanese soldiers.

In spite of the difficulties, we managed to get news about the progress of the war, particularly in Europe. One morning riding my bicycle into town to do some marketing, an unknown Filipino pulled alongside me. He was quite elated with the news he passed on that Italy had fallen to the Allied powers. In June, 1944, I heard in the news from Kunming about the Normandy landing. Even though it was after ten at night, I just had to go around to some of our missionary friends in the neighborhood with the good news.

We could also sense that things were not going well for the

Japanese, in spite of their propaganda. There were signs of increasing tension. It was a turning point when Saipan was taken by the Americans. It would put an air base within striking distance of mainland Japan. This was followed by a smashing defeat of their navy in Philippine waters. For us, prices were rising rapidly. A sack of rice cost us over seven hundred pesos. There would certainly be more inflation. Yet our trust was in the Lord and in the exceeding great and precious promises of His Word.

At the beginning of the occupation, one of the Filipino elders asked if we should stop making payments on the chapel land. Knowing there were sufficient funds for the next payment I said we should go ahead as long as the Lord supplied our needs for that. The former owner was the wife of a Supreme Court justice, and she expressed surprise that the congregation could still maintain their payments. Her other debtors had stopped paying. It was an opportunity for the elder to testify about the goodness and power of God even in those difficult circumstances. Later, I approached a Christian Chinese businessman about the possibility of him advancing the money to pay off the mortgage. The assembly would sign a note to pay off as they were able, particularly after liberation. He agreed to this arrangement and some payments were made to him but after the liberation he wiped out the outstanding balance as his gift to the chapel.

Can God? Yes, indeed he can! "Now to him who is able to do immeasurably more than all we ask or imagine, according to his power that is at work within us, to him be glory in the church and in Christ Jesus throughout all generations, for ever and ever! Amen" (Eph. 3:20-21).

15

LIFE IN AN INTERNMENT CAMP

"Be content with what you have, because God has said, 'Never will I leave you; never will I forsake you." (Heb. 13:5)

One afternoon in July, 1944, while a neighbor missionary was visiting us, we observed some Japanese officials going to the home of another missionary. Our visitor hurriedly left by a back way so as to be home if they should visit him. Soon the unwelcome guests were at our door. They ordered us to all stand before them while they read a proclamation, first in Japanese, then in English. The purport of it was they could no longer guarantee our safety because of the prevailing lawlessness. So for our own protection we were to be confined in an internment camp. There we would be provided with "protective custody," a euphemism we readily understood. We were to be ready at nine the next morning with one suitcase each with our clothing—everything else would be provided! Anna remonstrated that since our daughter was sick we couldn't possibly be ready at such short notice. But she desisted from further protestations when the Japanese officer waved his finger under her nose and said, "You be ready tomorrow morning or else . . ." Better let him have the last word under such circumstances.

As soon as they left, word was sent to the brethren in San Juan. They came out in force to help us. Our belongings, furnishings, and books were quickly taken away to their homes for safekeeping. They would have stripped the place bare; but since we were not supposed to remove anything, I persuaded them to leave some furniture in the house. In this way most of our personal belongings were safely returned to us after we were liberated. A chiming eight-day clock, one of our wedding presents, and a few books were lost.

The next morning the army truck arrived, already quite full with friends and neighbors. We interpreted "one suitcase each" somewhat liberally and quickly began to load things on the truck to forestall any objections. One of our friends had brought us a basket of fruit. The soldiers hindered Anna's efforts to get this on the truck—"No food!" But each time Anna had stopped a little closer to the truck. Finally she appealed to one soldier who seemed as if he might be a bit more friendly. "My little girl has been sick, she needs this fruit." Possibly thinking of a little girl back home, the soldier put the basket on, and my wife followed. Finally the boys and I climbed on the tailgate of the overloaded truck and hung on as it lurched its way to Santo Tomas.

There it was made plain to us that we would not have any opportunity to communicate with our friends already interned there. Roman Catholic priests and nuns and Protestant missionaries alike were crowded into the gymnasium for an overnight stay. The Japanese tried unsuccessfully to take a roll call and establish some order out of chaos. The first time they often couldn't hear the response when names were called. After calling a nun's name two or three times someone said she had died some months before. Then they said we should answer by giving our age. The name of a white-haired Methodist was called and at the top of his lungs he shouted "64." This brought forth a burst of laughter from the crowd so this method was abandoned. I don't know how the Japanese recorded our names in their characters but we got an inkling when they called for "Mr. Littlewood." There was no reply. I turned to our friend "Chips" Smallwood and said, "It's you they're calling." However, he declined to respond to "Littlewood."

A hard concrete floor with no bedding and hordes of mosquitoes were not conducive to sleep that night. At daybreak we were lined up in columns of four and counted, then loaded on

Life in an Internment Camp

trucks to take us to the railroad station. Then we were counted as we got off the trucks. Lined up beside a train—counted again. On the train—counted again about three times. Evidently they were having trouble getting the same count each time! Very frustrating for them but very amusing to us though we tried to hide our mirth.

That afternoon we arrived at the grounds of the University of the Philippine Agricultural department at Los Baños. There were about fifteen hundred internees there before us, and long buildings divided into cubicles had been erected. These buildings were thatched with nipa palm leaves. There was the privilege not found in other internment camps that the family could be together. Husbands and wives shared a cubicle instead of being segregated in separate buildings. Len and Ken had a cubicle a few doors away and Rose shared one in between ours and Pagets with the daughter of the Pagets, of the Ceylon and India General Mission.

A committee of internees had been formed to manage the affairs of the camp under the supervision of the Japanese. Japanese soldiers guarded the perimeter to be sure no one escaped and to keep away Filipinos who would gladly have brought food. So the rank and file of the internees had no direct contact with the Japanese. Work teams were formed for every able-bodied person to have some part in the maintenance of the camp. Anna was on the food preparation detail which principally consisted of removing from the rice most of the worms, grubs, and dirt. I signed up for maintenance and one of my jobs, along with one of the priests, was building a walkway between two buildings, roofed with nipa thatch. So I learned to tie on the thatch with rattan. The boys helped in the kitchen, but they also had some special classes and Rose was able to keep up some of her lessons.

For several months our end of the camp was segregated from the other; and since we were all religious workers, our end was dubbed "Vatican City" or "Holy City." Since the hospital was at the other end, one way for us to get down there was to be sent to the hospital. When I had an attack of dengue fever I spent a couple of days there. This enabled me to contact Mr. Dayton and pass on to him a few things his wife had asked me to take to him. His job was buying food supplies from Filipinos at the gate.

Later on Anna developed beri-beri from the insufficient diet so she needed to visit the hospital for injections. What vitamins were available were kept there for those who were badly in need of them.

At first the food was fairly adequate though quite plain. This didn't last long and soon was quite insufficient. We liked to think that a Japanese defeat in the war was followed by a cut in rations. Towards the last we averaged 700 calories a day per person. "Lugao" was rice boiled in a lot of water. That was the main dish. Once in a while a pig was killed—it didn't go far among two thousand people. There was an occasion when dried fish and salted eggs were available. Hunger spices up even eggs that are a bit "high." We tried growing greens or anything that seemed edible. By the cubicle of a friend was a banana plant. We fried the inner part of the stalk and the roots in rancid coconut oil. We got the oil by accepting a ration of cigarettes for trading purposes. On the rare occasions we got bananas we fried the skins and ate them too. From our camp we could see the hillsides around lush with banana plants and coconut trees.

Later on, the "middle wall of partition" was removed and we were free to mingle with others. The difference in behavior in the two sections soon became evident. Among the religious group, even if they were certainly not all believers, there was a spirit of friendliness, consideration, and willingness to help others. Although there were some missionaries in the other section, the majority were a miscellaneous group of businessmen, professionals along with the riff-raff of tramps, prostitutes, and some merchant seamen. The tension among them resulted in quarrelling, selfishness, and taking advantage of others. After we were liberated it was plain that some had hoarded food or sold it at exorbitant prices, for their greedy purposes.

People often asked us if those who were interned with us were more open to the Gospel. There was no indication that troubles softened the hearts of the unsaved. It is a common idea that calamities will cause men to turn to God. This may be true in isolated cases, but it generally does not happen that way. In the Great Tribulation, we are told, "Men gnawed their tongues in agony and cursed the God of heaven because of their pains and their sores, but they refused to repent of what they had done."

Life in an Internment Camp

One building had been set aside for a chapel by the committee of internees so regular services and Sunday school was carried on. The Roman Catholics and Protestants had separate services, of course. Since there were so many different groups, a committee was formed to make arrangements for services and rotate speakers. Sometimes a liberal preacher would lay stress upon man's love for his fellow. Personally it seemed rather hard to conceive of loving that Japanese guard with a rifle as he walked by outside. Once I was invited to give the morning message and chose to speak on the person of Christ from the first chapter of Colossians.

Those were opportunities to get to know each other better and to respect some with whom we did not agree theologically. The Episcopal Bishop Binstead earned our respect when he volunteered to help in an emergency in a temporary hospital. Emptying bedpans during an outbreak of dysentery was not a pleasant task. The Seventh Day Adventists adhered faithfully to their principles of not eating pork and observance of tithing and keeping the Sabbath. I told one of them, "I don't agree with some of your principles, but I do admire your living up to those convictions." Len and Ken worked out a deal with some of them to work in the kitchen on Saturdays to have time off on Sunday.

Almost everyone had brought in a few books for their own use, so it was decided to pool all these and put them into a library where they would be available to everyone. One afternoon I was looking over the books with an Anglican missionary from Japan. Looking at Papin's "Life of Christ" he glanced over and said, "That's a good book but you wouldn't approve of it." He knew where I stood theologically. It was there that I had the time and opportunity to read the trilogy "Mutiny on the Bounty," "Pitcairn Island," and "Men against the Sea." These were intensely interesting, and the second one presents the influence and change that came to the survivors through a copy of the Holy Scriptures.

Some of the internees who were teachers were assigned to teach the children though often they had to improvise since they lacked books and supplies. One of the priests took a special interest in helping Len with advanced mathematics. Rose took an interest for a while in sketching. One evening there was an unusually beautiful sunset. The sky was covered with delicate pastel shades that attracted the attention of many. I remarked to Rose that it would be nice to get that in a picture. She replied, "Dad, there is only one artist who could paint that!" I said, "Who would that be?" She replied, "The Artist who has just painted it in the sky."

During our time there our clothes and footwear were getting the worse for wear. What shoes we had wouldn't last long, especially in rainy, muddy weather, so generally we wore "bakya," the Filipino wooden shoe. Once I removed a piece of wood from the wall of our cubicle in order to fashion a pair of "bakya" for myself. Sometimes it was easier to go barefoot than attempt to walk through the mud in "bakya." One afternoon a number of the men were taken out of the camp by the Japanese to cut firewood in the hills around. We learned later that the Japanese included the cost of such firewood in their expense accounts. At one point they wanted us to work for them, offering the munificent wage of 25 cents a day. Our committee claimed exemption on the grounds of the Geneva Convention. That didn't mean anything to the Japanese, but they probably despaired of the quality of work we would produce.

One priest remarked, "We are developing a keen sense of RUMOR." That was true! Rumors that Red Cross supplies had arrived at Santo Tomas Camp in Manila; that they were at the railroad station in Los Baños; that they were in the Japanese Commandant's office. Rumors of American landings! In the evenings there were furious arguments that the thunder and lightning in the distance was the roar and flash of artillery fire.

Fortunately we also retained our sense of HUMOR too. Said one theologian, "Camp life puts us in a receptive mood. We are ready to receive anything—moldy mush, wormy rice, green water, meatless watery stew—anything that's called food. And what a cure for allergies—they have become ancient history to internees."

It was reported that Mr. Leith, a British missionary, mistook his stew for hot water and made tea with it—just like an Englishman. That report couldn't have been true—the stew was never that hot!

A lady reading the instructions for writing cards home, that they must be in English or Nipponggo, was heard to exclaim, "Oh, I shall write mine in Nipponggo. Mother and Father are so fluent in it!"

Life in an Internment Camp

Conversation overheard over the partitions:
Mr. G. "I hate to go to bed on such a full stomach."
Mrs. G. "Don't lie on your stomach, lie on your back."
Mr. G. "I do—but still my stomach touches the bed."

There were a number of Dutch priests brought into the camp, and they formed a glee club. So once in a while the monotony was relieved by putting on a concert. Some wrote parodies on oldtime songs concerning our conditions. "They'll be Coming Round the Mountain when they come" was a favorite. It had such references as to killing the old black bull (the only work animal) so that one day we would be full. The innuendoes about the Japanese were highly gratifying because they were subtle enough to escape the attention of those gentlemen.

It was during those days that I passed through a spiritual turmoil. It was bad enough to be perpetually hungry, but to also see my children hungry but not complaining was hard. Then to see my wife's feet and legs puffed with beri-beri, a malnutrition disease, was an added trial. We elevated the foot of her bed to help the circulation and she went frequently to the hospital for vitamin injections. At that time one verse came repeatedly to mind, "Be content with such things as ye have." It seemed I could not evade it. In the middle of the night I would wake up and "Be content with such things as ye have" would come to mind. But what did I have to be content with? An empty stomach, an ailing wife, hungry children, little strength or energy because of lost weight. My weight was down to 105 pounds and my wife's to 85. We had no idea what was happening to our home and few possessions. There was no communication with friends and loved ones; no certainty that we would come out of this alive. Be content with such things? I was too pious to voice the inward rebellion, but it did seem as if the Lord was asking a bit too much just then.

There flashed across the screen of memory what the Apostle Paul wrote, "I have learned to be content whatever the circumstances. I know what it is to be in need, and I know what it is to have plenty. I have learned the secret of being content in any and every situation, whether well fed or hungry, whether living in plenty or in want." The inward reaction was that Paul was an apostle, an exceptional Christian, which I am not; but then I had to face the fact that Paul wrote those words when he was in prison in Rome. "Be content with what ye have." It seemed as if there was a mental block which stopped the quotation at that point. "Such things as ye have," seemed to be mostly a minus quantity. Really, I did want to be content—but couldn't it be postponed until after our release?

No! I had to learn the lesson of contentment there and under those circumstances. This seemed to go on for some time until I just told the Lord, "If you want me to be content, you will have to do it, I can't." Then it seemed I was at the point where I could go on to the rest of the verse, "for he hath said, 'I will never leave you nor forsake you.'" Those familiar words then glowed with a new light. God wasn't asking me to be content with *things,* with circumstances, but with Himself. We can never be content with *things* for they are only temporary and transient. In this world we can never be satisfied with our circumstances. It is only in Christ that we can find contentment. That's how Paul learned this difficult lesson—"I can do all things through Christ who strengtheneth me." His grace is always sufficient. His power is made perfect in our weakness. Like the old hymn of our childhood days, "I have Christ, what want I more." No matter what the circumstances may be, Christ is enough the heart and mind to fill. He alone can satisfy. "Godliness with contentment is great gain."

16

LIBERATION FROM INTERNMENT

"Come and see what God has done, how awesome his works in man's behalf." (Psa. 66:5)

One day some duty, which I have now forgotten, took me to the gymnasium in the lower part of the camp. A large number of men were billeted there and on a cupboard beside one man's cot these words were written:
"Sept. 20—Worst slop I ever tasted.
Sept. 21—Sweetest music I ever heard."
The sweet music was not the strains of some symphony orchestra nor the march of a military band. That morning we heard the distant hum of a flight of bombers. In the clear sky and bright sunshine we spotted them away off in the distance, like a swarm of flies. Later there was the boom of bombs bursting in the distance. There was no doubt as to whose side they were on. To the dismay of the Japanese guards, the internees cheered in the excitement of the first sign of returning Americans. MacArthur's famous words were becoming a reality, "I shall return."

They were just a day late for our 22nd wedding anniversary! That evening as we sat outside our barracks and talked about the day's event, there was a brilliant flash of light. A few seconds later the sound of a terrific explosion reached our ears. Someone had the presence of mind to count the lapse between the flash and the sound and calculated it would have been somewhere near Manila. We were not sure whether it was an ammunition ship in the Bay or some large ammunition dump.

Later on whenever American planes were spotted, the internees showed their joy by waving, not handkerchiefs but sheets. This was very annoying to the guards. Some internees were slapped for this. So orders went out that whenever the air-raid alarm sounded, all should go immediately to their barracks and remain there until the "All Clear" sounded. This didn't make too much difference because by the time our camp authorities got the official word of an air raid, it was almost over!

The food situation was steadily deteriorating and becoming more critical. It was learned that the Japanese had a quantity of rice stored in a bodega as a reserve for future emergency. The Japanese guards had evidently been helping themselves and could not be depended on. So the Commandant asked the camp committee to provide men to guard the bodega, preferably missionaries. So there arose the ironical situation of internees guarding the supplies of which they were being deprived!

With blackouts every night, the evenings were spent by groups of people conversing together. The favorite topic? Food! What's the first thing you want to eat when we are liberated? All kinds of recipes were concocted and exchanged. Another topic was the progress of the war. Where would MacArthur make his first landings? In Santo Tomas Camp in Manila that was subtly announced over the loudspeaker. A well known news announcer had evaded the Japanese by using his real name instead of his radio name. He announced the work details each evening. One evening he concluded, "Don't be late! But better Leyte than never."

What did the future hold for us? We weren't even sure what was happening in the present, let alone the future. Air activity was increasing. Troop movements in the night were heard. Our loved ones at home, scanning the newspaper, listening to the radio, probably knew more about the war than we who were right in the midst of it!

Everyone was speculating on the strategy of MacArthur. Americans had landed on Mindoro and established an airbase at San Jose. What seemed likely to us was the Luzon landing would be in Batangas to approach Manila from the south. It

Liberation from Internment

seemed the Japanese had the same idea for at night we heard traffic moving south. If this should be the strategy we might expect an early rescue!

On January 7 in the small hours of the morning we woke up realizing that there seemed to be unusual activity in the building where the Japanese stayed, near the gate. Some of the American committee were called to hand over records. The commandant and his staff left before daylight. They told the committee that we would be on our own. However, since there were thousands of Japanese troops in the surrounding area, we should stay in the camp. At daybreak the Stars and Stripes and Union Jack were hoisted on bamboo poles. Someone borrowed Ken's trumpet to play the national anthems while everyone stood and saluted. That evening over the loudspeaker we listened to some news—the Americans had landed at Lingayen Gulf and were pushing south towards Manila. We even heard President Roosevelt speaking from Washington.

We soon realized that in our excitement we were acting unwisely. With Japanese troops in the vicinity it would be wise not to attract their attention. After that, news reports were passed out more discreetly. The Filipinos around soon learned that the Japanese had left and began bringing in supplies. Promissory notes to be redeemed after liberation were readily accepted. Immediately there were three meals a day instead of two, more variety, and more quantity. There is no doubt that this was of the Lord to strengthen us for days ahead. With more food we got stronger and instead of struggling around listlessly we felt like putting a little more zip in our step. The committee opened the bodega and distributed the rice, a quantity to each individual. There were two purposes for this action. One, they feared that if the troops heard about that store of rice they would confiscate it. Second, it was to be kept by each family as a reserve in case of future shortage. Another life-saving provision for many of us.

After six days, the Japanese staff returned, much to our dismay. They evidently lost face and were no doubt reprimanded for leaving us. Their strict and oppressive attitude was an indication of this. One internee had sneaked out in the night to get food and was crawling back under the fence. Apparently he misunderstood the signals of his buddy on the inside because he was seen by the guards and shot. For some hours the committee argued with the Japanese about bringing this man to the hospital for treatment. When the commandant gave consent it was too late—the man was dead. Another man was shot on the suspicion of trying to escape.

The news that had circulated in the camp convinced the Japanese that a radio was hidden in the camp. They cut off the electricity (that was before transistors and battery operated radios). Dr. Nance at the hospital demanded that they have electricity there to preserve what few medicines remained. Actually the radio was there too! One day we were ordered to leave our barracks and line up on the road. For hours we stood in the hot sun while the guards began to search our quarters. The internees remonstrated that they should not search our rooms while we were not there. Finally, they had to give in because many of us simply returned to our barracks. The Japanese were told they could go ahead with their search but we would stand outside and watch. Actually it was a bit amusing to watch. The partitions were of "sawali" (woven bamboo split very thin). The guard lifted a homemade paper motto to see what was behind it! Nothing but the thin partition!

There were further cuts in the rations. People were dying of starvation. It was necessary to give some men a bit extra so they would have strength to dig graves. Twice I served as a pallbearer—the simple coffin was carried to the grave on a small handcart used to haul garbage! One for whom I thus served was an elderly Presbyterian missionary, Mr. Blair, who had spent many years in Korea and was caught in Manila by the exigency of war. The other was Dr. MacGill, also a Presbyterian who had served in Lucena and had done a great deal in the revision of the Tagalog Bible. Another old friend for whom I acted as pallbearer was Leslie Wolfe of the Disciples, Church of Christ. He was also a Tagalog scholar and died a few days after we were liberated.

Increased war activity all around us convinced us that the situation was very critical. It was reported that American forces entered Manila on February 3, 1945, and headed directly for Santo Tomas Camp. Unfortunately, after their liberation, the Japanese shelled those university buildings and some were killed and others wounded. From our camp we could see towns burn-

Liberation from Internment

ing. The Japanese were furious that after all their propaganda the Filipinos still were welcoming the returning Americans.

Finally, the Japanese said that no more rice was available and we were given a final ration of "palay" (unhusked rice). Our doctors warned us not to eat it without removing the husks. With the delicate condition of our stomachs it would probably be fatal. Was that what our enemies hoped? There being no rice mill people tried various ways of removing the husks. We took small blocks of wood and rubbed these vigorously over the "palay" on a rough table and then fanned away the chaff. It took most of the day to prepare enough rice for the day. Clearly it was time to begin using the reserves which had previously been issued to us. One dear sister, an elderly missionary with a small appetite brought some of her rice to us. She wasn't so optimistic about the return of the Americans and felt we were unwise in using up our supply. However, the Lord had showed her she should share with us.

The afternoon of February 22 a number of missionaries felt the emergency called for a special time of prayer. Food supplies were almost exhausted. In our family there was just enough for two more meager meals the following day. After that, what would we do? Trust the Lord, for our times are in His hands. Shortly after the prayer meeting, our hearts were cheered by the sight of U.S. bombers attacking places around the camp. We could actually see the bombs falling from the planes. Waking up during the night, it seemed quieter than usual—What could that mean? While we recognized the possibility that we would not get out of that experience alive, we didn't really think that would happen. We were confident that the Lord would take care of us, and we rested on His promises that He would deliver us.

At dawn on the 23rd of February we were up to get a fire going under a tin can in which was half of our remaining rice. We could get that going before roll call at seven o'clock when we would all line up on the road to be counted. However, word came that roll call would be later that morning. After our rescue we heard that the Japanese had plans to turn machine guns on us when we lined up for roll call. One or two of the internees had managed to slip out of the camp a day or two before. Through contact with Filipino guerillas they got in touch with MacArthur's headquarters about the desperate plight in the camp.

Just about seven o'clock planes few over the camp and something was falling from them. First thought—they are dropping food supplies. But no—those are paratroopers. Then what excitement! One of the planes, after dropping his load, swung low over the camp and on the fuselage in big letters we saw "RESCUE." A couple of years later when I told this story in the southern U.S. an ex-G.I. came to me after the service and told me he was the one who painted that word. He was ordered to paint the word but never knew until that evening which rescue it was.

Then everything broke loose! Excitement made us oblivious of the danger from flying bullets. Len dashed in and said, "Put the rest of the rice in that pot!" We crouched low and fanned the little fire. Being police deputies Ken and I were ordered to go through the barracks and tell people to lie down in their barracks. It was an exercise in futility—people laughed at us! Anna and Rose ran hand in hand to the front of the barracks to see an American soldier. We didn't know they were called G.I's or why. One of them shouted, "Get in there and lie down, you are flirting with death!" An old man in a neighboring barracks patted a machine gunner on the back and cheered him on.

Guerillas cut the barbed wire fences and poured in from all sides. The paratroopers' jump was their signal for action. The Japanese were about to take their usual morning physical exercises, arms piled at the side. They didn't have a chance to fight nor to escape. As we hurriedly ate our rice, amphibious tanks were rolling into the camp. They had come across Lake Laguna de Bay. They were supposed to evacuate the women and children, but men too climbed aboard. Our barracks monitor tried to preserve some semblance of order, but that only delayed us from getting on to the tanks.

Grabbing a suitcase each we went to an open area; and I tried to persuade Anna and Rose to climb aboard, but they wanted us to all stay together. The soldiers shouted "Women and children only!," but when I saw priests in their robes climbing on I was disgusted. Perhaps their robes qualified them! A newsman got hold of Ken, got his name, and the name of his grandmother in Buffalo. She would be notified. Ken told him about the rest of

Liberation from Internment

us, but the news report only mentioned Ken. So for ten days Anna's folks thought that only Ken was left alive.

We were told to start walking out of the camp. A G.I. threw us a chocolate bar which we shared among the five of us. How good it tasted! Along the road Filipinos gave us some bananas and raw eggs which we ate as we trudged along. Some people too tired to carry anything just left suitcases on the side of the road. There was a typewriter sitting there! An officer urged us on, "Please try to hurry!" He took my suitcase and carried it for me to speed up the movement. Thousands of Japanese troops were in the vicinity and we were miles from the American lines. At the main Manila south road some soldiers directed us to go on towards the beach.

Later we learned that the original plan was to take out as many as possible in the tanks across the lake. The rest would march north on the main road and shielded by troops and guerillas would fight their way back through the Japanese lines to the American forces. However, the amphibs made such good time and met so little resistance, they offered to return to the beach and pick up another load.

As we stood on the beach and waited, Japanese shells were bursting only a short distance away. One internee had hoarded a jar of brown sugar and he was going down the line offering everyone a spoonful—the first sugar we had tasted in months. A famous LIFE photographer was taking pictures, but somehow I never made the pages of that magazine. Later on I tried to obtain some of those pictures from news agencies. I got some, but none were of ourselves or our friends. Also, I was able to get an army film of the rescue and for a fleeting moment there we were standing together just before starting off for the beach. It was only excitement that kept us plodding along on that three-mile hike.

After a while the amphibs returned and we boarded them. The baggage was left behind—it would be brought later if they had room. It really wasn't worth much but we did get it. Some of the amphibs were fired on as they went across the lake to a point near Calamba which was then behind American lines. As we waited on the beach a Filipino sold me some cooked rice at an exorbitant price. But never mind; we were free, safe, well, and all together. Soon trucks came to take us to Bilibid, a penitentiary at Muntinlupa. The former occupants had either been released or escaped. All along the way Filipinos cheered "Mabuhay" and made the victory sign. By late afternoon of that thrilling day we pulled into another prison, but this one with the Stars and Stripes flying overhead. Even though I was not then an American citizen, there was a thrill in looking at that flag.

I quote from a news item dated February 24 which appeared in a Buffalo paper. "Striking from the sky, by land, and over water in enemy territory at dawn Friday, American troops and Filipino guerrillas brought freedom to 2146 in the civilian internment camp at Los Banos. . . . Only two of the captives were wounded in the brief battle at the camp and in the running fight with snipers which followed. Two of the rescuing force were killed and two wounded . . . Nothing could be more satisfying to a soldier's heart than this rescue." said Gen. Douglas MacArthur. "I am deeply grateful. God was certainly with us today."

The military authorities had estimated that rescuing 75% of the internees under those conditions would be considered a successful mission. The rescue was 100%, and with a very small number of casualties. Two days later the chaplain conducted a thanksgiving service for both the internees and the rescuing forces. We certainly had a great deal for which to be thankful to the Lord. Of course we were thankful to those men who risked their lives to save us. The chaplain said that when the call was made for a dangerous mission, the whole group volunteered. But after paying due respect to the bravery of soldiers and guerrillas and the precision of the planning, we have to recognize the truth of MacArthur's words, "God was certainly with us today." One fellow told me that he had never been in action where everything went so much according to plan.

My bed that Friday night was a hard metal bunk—no telling how many criminals had slept there! I picked up my Bible and read Psalm 66; it seemed as if it had been written for that special occasion! "He turned the sea into dry land, they passed through the river on foot." David never dreamed about amphibs! "You let men ride over our heads; we went through fire and water, but you brought us to a place of abundance." Would we ever forget those planes, the paratroopers dropping into our midst? Yes, I know this is eisegesis and not exegesis, but it was

Liberation from Internment 151

real comfort to me that night. "Come and listen, all you who fear God; Let me tell you what he has done for me . . . Praise be to God, who has not rejected my prayer or withheld his love from me."

17

HOMEWARD BOUND!

"May the groans of the prisoners come before you; by the strength of your arm preserve those condemned to die." (Psa. 79:11)

The Lord indeed had heard our groans and had preserved us. Now we were to spend six weeks in Bilibid waiting for repatriation. The military authorities hadn't been able to prepare adequately for us. Anna and Rose slept on a hard cement floor for several nights before blankets were provided. The boys and I were on those hard metal bunks. Food was supplied, but it seemed to us somewhat limited. Then we learned that in Santo Tomas Camp food had been abundant. The Red Cross even brought in coffee and donuts. The hungry internees there gorged themselves and suffered for it. Many were quite sick. So at Bilibid they limited us at first for our own good. But the internees found the garbage dump—bright shiny cans were still considered treasures. Also in many of those cans some food remained! The G.I.'s couldn't understand their fellow-Americans. To us we couldn't understand why they would complain about the food. They turned up their noses at scrambled eggs made from canned powdered eggs—we thought it was gourmet. After all we hadn't tasted eggs for months. One day the fragrant aroma of newly-baked bread assailed our nostrils—we hadn't smelt anything like that in years! To our dismay they wouldn't let us have any until the next day. At the first they needed to fly in food by parachute drops as the trucks couldn't get through fast enough.

The second day an MK (missionary kid) told me some fellow was asking about "Plymouth Brethren" missionaries. I soon located Homer Grob working with the hospital unit set up there. Homer was from Cleveland and in later years came back to the Philippines as a missionary for a while. Through him we met some other Christians and had some good fellowship together. In the evenings we would spread a blanket on the ground and have a time sharing the Word together. Sometimes we also shared some of the goodies they could obtain. Those were refreshing times of spiritual uplift for all of us.

A number of wounded Filipino civilians were being cared for in the hospital, and we learned that our good friend Maria Calica was a patient there. Mr. and Mrs. Calica and their family lived on the Canlubang Sugar Estate in Laguna. We had come to know them through Mrs. Dayton and her family who also came from there. In May, 1941, the boys and I with a Filipino evangelist had made an evangelistic trip to a number of towns. We spent a night in Canlubang then, had a gospel meeting, and stayed in the Calica home.

In the hospital in Bilibid she told me her story. In the fighting around Canlubang, a shell had demolished their house and her son had been killed. She and other members of the family had been injured, and they had lost all their earthly possessions. She had saved her Tagalog Bible and showed me how many pages were stained with her blood. What could I say to comfort this dear sister? It was she who comforted me! Through her tears she said, "But we know that all things work together for good to them that love God." She was a woman of much prayer and triumphant faith. Up until the time she passed away some 35 years later she remained a faithful prayer partner. There in the hospital she asked me to get her some Testaments or gospel portions from the chaplain if possible. She was having a Bible class and witnessing to other patients as they gathered around her bed. In the 1950's it was in her home in Canlubang that we had a part in helping in the formation of a local church.

Naturally we were concerned about the believers in San Juan, the chapel, and our home. Some news came to us through meeting Ismael Alfonso, one of the young fellows from San Juan. He was driving a truck for the Americans. Manila was still not safe as many Japanese snipers were holding out in big buildings and the Walled City. With the help of the chaplain we got passes for the boys and me to ride into Manila with the chaplain in his jeep. What a scene of ruin and destruction as we drove through the south side of the city! For blocks and blocks there was nothing but ruins. The retreating Japanese had gone on a rampage as they realized that only a small minority of Filipinos had been won over by their propaganda. We heard many stories of the atrocities. Some Spanish and better-class Filipinos took refuge in the chapel of the La Salle College; it was no safe sanctuary for most of them were brutally murdered there.

Most of the bridges across the Pasig had been blown up and replaced with temporary "bailey" bridges. The chaplain took us to Santo Tomas and warned us to be back there by five o'clock as there was a curfew from dusk to dawn. Anyone on the street would be shot, either by Japanese snipers or by patrolling troops. There were no kinds of transportation so we walked out to San Juan and called on some of the Christians. Some were still in their homes for there had been little destruction in that area. Others had fled to the provinces and generally had suffered loss. One sister and her child had died from sickness while they were fleeing. An American Bazooka bomb had exploded in front of the chapel. The building was riddled with holes from the fragments, but we could not see any structural damage. Our home was intact and empty with some damage to fixtures by previous occupants.

Returning to Santo Tomas, we spent the night there and met some of our friends who related their stories of God's preserving care for them. The next day we returned to Bilibid. In our walking through the city there had been times when we hardly recognized where we were. It was helpful to assess the situation there as we prayed for guidance from the Lord about our future. Should we stay on and re-establish the work at San Juan? Or should we go home for a badly needed and much delayed furlough?

There was an obvious need to help the Filipino believers through the time of re-gathering and rebuilding. The chapel needed extensive repairs and the work needed to be reorganized. Also, it was necessary to see about our home, involving legal matters and repairs. On the other hand, we hadn't been home for over seven years. Our health had been seriously impaired by months of starvation diet. The children needed to resume their education. Our loved ones were anxious to see us.

The authorities gave us a choice. They would take us home then by troopship or we could stay on. If we stayed, it would be months, perhaps years, before other shipping would be available. Also, it was uncertain how soon normal mail service and banking facilities would be available. As we prayed about this matter with a sense of urgency because we had to sign up for one or the other, we felt led to decide that if our home could be disposed of that would be an indication we should go home.

We were able to make another trip into Manila. Len's Spanish friends had been living in the home of other American friends. The latter was an electrical contractor and on his release from Los Baños foresaw big business opportunities in the rebuilding ahead. He wanted his house back, and the Spanish friends were therefore looking for another place to live. Naturally there was a housing shortage, so they asked Len if I would sell to them. The offer they made was not excessive, and it would probably have been possible to ask for more; but it was reasonable and later I calculated it covered all I had ever put into that house. Also the arrangements were made for them to assume the remaining small mortgage, pay off loans owed to Chinese who had befriended us in our need, and deposit some in the bank for a future home. All of this added up to a clear indication that we should return home.

What about the work in San Juan? God provided for that also. Homer Grob was transferred to a medical unit close to San Juan. With other fellows they helped repair the chapel and encourage the believers. Regular services were resumed and the testimony continued. Some of the older Christians still remember with affection the friendship and loving service of these servicemen. This happened in a number of places. Christian G.I's fellowshipped with the small groups of Filipino believers and helped rebuild their chapels and homes. This was much more obvious with Protestants than with Roman Catholics. It was one factor that paved the way for times of blessing and

Homeward Bound!

outreach with the gospel in the post-war years, but it did not benefit the Filipinos alone. Many of those servicemen saw the spiritual need and the opportunity for missionary work. Some years later I estimated that more than half of the new missionaries were ex-chaplains and ex-servicemen.

On April 9 it was our turn to leave Bilibid by truck. We had been given some Red Cross kits with toothbrushes and toothpaste, safety razors for men, and toiletries for women. Also, we had been issued some army fatigues and boots. Prior to that, we had one pair of shoes left. It wasn't a case of "Can I have the car this evening?"

On the way, we marvelled at the huge stocks of supplies piled high on vacant lots. There were no warehouses to hold them. To Filipinos who had been deprived of so much for years, these supplies presented a big temptation. Many of those items were being sold in the black market. Hundreds of jeeps were stolen and converted into the famous Manila jeepney. The U.S. Navy traced one jeep to a body shop where it was being converted. As soon as the work was completed they confiscated it. Shortly after they were presented with a bill for the work done! Whether it was ever paid, I don't know.

In the Manila North harbor we boarded a large troopship, S.S. Admiral Eberle. The women were segregated in the forepart and men towards the stern. We were in canvas bunks four deep, so if we drew up our knees we bumped the fellow above. The air conditioners didn't cool it but did keep the air fresh. The ship was clean but hot. No one was allowed on deck after dark, so we lay on our bunks with the perspiration running off us.

After a couple of days we pulled into anchorage in Leyte Gulf. Flags were half-mast and we learned President Roosevelt was dead. Then who succeeded him? Some of the crew said, "Harry Truman." "Who's he, never heard of him." We had been completely out of touch with what had been going on. We left Leyte in convoy with destroyer escorts. Each morning one member of the family stood ready with a blanket when the hatches opened, then dashed to claim a spot on the deck for that day. With 3000 internees, rotating troops and crew, there were over 5000 on that ship. Deck space was not for promenading but for sitting, as there was no room for anything else. Woe betide the hapless individual caught by the Marine guards without a life belt around his or her waist. Those belts would have been good for reducing except we didn't have anything to reduce.

We ran through a storm and felt sorry for the crews of the destroyer escorts as they wallowed through the waves. That night the ship rolled and pitched and we had to hold on to stay in our bunks. A fellow across from me had put his dentures in a tin plate under his bunk and with fascination we watched his dentures sliding back and forth across the deck.

One evening we pulled into the reef-bound island of Ulithi in the Caroline Islands. We looked with amazement at the fleet of ships being assembled there for an assault on the mainland of Japan. After replenishing supplies, we pushed on across the Pacific in beautiful weather. Usually two meals a day were served on those ships, but because of the needs of the internees they served us three meals. That meant the chow lines were almost continuous. After our years of deprivation it hurt us to see so much food wasted and left on the trays. To this day the customary waste of food in the average American home or restaurant is still most deplorable. In boyhood days we couldn't leave the table until our plates were clean. With millions around the world starving to death it is high time Americans awoke to the sin of waste.

A Coast Guard combo played what is called "music" on deck each day to the delight of some and boredom of others. Some years later in Manila, we met Redd Harper or "Mr. Texas" of one of the early Billy Graham films. We learned then that he was in that combo but not yet saved. After he was saved he would not play any of the worldly music. His talents were devoted to the Lord to sing his praises.

One Sunday evening a chaplain held a service in one of the dining halls. He announced his text was Acts 16:31 so we really expected a good gospel message. After all, how can one preach on that verse and not proclaim the way of salvation? That chaplain managed to do just that. Never once did he tell his audience what it meant to believe in Christ. I was just wishing he would give me five minutes!

One day the ship pulled into the bay off Honolulu, just long

Homeward Bound!

enough to pick up a number of customs, immigration, and FBI officials. They were to process the civilians for landing in Los Angeles. The original destination was San Francisco but was changed because of the conference for the formation of the United Nations organization then being held in San Francisco. Ken saw these officials in suits, white shirts, and ties and came to us, "Did you see those fellows? They sure look spiffy!" Quite a contrast to our shabby apparel. We realized we were facing a cultural gap even though we were coming home.

Between Honolulu and Los Angeles we were screened by those officials. We still had our British passport. Our original Canadian passport had been cancelled because we had lost our Canadian status by being out of that country for more than five years on our first term. Holding a British passport, it was presumed that we would be proceeding to Britain. Although I had my brother George in England, I had no intention of going there under war conditions. The FBI men showed considerable interest about the U.S. dollars in my possession and that was quite natural. They seemed satisfied with my explanation. Some dollars were given to us by the British authorities in Manila for travel expenses to be repaid on demand. There has never been any such demand. Then the rest were U.S. dollars given as a downpayment on our house. I had no idea where the Spanish buyers obtained dollars. We were questioned again about this on our arrival in Los Angeles where again they accepted my explanation.

Because of the crowded conditions and strict discipline on the ship there were no opportunities to gather together for services or Bible study. There was no privacy even for family devotions. So our spiritual exercises were mostly limited to our own private devotions and Bible reading. But it was also a restful time to review all the way in which the Lord had led us. Not only to review the past but also consider what the future would hold for us. Of one thing we were very sure: the Lord would not fail us. For three years we had been cut off entirely from contacts with the homelands. There had been many trials, many dangers seen and unseen, many testings of faith. The Lord was faithful through it all. So we could face the future with confidence in Him.

When we got home, that absence of news about folks at home

proved very embarrassing at times. With older friends we were embarrassed to ask about their partners for fear they might have gone home to be with the Lord. On one occasion I was greeting a lady who had graciously entertained us in her home some years before. Then she and her husband had a delightful little boy. Innocently, I inquired about her son and the dear sister burst into tears. Then I learned that this only son had passed away some time previously. It was most embarrassing for her and for me, but I thought I could safely inquire about a young boy.

It was on May 2, Anna's birthday, that our ship docked at Long Beach. What a birthday present—also for Ken whose birthday was the previous day. Excited troops and internees lined the rails. Not many relatives would be there because our arrival was not announced until we had safely arrived. As soon as the gangplank was in place, one G.I. rushed down to kiss the soil of the good U.S.A. No doubt many times he had wondered if he would ever see it again.

It didn't take long to clear customs, for none of us were weighed down with baggage. That morning Anna had turned her ankle so was somewhat crippled. When the Red Cross ladies noticed this they took special care of us. We should not go on the buses to Los Angeles; they would provide a car and driver for us. This took a bit of time and then on the way we had a flat tire. We helped fix this and finally arrived at the Elks Club, where we were to be processed, in the early evening.

Perhaps the most impressive sight as we drove along were the stalls of fruit in apparent abundance—how different from what we had left behind. Yet people grumbled about shortages and rationing of some items. Many evidently hadn't faced up yet to the realities of war. The Red Cross had taken over the Elks Club facilities to care for the needs of internees. They were ready to provide hotel accommodations, travel arrangements, communications with loved ones, and even ration books were on hand. While I took care of such business, Anna was taken upstairs to a lounge where she could rest. Rose came along with a big orange which someone had given her. I asked her why she hadn't eaten it. She was waiting until we could all get together so she could divide it equally. For months everything we had had been divided that way, but those days were over! She could go ahead and eat it all herself. We would get ours in due time. We were home at last!

> "And though by storms assailed, And though by trials pressed, Himself our Life, He bears us up, Right onward to the rest."

18

HOME AT LAST

"They were glad when it grew calm, and he guided them to their desired haven." (Psa. 107:30)

Back in the 1920's, two brothers, Fred and John Murset, with their families, moved from Buffalo to Los Angeles. Leaving a missionary-minded assembly like Assembly Hall, they were disappointed at the lack of missionary interest in southern California. The wives, Hattie and Dora, missed the monthly sisters' missionary meetings they had enjoyed in Buffalo. With a few others who were like minded, they endeavored to start a monthly ladies' missionary meeting. They encountered opposition. Some of the older brethren thought such an activity was unscriptural. In fact, in one elders' meeting, a brother had a fatal heart attack while speaking against such sisters' meetings. Eventually a monthly meeting was commenced and for several years Hattie Murset was one of the most active. It is safe to say that the awakening of missionary interest in southern California was largely due to the untiring enthusiasm of a number of sisters.

Late in the evening of May 2, 1945, the phone rang in the Murset home; the Red Cross was calling. Immediately, Hattie guessed it was the Brooks for she had heard a report of internees arriving. It didn't take them long to get downtown to the Elks Club. Len was standing near the information desk when he heard a lady ask where she could locate the Brooks family. He introduced himself, and it wasn't long before we were in the hospitable home of the Mursets. The two brothers lived next door to each other and they had room for the five of us.

The next day was the monthly meeting of the ladies' missionary group, so Hattie was delighted to take Anna as her special guest. The ladies, of course, were delighted to see one for whom they had been praying so much. That meeting was the beginning of an outpouring of love gifts.

The rest of us went downtown window shopping; but, unfortunately for Rose, the menfolks rushed by the things she wanted to look at. Passersby soon recognized us as returned internees by the shabby way we were dressed, but this was to our good in the stores. Rare items like white shirts were brought out of the back room, so we got priority on things which were in short supply because of the war. When I explained that I would need my suit by Saturday because I was to preach on Sunday, the order was marked RUSH.

While in the Los Baños internment camp, I broke the crystal on my watch. Dr. Widdowes, a United Brethren missionary, had set up a watch repair shop there and he made a new crystal from discarded eyeglasses. It was a good fit but wouldn't stay in place because we had no glue. For months I had been carrying it around in a matchbox. When I went to a watch repairer, he was curious to know why I was carrying the watch in a matchbox. When he heard my story, he had the watch cleaned and the new crystal installed in a few days and refused payment. Apparently he was not a Christian but thought we had suffered enough!

Since several of the servicemen we knew in Manila were connected with the Navigators, Dawson Trotman invited us to his home in Pasadena on Friday evening. Suspecting there would be young ladies present, Len announced he was not going since he had nothing decent to wear. However, we prevailed upon him because all would know the circumstances. The Western Assemblies Home was then right across the street from the Trotman home, so we visited there first. This Navigator home had been built by a lumber merchant with beautiful woodwork and the bedroom closets were all of cedar. After dinner Daws took us upstairs, threw open a closet, and told us to help ourselves to what would fit us. Many fellows going overseas

Home at Last

had left their civilian clothes with Daws. Some of them would never return. So we came away with a load of clothes and shoes. Len was glad he went!

We still had our British passport and would have been provided transportation to Britain, but we had no desire to go there. VE day came while we were in Los Angeles. I lost my Canadian citizenship by being gone too long during our first term. Even though I had been four years in the Canadian army during World War I, the Canadian consul wouldn't allow us to go to Canada unless we had a re-entry permit to the U.S. This we couldn't obtain because we were visitors in the U.S. We tackled the consul in San Francisco to no avail and finally went to the one in Seattle. All the way we were praying about this because naturally we wanted to visit our relatives and friends in Victoria. It turned out that the Seattle consul was Irish from Belfast, and he noted that Anna was born there. He then called the Commissioner in Vancouver and got permission for a visit to Victoria.

Heading north we stopped a couple of days in the San Francisco Bay area. There we met Eldon Durant who had been in our home in Manila. He had been wonderfully preserved by the Lord through the Pacific war, serving on a submarine which sank a number of Japanese ships. He tried hard to get airline reservations for Anna and Rose north to Portland, but even internment didn't confer any priority in that. After an evening meeting at Bethany Chapel we travelled north by bus and had seats most of the way. We stayed overnight for a meeting in Portland and then went on to Seattle where my sisters were waiting for us.

Three weeks were spent in Victoria trying to get some rest between visiting with friends and having meetings. Naturally everyone wanted to hear our story of God's goodness and preserving care. Then it was back to Seattle to take a train across country to Buffalo. In Chicago, we had to change trains and found a vast crowd waiting for the train east. "Servicemen and dependents first" was the call as the gate was opened. A sailor standing beside Anna said, "I'm going to get on that train; I haven't seen my Mother for three years." Anna replied, "I haven't seen mine for almost eight years." Learning the reason for this, he said, "You come with me as my dependent. You come on as my wife." He acquired not only an instant "wife" but also her husband and three children for the few moments it took to board that train. We never saw him again! Amazingly we also got seats with Rose sitting between us. As the train left Chicago, a dining car steward came through—"Someone left his teeth in the dining car!" That, of course, was greeted with a roar of laughter—did someone take out his teeth to eat? Shortly after he returned with a sheepish-looking G.I. in tow.

What a great welcome we had in Buffalo, first at the station and then by Anna's parents at home. Those years had been an anxious time for them, harder on them perhaps than on us. The Christmas package they sent in 1941 had been returned months later and put in a cupboard to await our return. While we were celebrating Christmas, 1941, in June, 1945, a newsman and photographer arrived for an interview. The picture taken on the front steps was so clear that people recognized us on the street.

Shortly after our arrival in Buffalo, there was a special Sunday afternoon rally where we gave our testimony in the Statler Hotel Ballroom. Some friends took us to lunch there before the rally. Our host told the waitress to take good care of us since we had just been released from a Japanese internment camp. "Oh, I bet you said your prayers there," she said. I replied, "No, we didn't say our prayers—we prayed. Do you know the difference?" People thought we were very thin, not realizing that we had regained a lot of lost weight even before we left the Philippines. From not having enough to eat, our problem was the reverse—too much rich food!

After the hassle about getting into Canada, Anna decided to reclaim her American citizenship lost when she married me. The law was changed two days after we were married and she would not have needed to lose her citizenship, but we didn't know that then. At the same time she was getting her papers together, I established residence so I could acquire American citizenship. There would be some advantages in this when we returned to the Philippines. However, all this took rather longer than we had anticipated, so it was four years before we returned to the Philippines.

This was probably of the Lord because of the needs of our family. Leonard was drafted into the army in spite of the internment experiences. When we were released from internment, Gen. MacArthur authorized all civilian internees to wear the

Home at Last

Pacific War Ribbon. So Len wore a campaign ribbon while in basic training, calling forth more than one question from officers. He was sent to Germany as part of the Occupation Forces. On Decoration Day, 1946, at a conference in Chicago, I learned about an army order authorizing release of ex-internees. When I sent this information to Len, I thought that with the ways of bureaucracy, he might be home for Christmas. He found a copy of the order in the office where he was working and arrived home on July 4, in time to accompany us to the Guelph Summer Bible School.

Kenneth was busy in high school when he received draft board orders. One of his instructors took a personal interest and argued with the draft board that Ken needed to complete his much-delayed high school, so he got exemption. Rose was finishing up elementary school and was in high school when we left for the Philippines.

Those were busy years as invitations for meetings and conferences came from many parts of the country. Thanksgiving Day, 1945, I spoke at the one-day conference at Assembly Hall in Buffalo, then took the night train to be at the longer conference in Chicago. There I had a reminder that the years had taken a toll physically for I came down with a very bad cold. By resting in between, I was able to keep up with speaking engagements, which included giving a devotional message over WMBI radio each morning for a week.

Friends took me into their homes instead of staying in the missionary home where I would have had to fend for myself, and I was most grateful for their consideration. After the conference meeting one night, Mr. and Mrs. Bill McCartney graciously took me home and put me to bed in their own double bed. In the early hours of the morning I became aware of a child beside the bed. I threw back the covers for a moment while a little girl crawled in beside me without a word, not even realizing it wasn't her Daddy and Mommy. When I woke after daylight, she was still sleeping so I lay quietly until she would wake up. When she did, I greeted her with a cheery "Good Morning!" She contemplated me for a few moments and then without a word ran out of the room. Then it was back to Buffalo for Christmas, the first in eight years with the family there.

The next spring, Anna was speaking at a ladies' conference in

Flint, Michigan. Some of the sisters from Detroit rented a bus to go. The Flint brethren who took care of the meals at the conference talked with the bus driver and learned that he was one of the paratroopers who made the jump at Los Baños. It was an interesting opportunity to thank him personally for his help in our rescue. I bought two 16 mm black and white news films of the bombing of Manila by the Japanese in 1941 and the liberation by the Americans in 1945. While purchasing a projector I also learned the possibility of purchasing a film from the military. We got a film of the rescue, and for a few fleeting moments there we were in a group waiting to be evacuated from Los Baños. These, of course, added interest to the accounts given about our experiences.

For three summers we had some most enjoyable times of fellowship and ministry at the Guelph Summer Bible Camp. It was indeed a privilege to meet with many men of God there. Some of them have since gone home to be with the Lord: Dr. H. G. Lockett, Alfred P. Gibbs, and my fellow-Victorian, John Smart. On Lord's Days we went out to nearby assemblies to minister the Word. One of my responsibilities was to organize groups of students to canvass the town of Guelph with literature.

During the 1948 session, I had to make a trip to Buffalo in connection with my application for naturalization; so I became the butt of the Friday evening skit that week. Spearheaded by Ernie Woodhouse, I was charged with treason by a mock court, noted more for hilarity than sobriety. Found guilty, I was "shot" and then laid out for burial on the pingpong table. Then a large trunk was hauled off to the garbage dump with my "corpse" supposedly in it. One little boy observing the proceedings had seen that I was not actually in the trunk and hastened to reassure my wife of that fact!

We used to go swimming in the pool at Fergus. On another visit to Guelph, I accompanied A. P. Gibbs to that town. He wanted to take a picture of a grave in the cemetery beside the Presbyterian Church there. We found the grave marked with the name Clephane. He was the ne'er-do-well brother of Elizabeth Clephane who wrote the hymn:

> "There were ninety and nine that safely lay,
> In the shelter of the fold

Home at Last

> But one was out on the hills away
> Far off from the gates of gold."

Because of his dissolute character, the brother had been sent by the family to Canada and no doubt Elizabeth had him in mind when she wrote the hymn. Mr. Gibbs and I wondered if his burial in the churchyard indicated that he had at last been brought back to the fold.

As our stay at home was longer than we had anticipated, we were glad to help in the Lord's work at home. For three months in the spring of 1948, I took a series of meetings in the Buffalo area: Four nights each week in four different assemblies and rotating the Sundays between these places. Some of this was combined with afternoon visitation in the neighborhood. Feeling there was a lack of teaching about the church and why we meet as we do, I endeavored to present the New Testament teaching on this important subject.

It was a great joy to us when Leonard and Kenneth decided to attend Emmaus Bible School in Toronto. At first, Len intended to go for the one year course, but soon decided to stay on for three years. It was there that he met Esther Christiansen and they were engaged shortly before we returned to the Philippines. Kenneth and Elaine Petersen were engaged and both attended Emmaus. They were married in Buffalo in September, 1948. Len and Esther were married the following August, but by that time we were back in Manila. Rose was in high school in Buffalo, and it seemed best to leave her there to stay with Anna's sister and her husband, George Gibson. After finishing high school, she took a nursing course at the Deaconess Hospital in Buffalo.

We left Buffalo in the spring of 1949. I had acquired my American naturalization a few months before. We were all together for the last weekend, and it was not easy to say goodbye to Len, Esther, Ken, and Elaine as they returned to Emmaus on Sunday afternoon. It was still harder to leave Rose and Anna's relatives a couple of days later. They were all standing on the porch waving as we drove away and turned the corner. There came to my mind the words of Christ, "Everyone who has left houses or brothers or sisters or father or mother or children or fields for my sake will receive a hundred times as much and will inherit eternal life" (Matt. 19:29). Anna said later that she recalled the same verse. As we left three children behind, I dared to ask the Lord (though with feeble faith) to grant us 300 spiritual children.

Our first stop was with friends at Cleveland who had a special meeting for us that evening. The Hough Bakery, managed by the Pile brothers, had a beautiful large book cake for us. As they had plenty of other goodies, they kindly offered to send the cake back to Anna's folks in Buffalo. They were so fond of showing it off that it risked getting stale before they ate it!

After visits to Victoria, we made our way to San Francisco. Shortly before boarding the ship there, we had a call from Kenneth to announce the birth of our first grandchild, Dale, born on July 17, 1949. So in the midst of parting from loved ones, there was the joy of knowing that another generation had begun. We constantly praise the Lord for all his great goodness to us as a family. In His wonderful grace we have ten grandchildren, all of them know the Lord and are going on for Him. As of May, 1982, we had 14 great-grandchildren. We praise the Lord that the grandchildren who are married all have fine Christian partners. We take no credit for all this, though we feel we owe a great deal to our Christian parents. When we see the tragedy in many Christian families, we just wonder why the Lord should have been so good and gracious to us. Like Jacob of old, we say, "I am unworthy of all the kindness and faithfulness you have shown your servant" (Gen. 32:10).

Crossing the Pacific, we had time to contemplate what lay ahead of us. Finding a home to live in; back to the work with all its needs and challenges; to recoup the losses and regather those who had been scattered; to plan for expansion of the work and pray about the future. A great challenge lay ahead of us. After the havoc of the war years, things would not be the same. Well we knew that we were not sufficient for these things, but we also knew that our sufficiency is of God and His grace is always sufficient.

19

POST-WAR RELIGIOUS AND POLITICAL CONDITIONS

"Because a great door for effective work has opened to me, and there are many who oppose me." (1 Cor. 16:9)

Before writing about the Lord's work in the Philippines after World War II, it might be well to review both the political and religious background in these islands. These conditions do have a bearing on the development of the work.

When we arrived in 1922, the Philippines was a dependency of the United States. The country had its own legislature and the two most prominent Filipino leaders were Manuel Quezon and Sergio Osmeña. However, the final authority was in the hands of the American governor-general. The American intention was to gradually turn over the control to the Filipinos. On our arrival, General Leonard Wood was governor-general. Being a military man he was strict in abiding by the laws and was authoritative. He was not popular with the politicians who had pretty much their own way with the previous governor-general. He had been an easy-going man and, according to reports, shared in the loot that many acquired. Naturally the Filipinos felt the process of becoming independent was too slow and that the Americans were seeking their own advantages. While there was no doubt some truth in this, American rule had brought many benefits which they had not had under the Spanish regime. One of the most prominent of these benefits was the public school education. This was signalled by the arrival of many American teachers who were known as "the Thomasites" because they arrived on the S.S. Thomas soon after American troops landed in 1898.

In 1935 the Commonwealth Government was inaugurated with Manuel Quezon as President. Being an historical event I took the boys downtown to see the inauguration ceremonies. The Presidential Palace, Malacañang, previously the official residence of the governor-general and before that of the Spanish governor, was turned over to the Philippine President. The United States was then represented by a High Commissioner. The Commonwealth was a transitional government for ten years. During the period the tariffs would be adjusted gradually so that by the time the Philippines became a fully independent republic it would no longer be dependent upon trade with the United States.

Unfortunately, these plans were interrupted by the war in the Pacific and the invasion of the Japanese. The leaders of the Philippine government were evacuated to the United States; President Quezon later died there after a long-time illness with tuberculosis. He was succeeded by Sergio Osmeña who had the assistance of men like Carlos P. Romulo. Some of the Filipino leaders left behind joined the guerrilla movement in their continuing opposition to the Japanese. Others believed they could serve their country and people by a measure of cooperation with the Japanese. Still others were apparently opportunists who felt they could advance their own cause by collaboration with the Japanese. It was difficult to determine at times the difference between these two latter groups. Jose P. Laurel, a prominent politician, was appointed President by the Japanese when the Japanese ostensibly forestalled the American plan of granting full independence. Laurel was wounded in an assassination attempt on a golf course near our home.

President Osmeña and Carlos Romulo came ashore with Gen. MacArthur in the first landing in Leyte in the fall of 1944. The Japanese were finally defeated in 1945. The following year on July 4, 1946, the Republic of the Philippines was inaugurated. In later years the date of Independence Day was changed to June 12 to conform to an earlier independence movement in 1896 during the time of the Spanish regime.

Post-War Religious and Political Conditions 173

It was a most difficult time for the birth of the new republic. Most of the country lay in ruins because of the bitter battles against the Japanese. One-sixth of the population had been decimated by the horrors of war. The country had been stripped by the Japanese of many of its assets. Like a Phoenix arising from its ashes, the country made great strides but with great effort and expense.

Yet there were many problems remaining. Graft and corruption was rampant. Some of the political leaders gained great power in their own bailiwicks through their bodyguards and private armies. In Central Luzon even before World War II, there had been unrest among the farmers, most of whom were oppressed tenant farmers for absentee landlords. These warred as guerrillas against the Japanese as the Hukbalahaps or Huks which was an abbreviation for the Tagalog of "Army fighting against the Japanese." This movement was infiltrated by Communists and to this day have continued as dissidents against the government, but more generally known now as the New People's Army. In the south, the Moslem Moros also wanted an independent government and this antagonism of the Moros goes back even into Spanish times. In recent years they have formed the Mindanao National Liberation Front, though many of the Moros are not in favor of this organization.

In the 1950's President Ramon Magsaysay took a firm stand against the Huks. For those who surrendered to the government, he offered land and farming utensils in virgin land in Mindanao. For those who rejected this offer, there was relentless fighting. He was very popular and was fondly called "The Guy." Unfortunately, he died in a fatal plane crash near Cebu and his loss was keenly felt.

From 1968 to 1972, the Communists became bolder in their attacks. There was a great deal of student unrest and many demonstrations. These took on an anti-American tone as students gathered outside the U.S. Embassy. Crimes such as bank robberies and arson became common. We wondered what the outcome would be. While on furlough in 1969 (to 1970), we were questioned by Ken if we should return. As we prayed about it my thoughts turned to Revelation 3:8, "See I have placed before you an open door that no man can shut." LeValley's were also on furlough at the time and Jim called to ask what our plans were. I mentioned this verse as the Lord's leading to us and he agreed that they felt led the same way.

The folks had a celebration for us on our fiftieth wedding anniversary in September, 1972. In connection with that, Hahn Browne of Far East Broadcasting Company arranged for us to be received by President Ferdinand Marcos at Malacañang. He granted us 15 minutes of his time in a very interesting interview in which Ken and Elaine and Rose shared. At that time there were many rumors of impending martial law. As we left the President's study, Hahn asked if any decision had yet been made and was told that the matter was being studied.

The following week our mission group was greatly saddened by the death of Teddy St. Clair, the second son of Steve and Dot, who were houseparents at Faith Academy. Teddy had gone outside and had apparently fallen into a small, shallow fishpond. The funeral was held two days later from the San Juan Gospel Chapel. In the Saturday of this weekend, we got up and found that no radio station was on the air nor was our morning paper delivered. The report was that martial law had been declared— all radio and TV stations closed down as well as all newspapers. All airports had also been closed overnight. Ken called the U.S. Embassy to ask if they had any instructions for U.S. nationals. We were told that we could go about our usual business and not be alarmed as we waited for further developments.

We didn't see such things as tanks rolling down the streets nor much evidence of the military. Gradually radio stations were permitted to resume operations under certain regulations. Far East Broadcasting Company was one of the first to be granted this permission. Also, papers resumed publication though obviously under censorship. The immediate outcome was the cessation of outward dissent. There was no restriction on our religious liberty nor any hindrance to our spiritual ministry. (In any case, it is not our policy to participate in political affairs.) It was undoubtedly a form of dictatorship against which the opposition rallied continually. Martial law was lifted just prior to the Pope's visit in early 1981.

Through all these different forms of government there has been religious liberty. Prior to World War II the Roman Catholic Church was the dominant religious force. They were in the majority and boasted that the Philippines is the only Christian

Post-War Religious and Political Conditions

nation in the Orient. Naturally they had advantages which were not shared by the Protestants who were and still are in the minority numerically. However, there have been many changes in these post-war years. There has been a greater openness to the Gospel, and these have been days of great opportunity in the work of the Lord. It may be worthwhile to consider some of the factors that have made this possible.

First, there is the factor of population growth. The population had increased six-fold during the period of Protestant missions, from about eight million at the turn of the century to over 48 million as of 1982. The population has more than doubled since World War II. There are just that many more people to be reached. Missionary effort always seems to lag behind the growth of population. It was only natural that in early days missionary work was carried on in the more accessible areas. The Bible was soon translated into the larger languages which had already been put into Roman script by the early Roman friars. In these early days there just weren't enough missionaries to penetrate the tribal areas which were not so easily reached. The training of national missionaries was also going on at a slower pace. Since World War II, there has been more outreach into tribal areas by groups like Summer Institute of Linguistics, New Tribes Mission, and Overseas Missionary Fellowship.

A second factor in the growth of missions was an outcome of the war itself. As the liberation forces poured into this country, there were among them Christian servicemen and godly chaplains. For the first time in their island-hopping conquests, they came to a land where many could speak English. Thus, they found fellowship with Filipino Christians. As it had been in San Juan, so it was in many places; chapels were damaged or destroyed and believers scattered. Christian G.I's helped to rebuild in many of the small evangelical congregations. It did not escape the attention of many communities that this voluntary help was more prevalent among Protestants than Roman Catholics. These practical demonstrations of Christian faith added prestige to what had been despised and insignificant minority groups.

Yet it also worked in another way. As the G.I's and chaplains worked with Filipino Christians, they were getting a first-hand experience of the missionary work. They saw the need, had a vision, and were challenged by the future possibilities. The most marked example of this is the Far Eastern Gospel Crusade, whose name is now SEND International. It was born in a servicemen's center in Manila in September, 1945, and has reached out to other lands as well. There was a time in the late 1950's when it seemed as if the majority of new male missionaries were ex-chaplains or ex-servicemen who had been here during the war.

A factor in the progress of missions has been the change in the Roman Catholic Church in recent years. Since the time of the Second Vatican Council and days of Pope John, Protestants are no longer labeled as heretics but are viewed as "separated brethren." In March, 1937, Testaments and Gospel literature were publicly burned in a plaza in Zamboanga. In recent years, priests have had a part in preparing new Bible translations in various languages of the Philippines. The people are being encouraged to read the Bible, though at one time it was banned for the laity. On Billy Graham's first visit to Manila some years ago, the archbishop forbade Roman Catholics to attend. On a more recent Crusade it is reported that 60% of the inquirers put themselves down as Catholics. Nowadays, a Bible verse is often seen in the obituaries of those who are evidently Roman Catholics.

In the early days of Bible School of the Air, priests and nuns forbade students to receive our courses. In later years, we have had requests from priests and others for Emmaus Courses to help them in teaching about the Bible. There have been many Bible study groups for Catholics. The charismatic movement has had a great influence among their clergy and laity. Questions have arisen about papal authority. Chinks have appeared in the monolith! The present openness to the Gospel was unthought of a few years ago.

A fourth factor in the progress of missionary work since World War II has been the increase in the number of different missions in these years. One reason for this was the closing of the door for missionary work in China and in what was Indochina. As the missionaries were forced out of these lands they looked for other fields of service. It was our privilege to entertain in our home the first survey team of the then China Inland Mission, now Overseas Missionary Fellowship. The stay of Raymond Frame and Stephen Knight with us was a refreshing experience for us, and we were happy to share what information we had and to help in this new outreach. About the same time we enjoyed fellowship with Dick Pittman who stayed with us for a time while on a similar mission for Summer Institute of Linguistics. (In later years Dr. Richard Pittman was honored with the prestigious Magsaysay Award as representing SIL.) There were other groups too that came here because of the open door. Here was a field with religious liberty and not too much difficulty in obtaining visas.

Of course, this same freedom also provided an open door for some cults that, for us, were not so welcome. Seventh-Day Adventists had been here before the war. However, in recent years the Mormons and Jehovah's Witnesses have been very active. There are also cults which are indigenous. "Iglesia ni Kristo" (Church of Christ) founded by Felix Manalo at the time of World War I has grown rapidly. With a distinctive type of church architecture, they aim to rival the Catholic Church. Since their adherents follow their leaders, they have been able to wield some political influence by telling their people for whom to vote. Also, faith healers linked with spiritists have attracted considerable attention. People have come from other countries in the hopes of getting healed.

A fifth factor has been the modern methods of evangelism through radio and television. While we used the radio commercial stations prior to the war, it was in 1948 that the Christian station of the Far East Broadcasting Company began operations. The impact of this radio effort has reached all over the Islands as local stations have been established in various places besides the main station just north of Manila. The wider use of radio has been facilitated by the invention of tape recorders and transistors. Back to the Bible Broadcasters have had an extensive ministry in the Philippines with its radio programs and also literature. Others have used television programs with advantage though the expense has been a limiting factor.

Finally, there is the factor of increased participation by national believers in the spread of the Gospel and in church planting. This, of course, is the goal of most missionary work—the indigenous church. So in local churches and in the Bible Schools and seminaries the nationals are carrying the burden. Foreign missionaries are here to help and serve as partners, leaving the administration to the nationals. This has gone a step further in that Filipinos from various Christian groups have gone to other lands as missionaries. One couple from the San Juan Gospel Chapel has been serving in Thailand with OMF and have done a great work there. It is a tremendous thrill to see the church in the Philippines not only receiving missionaries but also sending them forth, to their own people and to other lands.

20

REHABILITATION IN SAN JUAN

"It was he who gave some to be apostles, some to be prophets, some to be evangelists, and some to be pastors and teachers, to prepare God's people for works of service, so that the body of Christ may be built up." (Eph. 4:11-12)

During the four years of our absence from the Philippines, some rebuilding of the work had been done with the help of visiting servicemen. Some of the believers who had been scattered returned to San Juan and to their homes. Services had been resumed in the damaged chapel and preliminary repairs had been made. A small amount of money was released by the government for war damage, which helped in making some repairs. Soon after our return, a number of men gathered one evening to lay down a cement floor in the chapel. During the first few months, there was a great deal that needed to be done. Visitation of former church members and interested friends needed to be done and also services needed to be arranged and the Sunday school organized. We were thankful to have with us at that time Dr. and Mrs. Thomas Parks. They came here on a business project with a Chinese businessman but also with a view to help in the Lord's work. To our mutual disappointment, this venture could not be pursued (though no fault of theirs), and they returned to the United States. However, their presence and fellowship meant a great deal to us at that time.

Having sold the house we lived in before, there was the need to find another home. Mr. and Mrs. Dayton kindly allowed us to stay with them while we were house hunting. This took longer than anticipated, due first to the difficulty of finding a suitable place. Then once we were assured of the Lord's will in our choice, there were legal problems concerning the property. Many records had been destroyed during the war, and it wasn't always easy to get these things straightened out. After the deal was settled and before we moved in, there was a need for new electrical wiring and changing the meter. Saturday afternoon when this had been done we had a very heavy shower of rain, which caused a short in the meter, starting a fire. In the goodness of the Lord, we were able to break the wires with the help of a serviceman who was visiting us. In the drenching downpour this was a risky operation, and I had visions of our house being burnt down before we even occupied it. Our friend's quick action limited the fire to the meter and the immediate wiring.

With regard to the chapel itself in San Juan, I might add here some late developments. Through the years, the steady growth of members attending necessitated a number of enlargements and improvements in the building. Now we wish we had more land on which to expand. For a while we thought we might be able to purchase the lot, or part of it, adjacent to the chapel. That deal fell through and in any case it would have been quite expensive. The most recent renovation was in 1976, but by 1982, plans were being drawn not only to enlarge the chapel but also to increase the number of Sunday school rooms. There were not enough rooms for all the classes with an average attendance of about 250. The chapel is well filled for the preaching service every Lord's day morning with around 250 to 300 attending. Although almost all of the members speak and understand English, the bulk of the services are in Tagalog.

At the back of the chapel is a two-story building. On the upper floor are apartments for the caretaker and for a national worker with their families. On the ground floor is an office which also serves as a conference room and an apartment for transient workers, and library and reading room. Some of the national workers from the provinces need to come to Manila occasionally, so there is a place where they can stay overnight. The library is well-organized and well used, too.

Rehabilitation in San Juan

The larger task before us in 1949 was the spiritual rebuilding of the work of the Lord. In one of my trips while on furlough I had been on a train in Canada going to Ottawa. A Roman Catholic priest took the seat beside me. As we started up a conversation, he noticed the book I was reading, "Divine Principles of Missions," by W. E. Vine. I told him its main thrust was that the New Testament principles and patterns of missionary work were quite adequate in this modern age. Then I also pointed out that in Communist countries there are many small local churches meeting in homes. They continued to function because the authorities found it difficult to deal with them since they had no central organization or leaders. He seemed interested, but I don't know if I made any real impression on him.

However, during the years there have been many opportunities to observe different missionary methods and operating principles. There is no doubt in my mind that in the Word of God we have a sufficient guide regarding our service for the Lord. The record of the early church's missionary outreach in the Book of Acts gives us clear guidance regarding missionary work. Luke's inspired record in Acts is not merely an historical record; it is a pattern that we should analyze and follow.

In recent years a great deal has been said and written about church planting and church growth. This is commendable. However, some of these writings give the impression that the exponents of church growth feel they have just discovered something new. But it has been there in the New Testament all along! It is this principle that the preaching of the Gospel and the salvation of souls must result in gathering the saved into a local church fellowship. The effectiveness of much modern evangelism has been weakened because of inadequate follow-up. It is not enough to tell converts to go to the church of their choice; they don't know enough of the truth to make the right choice. They need to be guided into a local church where they will find the truth of God's Word, the fellowship of God's people, and the opportunities in God's service.

There are, unfortunately, many churches today where the Word of God is not being expounded and where many members have no opportunity for service, other than attending services. Because of this, many earnest Christians lose interest in their local church. They turn to para-church organizations to find fellowship with like-minded Christians and to seek outlets for serving the Lord. There is no doubt that many of these para-church organizations do an excellent work in ministering to specific groups and for special purposes. However, there is an inherent weakness in many of them because they do not contribute to the building up of local churches. The writer of the Epistle to the Hebrews wrote, "Let us not give up meeting together, as some are in the habit of doing, but let us encourage one another—and all the more as you see the Day approaching" (Heb. 10:25 NIV). There is no doubt that the writer had in mind the meetings in the local church. There may be value in businessmen, students, those of the medical profession, etc., getting together; but it should not be at the expense of the regular church services.

The Scripture teaching is that local churches should be indigenous and autonomous. While remaining self-governing under the Lord's direction, each church is free to have fellowship with other like-minded churches. In order to be indigenous, each local church needs spiritual leadership through elders and deacons. On the return phase of their first missionary journey "Paul and Barnabas appointed elders for them in each church and, with prayer and fasting, committed them to the Lord in whom they had put their trust" (Acts 14:23). In a new work like that, it was necessary for the pioneer missionaries to point out men they considered fit to be elders. Later on in the Pastoral Epistles, Paul wrote about the qualifications needed for elders. We cannot help wondering if the men appointed by Paul and Barnabas had all these qualifications, for some of them must have been young in the faith.

So in any new work today it is necessary for the missionary to point out some men to be elders. In the early days of the assembly in San Juan, we invited some of the brethren to share in the responsibility of caring for the assembly. We were well aware that they didn't have all the qualifications for elders and, of course, there were some disappointments. However, we hoped to develop spiritual leadership by practical teaching and, as it were, on-the-job training. Naturally, in knowledge of the Word and in spiritual experience, the missionary would exceed these new elders. They would tend to follow him and let him make the decisions. However, we tried to get them to express themselves as to the right procedure in the various situations that arose. Also, it was important that we learn how their cultural outlook influenced their thinking.

It was important that decisions in the affairs of the church be based on the teaching of God's Word. This became a challenge too for it was necessary to distinguish between what the Scriptures teach and what was simply "brethren" tradition. It was out of place to say, "This is the way we do it in our country." If there is no clear guidance from the Scriptures we need to seek the guidance of the Holy Spirit in the light of present circumstances.

For example, we were using a piano at all the services in San Juan except for the Lord's Supper. The Filipino brethren in San Juan were not musically inclined, so they had great difficulty in starting the hymns when the missionary was absent. The tendency was to pitch it too low and sing it too slow, and sometimes the tune was hardly recognizable. "Why don't we use the piano at the Lord's Supper?" they asked. I had to admit it was not a matter of Scriptural teaching but of "brethren" tradition. As a matter of fact, I then recalled that in my childhood days in Lingfield, a small pump organ was used. Using the piano has improved the singing and I don't doubt but that harmony in our praise would be more pleasing to the Lord.

So, through the years following World War II, a great deal of the growth in the assembly has depended upon the spiritual leadership that God has raised up. This spiritual leadership has been sustained in spite of a number of losses. One tragic loss was the death of Sergio Mercado. As a government official with the Bureau of Health on malaria control, he travelled a great deal. Away from home on such trips, he would spend his evenings in the study of the Scriptures. The Lord gave him a good understanding of the Word. After one such trip to Isabela and Nueva Vizcaya in northern Luzon, when he was on a bus returning to Manila in the small hours of the morning, this bus was ambushed by dissidents and Sergio was among those who were killed. Other elders have left to reside in the United States and Canada. Each time we wondered how we should manage without the help and counsel of such elders. Yet the Lord in His goodness has raised up others.

In the early days it was inevitable that the missionaries had to do most of the preaching and teaching. In spite of the language difference, the missionary was better qualified. The question often arose in our minds—should the missionary continue to lead, or should he get the national brethren to take the responsibility, even though it seemed they were less capable? The answer was obvious if we desired the work to be indigenous. They would learn through their experiences, even through mistakes. Sometimes the process seemed painfully slow, but in the end it has been richly rewarding. Today there are gifted and godly elders who have a care and concern for the spiritual welfare and growth of the assembly. Now, at their request, we meet with them in their meetings as advisors and rejoice in the privilege of fellowship with them.

It may be helpful to mention the procedure they have developed regarding the choice of new elders. Often it is necessary to replace those who have left or who are no longer able to serve as elders. When one of the elders suggests the name of a brother as a potential elder, that suggestion is considered by the elders. For a month or perhaps longer they will pray for guidance and discuss among themselves the qualifications or disqualifications of the brother suggested. When the elders as a whole are satisfied and prepared to invite the brother to become an elder, then his name is announced to the assembly as a prospective elder. If anyone in the assembly feels they have a valid reason against his becoming an elder, they have a month in which to voice their objection to one of the elders. If no objections are received by the end of the month, the elders in their next meeting will confirm this decision. When it is announced that this brother is recognized as an elder, sometimes the elders will lay their hands upon him while one of them prays for him.

In the early days when the assembly was small, the elders were able to take care of both the spiritual and material needs. However, as the numbers increased a need for deacons was felt. These men could relieve the elders of much of the material business in the assembly. The word "deacon" is taken from the Greek for "servant," so in one sense all who serve are "deacons." In 1 Timothy 3, after defining the qualifications of elders (bishops or overseers), the apostle Paul gives the qualifications for deacons. This indicates that some are specially recognized as servants. An example of this are the men chosen to distribute relief funds in Acts 6. While they are not called "deacons" there, the verbal form describing their service, is related to the word from which "deacon" is derived. In San Juan the deacons serve in a number of practical ways so that "everything should be done in a fitting and orderly way" (1 Cor. 14:40).

As the population of the Philippines has expanded rapidly in recent years, it has resulted in a preponderance of young people. A considerable majority are in the under-30 bracket. Naturally, this is reflected in the make-up of the local church. Senior citizens are decidedly a minority group. The Sunday school with an attendance of about 250 has classes for all ages. There are various activities for the young people. High schoolers and teenagers call themselves "Young Builders." Besides meeting every Lord's day afternoon, they help in the children's extension classes in different districts and also in literature distribution. The older young people, the college and career group, call themselves "Young Adult Fellowship" and also meet each Lord's day. Young married couples get together once a month, usually in some home. The Lydian Fellowship ladies group meets twice a month, and also go as a group to visit the sick and shut-ins. The young people also meet to prepare choral numbers, and besides the regular choir there is also a children's choir.

In the 1959's Ken Engle and Ken Brooks, with the help of some U.S. servicemen, started a Boy's Brigade. This has been a real blessing in the lives of many as the boys have grown into spiritual as well as physical maturity. Some of the elders and deacons were formerly helped in the Brigade. This work still continues under the direction of Filipino young men. Among the first to win the award of "Herald of Christ" outside of the continental U.S. were two from San Juan. There has also been a similar work among the girls through "Pioneer Girls."

In addition to the Sunday school there have been children's classes held in homes in different parts of San Juan. Each hot season, a two-week Vacation Bible School is conducted for the purpose of reaching children who don't attend Sunday school. One of the great opportunities for service these days are the home Bible studies. It is often easier to gather people informally in a home than to get them to come to the chapel. Where there is an evident interest in a district, an open-air film showing affords wider witness and fresh contacts.

Considerable thought and prayer have been devoted to the

project of a hive-off but this has not yet materialized. This is due to various factors: Many of the believers live relatively close and have grown up in the atmosphere of the present chapel, and those who live farther away are scattered in different directions. So while there have been home Bible studies in those districts, there has not yet been the potential for a local church.

Some people wonder why there is no assembly in the city of Manila. The city of Manila is distinct from but part of Metro Manila which includes five cities and thirteen municipalities, of which San Juan is one. The two small pre-war assemblies in Manila were scattered during World War II. Efforts to revive one of them were unsuccessful. Another problem in building up a work in Manila is the very high cost of land and rentals. For a small and struggling assembly this would be prohibitive apart from a lot of outside help. As much as possible we like to see new churches standing on their own in their building programs.

It is only natural that San Juan should be a sort of parent assembly to which others look as a pattern. The elders at San Juan are often approached for help and counsel in problems that arise in other assemblies, and they are often invited to minister in these other places. So they have tried to be a help and yet not hamper the autonomy of each church. It has been helpful to conduct elder's and men's conferences for the sake of fellowship and teaching. To some it has seemed desirable to have a central association to preserve uniformity and a common purpose. While we encourage fellowship between local churches, we also resist any attempt to set up an authority which could interfere with the autonomy of those local churches. It is not easy to always maintain that balance. While some desire the formation of some kind of association, others tend to the opposite extreme of isolation. In all of these situations, we need to abide by the teaching of the New Testament and the guidance of the Holy Spirit.

Some years ago I was meditating on Colossians 3:16, especially the words, "teaching and admonishing one another in psalms and hymns and spiritual songs." Often we have felt the need for an understanding of what it means to worship, especially at the Lord's Supper. I began to realize the teaching value of hymns, especially in this area of worship. The Tagalog hymnals we were using, published by some inter-denominational groups, were

Rehabilitation in San Juan

lacking in hymns of worship. One of the outstanding features of the "brethren" movement has been its wealth of worship hymnology. A practical way of teaching about worship would be to have some worship hymns. Brother Geronimo Mercado translated some and also composed some hymns. With the help of others we collated a small number of such hymns which were mimeographed, without music, in a small booklet. This has been revised and enlarged several times. Now with hymns of a more general nature there is a hymnal with 200 hymns. This is being used in many of the assemblies.

When we first arrived in the Philippines we were handed hymnals and expected to sing along. Since Tagalog is a phonetic language with only four vowels of one sound each, it was fairly easy to blend our voices with others, even though we were not singing with understanding! However, this started a bad habit—to sing without fully understanding what was being sung. Later on, we discovered that we were sometimes singing things with which we did not agree theologically. The most glaring of these was in the translation of "I know not how God's saving grace." One verse actually meant "I don't know I am saved."

When a Baptist group which had a printing plant was about to publish a new Tagalog hymnbook, I was asked along with some others if I would give some time to revising some of the hymns. There are many pitfalls for the unwary in translating hymns. In one hymn the word "bagong" (new) was used. Unfortunately, the second syllable came on a slurred note so that it came out in singing as "bagoong" which happens to be the word for a kind of anchovy paste!

Today in San Juan there are about 150 in assembly fellowship, with eight elders and six deacons. The Lord's Day services begin with the Lord's Supper at eight o'clock, followed by the Sunday school at nine and the preaching service at 10:15. At this service there are no vacant seats—even the front row is full! Latecomers may have to stand at the back! This is why the brethren are concerned about hiving off since no further enlargement of the present building is possible. In the afternoon, the young people and the ladies have their meetings. There is no regular evening service but occasionally there are special activities such as special evangelistic effort, a film showing, or a musical presentation.

21

CHURCH GROWTH

"So the churches were strengthened in the faith and grew daily in numbers." (Acts 16:5)

What a great deal of missionary effort lies hidden under this brief statement. How much preaching and teaching by Paul, Silas, and Timothy must have been involved in this remarkable church growth. Remarkable indeed—for seldom have churches grown *daily*. No doubt most of the growth in this verse was in individual believers added to the churches. Nevertheless, such growth would lead to growth also in the number of churches. Whether it be in the size or number of churches, church growth rests upon their being "strengthened in the faith." Physically or spiritually, where there is no strength there will be no growth. Undoubtedly the lack or slowness of church growth is due to weakness in the faith.

In the Philippines church growth was slow in the years prior to World War II. For one thing most of the population was either indifferent or antagonistic to a "religion" which was new and different. Why should they leave the Roman Catholic Church in which they had been brought up? The Protestants were attracting mostly poor people and most of their chapels were not impressive. In our own case there was a shortage of workers. Due to his printing business, Brother Wightman was pretty much limited to the assembly in the Walled City, which later moved to Legarda Street in Sampaloc. For ourselves, the new work in San Juan required much of our time. During those years there were no full-time national workers, only part-time helpers in the work with us. In an earlier chapter I have mentioned the labors of Brother Geronimo Mercado in the Paco district of Manila and also in Tanay and surrounding towns in Rizal province. During the Japanese occupation, he gave up his work in the Bureau of Health and confined his energies to Tanay mostly. In this he was joined by Brother Candido Aguilar, who had been saved through our contacts when he was a patient at the Santol Sanitarium. These two men of God had a vision of establishing assemblies in many of the towns of Rizal. Brother Geronimo went home to be with the Lord during the war years, but members of his family are still with us in San Juan.

Brother Aguilar suffered at the hands of the Kempetai, or Japanese Military Police, because of his contacts with the guerillas. In spite of weakness of body he bravely continued serving the Lord and established a work in Binangonan. Shortly after our return in 1949 we drove out there. The chapel was easily located as it was on the main street beside a hand pump where the townspeople drew most of their water. From there we were directed to the home where Brother Aguilar was staying and he welcomed us with open arms. He was a man of considerable ability and devoted to the Lord and His Word. He was living with some of the believers because his own family in Manila had no interest or sympathy in his stand for Christ. He was able to minister the Word with profit, even though he seldom specifically prepared a message. He had an ability to refute the errors of cultists in discussions. They were frustrated by his ability to expose their errors from the Scriptures. On one occasion some from the "Iglesia Ni Cristo," a cult started by Felix Manalo, were reported to have said, "We'll never accomplish anything here unless we get rid of that old man." Brother Aguilar heard of it and publicized the threat so that people would know who to blame if he was liquidated. However, he continued to serve the Lord until his home call in 1954. His brother, Severiano, continues faithfully in the fellowship at San Juan.

The location beside the well was so noisy that a move was made to a side street where a chapel was erected on rented land. After the war they got some crating material left behind by the

Church Growth

Japanese to make benches. Those benches were noted for their extreme discomfort—it was a relief to stand up and preach! Another move was to a piece of land purchased by the assembly, and there continued to be some growth. In 1980, due to some personality problems, some withdrew and started another assembly in another part of town. The leaders left behind were younger men, and they moved the chapel to a more suitable location. So there has been growth in both places. In 1983, a new assembly was established in Bilibiran, a barrio near Binangonan.

Small assemblies had been established in Tanay and Pililla, a few miles east of Binangonan through the ministry of Brother Geronimo Mercado. His home call during the war was a great blow to this work. Intermittently there have been times when a few believers met together in Pililla, but there has been little growth there. In Tanay the Mercado family had donated a piece of land and built a chapel. Most of those who met there were older men. Though they had some knowledge of the Word, it seemed to have little effect in their own lives. They seemed complacent with the situation even though their own families were not being won for Christ. They blamed the lack of response on the difficulty of witness in that town. There seemed to be a measure of truth in this excuse because other groups had little success there. There were no young people and no Sunday school. It was quite disheartening trying to help those men. On one occasion Jim LeValley stopped in the middle of his message, hoping that would awaken a couple who were sleeping!

Something drastic had to be done. Dennis and Elaine Carter (from New Zealand) were willing to help there and a fresh beginning was made. As there was evidently no hope of cooperation from the few old men, the Mercado family intimated they would reclaim the land unless the chapel was put to better use. The men found some place else to meet and since then the work in the chapel has been revived, mostly among young people.

Through the years there had been efforts to revive the work in Pililla. Meetings have been held in homes and in the open air. At different times a few believers have met together in a home as a small assembly. Since there were no men with the knowledge and ability to lead and show potential of becoming elders, efforts have petered out. For a time there seemed to be a possibility of starting a work in Jalajain, a barrio beyond Pililla. Children's meetings and home Bible studies were held for a time but this was not sustained. This was partly due to lack of workers.

In the early 1960's one of the elders from San Juan with his family moved to Taytay, a town midway between San Juan and Binangonan. He began meetings in his home and also a small Sunday school. Jim LeValley and others helped canvass this town with Gospel literature. Some churches in the New Testament were started in homes. We don't read about chapels being built in early church history in the book of Acts. However, while a home is a good place to start a home Bible study, it is not always best for the building up of an assembly. So in Taytay they rented a two-story apartment which served for Sunday school downstairs and for meetings in the upper floor. Later on, the assembly was able to purchase a lot and erect a chapel where the work has continued.

When the first Literature Crusade team was here about 1965, they made contacts with a family living in the slum area of Tondo, Manila. Some were saved, and some meetings were held in their home. Later, they moved to Cainta, a neighboring town to Taytay. They fellowshipped with the believers in Taytay for a time but later wanted meetings to be held in their home. Brother David Harvey helped in this work and the group there was able to buy a lot and build a chapel. The spiritual growth of the work there has suffered because of a lack of men who are spiritually able to lead and feed the flock. Yet souls have been saved and a goodly number gather there.

On the other side of Taytay from Cainta is a town called Angono. Home Bible studies and open-air meetings have also been held in this town, and a few have professed faith in Christ. However, no established work has been maintained. Up in the hills beyond these towns is Antipolo. This is a staunchly Roman Catholic community, largely because in the church there is a famous image of the Virgin Mary. It was reputedly brought from Spain by way of Mexico in the days of the galleon trade and was "miraculously preserved." So this image is greatly venerated, and in the month of May thousands of pilgrims flock to Antipolo. Some attempts have been made to begin a work there but with no success as yet.

Church Growth

Soon after we returned to the Philippines in 1949, Mrs. Tiongco, the mother of Mrs. Dayton, was visiting San Juan. She invited us to go to Floridablanca, her home in Pampanga, to preach the Gospel there. At the time this was not possible for too much needed to be done in San Juan. Mrs. Dayton had been praying that her husband could get some other work so the family could have more time together. His work then was in Canlubang and their home was in San Juan. So he was home only on some weekends. Later on, in January 1952, he was offered a position on the Del Carmen Sugar Estate near Floridablanca. This position included housing, so they moved there. It was a disappointment to Mrs. Dayton to be away from the fellowship in San Juan, yet this became the opening for a work in that area. Mrs. Dayton was anxious to serve the Lord and to witness to her many relatives in Floridablanca. She began classes at the home of her mother, Mrs. Tiongco, and another relative, Mrs. Isip. Mr. Dayton had the carpenter make some benches for these children's classes which were usually held outside. The classes grew and were often attended by older women and some men at times.

In April, 1954, they were able to hold VBS at Floridablanca and at Del Carmen with the help of some from Manila. Then in August Mrs. Dayton invited Ken Brooks to go there for some meetings which were held in homes over the weekend. These were followed by monthly visits in September and October. In November, after much prayer, it was felt a more intensive effort should be made. Jack LaBuff, who had to leave the work in Laos for a time, shared in this effort. Meetings were held every weekend, not only in Floridablanca but also in surrounding barrios.

In San Jose, Ruben Nanquil and his wife were saved and meetings were begun in their home. Later on a small chapel was built beside their house to better accommodate those who attended. However, San Jose was part of a large sugar estate and later on pressure was applied by the estate owners. So in later years the chapel had to be torn down and the few believers joined with those in Floridablanca. A few miles beyond San Jose there is a river at the foot of a range of mountains. Some were baptized in this river and meetings were held in barrios like Pandergirig and Pabanlag. The outreach at the latter place continued intermittently for several years.

After our return from furlough in 1954, we also helped in

this work. Two brothers, Eugenio and Daniel Tique, also gave valuable help because they were Pampangans who could preach in the language of the people. Most of the people understood Tagalog which we used, but there were a few older folk who did not. While there are some similarities in the two languages, they are distinctly different. One peculiarity of Pampango is that it has no aspirates while Tagalog does. It was rather amusing to hear a Pampangan preaching in Tagalog, dropping an "h" where it belonged and putting it on where it did not, just like an English cockney.

The outreach from Floridablanca in another direction included meetings in other barrios. One was a place called Valdez where some years later a large house served for some young people's camps. For a while there was some interest in Mayquiapo and Seran with one or two families in each place evincing some interest. However, between these was the barrio of Dau where there was a good interest and some conversions. In fine weather the meetings were held under the shade of large mango trees, with children's classes nearby. Some young ladies from San Juan would go along to help teach these classes. It was not unusual to have six or seven meetings in different places between Saturday afternoon and Sunday afternoon.

The few believers in Dau decided to build a small chapel with bamboo walls and cogon grass roof. The week after it was built someone set it afire at night. Of course, in a few moments it was gone, but the enemies of the Gospel did not have the last word. The believers decided to rebuild with materials which would not burn so easily—hollow block walls and galvanized iron roof. The work there still continues and the group are reaching out to nearby places.

Up in the hills beyond Floridablanca there are some hamlets of Negritoes, called "Baluga" by the Tagalogs. They are considered by some to be the aborigines and are a short-statured people, rather like pygmies, with short kinky hair. Ken Brooks and some others made some trips into the hills to reach these people and on occasion even spent the night in their little huts. The unsaved Pampangans did not look with favor on such efforts as it might interfere with their ways of oppressing and taking advantage of these poor people. In any case it was not possible to follow up this work for lack of personnel. It would

Church Growth

need someone who could devote all their time and learn their language.

In 1958, Mr. and Mrs. Milton Haack joined us in the Lord's work here in the Philippines. Milton had been here during World War II as a serviceman but was not then a believer. The Haack's went into that work in Pampanga and for several years have lived in San Fernando, the capital of that province. While they were on their first furlough, there was an invitation to help hold services at Basa Air Force Base (of the Philippine Air Force) which is a few miles from Floridablanca. Sunday morning services were begun there with the help of Howard Eppler who was then here with the Back to the Bible Broadcast. This work was taken over by Brother Haack after his return from furlough. Meetings are still held there.

The group at Floridablanca built a small chapel beside the home of one of the believers there. Later on, they were able to purchase a lot in a subdivision and have since built a larger chapel. Brother Stimson Alviar lives in that area and has been used of the Lord in the spread of the Gospel.

Brother and Sister Haack have also opened up work in several other places in Pampanga nearer to San Fernando. So that there are about eight small assemblies in and around the towns of Guagua, Sexmoan, and Bacolor.

Across the province of Pampanga, in the eastern part, the Lord has done a great work. About 1958, some interesting letters came to the office of the Bible School of the Air (more about this work in a later chapter). They were from a young lady who lived in Bahay-pare (meaning "Priest's house"), in a low-lying swampy area known as the Candaba Swamps. Though in Pampanga, it was close to the border of Bulacan and was reached through Baliwag, a commercial town in Bulacan.

One Saturday afternoon in 1959 we drove up there for a visit and met Miss Teresita Castro. As we drove into the barrio we noticed the Roman Catholic Church. Tessie told us she had been brought up as a Roman Catholic and was very devout in that religion. After finishing high school she developed a bad infection in one ankle and as we talked with her she had one leg in a cast and was using crutches. She was rather bitter when this happened because the prognosis was that she would be permanently crippled. So what were the prospects for college, for marriage? Why should this happen to her when she had been so devoted to her religion?

A missionary travelling on a bus going to Batangas witnessed to his seatmate, a young Filipino. He gave him some literature and enrolled him for an Emmaus correspondence course from the Bible School of the Air. The young man happened to be a cousin of Tessie. She decided to go to Batangas to seek help from a faith healer and visit her relatives there. While visiting him she saw the first two lessons of "What the Bible Teaches." Casually her cousin said, "If you want that, take it! I'm not interested." It was that course that was the means of her conversion and of an entirely new outlook on life.

Looking out of the window as we conversed with her, I realized that this was a rather remote place. Also I knew that it was an area where the Huk dissidents were quite active. Turning to Tessie I asked, "I noticed the church as we drove in. Tell me, does anyone ever come here and preach the truths you have learned through this course?" She replied, "No! No one has ever preached these truths here." She mentioned that the cults Jehovah's Witnesses and Iglesia ni Cristo, had been there. I told her that we would like to preach the Gospel there. However, it would be easy for us to preach there and go home again; but if there was opposition or persecution, she would be the one to face it. So we asked her to pray about it and let us know when she felt that the time was right. Her family was friendly and those we met were hospitable, as is customary with Filipinos; but we didn't think they were really interested.

Tessie took a short course with Child Evangelism Fellowship in Manila so she would be able to teach the children in her home. Then she attended Far Eastern Bible School and Seminary, in spite of her handicap. In the goodness of the Lord she was healed while she was in Bible School. After the first year, in 1963, she told us that her mother and sister had trusted in Christ and her father was willing. (Later we learned he consented to having a meeting because he thought he would prove that we were wrong.) Would we go and have a service in their home? Since it was not safe to travel those roads at night because of the dissidents, we arranged to stay overnight with the Castro family.

What a memorable meeting that first one was! Arriving about three in the afternoon we were served a cold drink of pineapple juice. As we rested and enjoyed our drink, Tessie went out to

Church Growth

invite people to come. She had previously informed the people that we were going to be there. Soon 25 to 30 people were gathered. With a silent prayer, I began by introducing ourselves and then told why we were in the Philippines. This naturally led to an explanation of the good news of salvation. For an hour everyone listened intently to this old message which was entirely new to them. Then I asked if they would like to ask any questions and they began to open up. As the daylight faded, oil lamps were lit but still they talked. It was getting to be around seven o'clock for the meeting lasted over three hours. I was getting hungry and wondered when supper would be served! Yet what a thrill to present the Gospel for the first time.

One statement I shall not soon forget. One man said, "Do you know why we are interested in hearing what you have to say?" I replied, "No, I don't, but I would surely like to know." "Well," he said, "we have noticed a change in the life of Tessie and we want to know what it is all about."

Soon after that I was quite ill and had to return to the U.S. to recuperate. However, Leonard, Kenneth, and others continued the work at Bahay-pare; and soon Felipe Castro, Tessie's father, gave clear evidence that he too was a believer. It was in June, 1965, that the few believers there first remembered the Lord in the breaking of bread. After a few years Brother Castro donated a piece of ground beside his home and a chapel was built. In the early days they didn't have a ceiling, and it was not uncommon to see a rat running across the rafters while we were preaching. Soon contacts were made in a neighboring barrio, Dulong-ilog (River's End), and services were started there. The road was either inches deep in dust or in mud, depending upon the season of the year. The services were held in a home for some time and then they received help to build a chapel there. In the opposite direction from Bahay-pare is a place called Pansumalok where there has been another hive-off. On the road from Baliwag to Bahay-pare, we used to pick up a man at a place called Tangos and take him to the meetings at Bahay-pare. Now there is a small chapel and company of believers there too. Another outreach was a bit further away in a place called San Roque where another assembly has been established. Yet in spite of these hive-offs, the work continues to prosper in Bahay-pare.

The first baptism of believers from there was held in a river near the town of Baliwag. The river was clear water running over a gravel bottom but rather shallow. One of the brethren from San Juan did the baptizing, the first time he had ever done this. Another brother who went with us was afraid the folks were not being "buried" in baptism. So he was calling out from the river bank, "Put them under, put them under!" One of those baptized was an old lady of uncertain age. The uncertainty about her age was not due to feminine diffidence; she had been born in that country area when the keeping of vital records was considered unimportant. The best clue we got was that she was already a young lady when the Americans first arrived which was in 1898. For her age she had remarkably good eyesight but was a bit hard of hearing. In the services she always wanted to look up the references. Filipino preachers are expected to give the reference when they quote Scripture. Having ascertained from a seatmate the reference, she would look it up and read it. That meant, of course, reading it aloud. She was quite oblivious of any comments the speaker might be making and to any inconvenience to those around her.

One of the brethren at Bahay-pare is very faithful in attending the services even though it means a walk of four or five kilometers across the rice fields each way. Perhaps one reason for the faithfulness of Tomas Carpio has been the unusual nature of his conversion. Like the majority he had been brought up a Roman Catholic. On one occasion he became ill and went into a coma. Without adequate medical help, his family and neighbors thought he was dead. He himself inclines to the idea that he died. Perhaps it was similar to the Apostle Paul, "Whether it was in the body or out of the body I do not know—God knows." At any rate, while in that condition Tomas had a dream or vision in which he saw himself standing before the gate of heaven. To his consternation, the person at the gate refused to let him in; with his Roman Catholic ideas he supposed it was Saint Peter. He remonstrated that he had been a faithful Roman Catholic while on earth and on that basis pleaded to be admitted. When Peter (or whoever it might have been) still refused, Tomas asked what he could do to gain admittance. He was told to return to earth and look for someone with a Bible, to tell him what was needed. At this point the family and friends who were making a coffin and were about to prepare him for burial, got the shock of their lives. (Where there are no embalming facilities, burial has to be within 24 hours.) The supposedly dead Tomas sat up and began to talk. Relating what had happened, he said he must find someone with a Bible as soon as possible. Someone recalled that Felipe Castro in Bahay-pare had a Bible. So as soon as he was able Tomas set out to visit Felipe who had the joy of showing from the Bible how he could be sure of getting into heaven. How true are the words of William Cowper, "God moves in a mysterious way, His wonders to perform."

22

MORE CHURCH GROWTH

"Then the church . . . was strengthened; and encouraged by the Holy Spirit, it grew in numbers, living in the fear of the Lord." (Acts 9:31)

Here are three basic factors in church growth. First, churches must be strengthened. In the introduction to the previous chapter, we say they were strengthened in the faith. For church growth there must be good, solid teaching from the Word of God. The edification of the believers leads to the strengthening of the church. Second, the encouragement of the Holy Spirit is needed. He encourages as He guides into new areas of witness and as He empowers the witnesses. Third, believers must live in the fear of the Lord. Growth of individual believers and their obedience to the will of the Lord will result in growth in the church.

A few years after we began the Bible School of the Air we heard reports that somewhere in Tarlac people were meeting for Bible study, apparently as a result of getting the Emmaus course. It was difficult to get any specific information, and once we wrote offering help to what seemed a likely contact. Then one of the workers was helping Every Home Crusade in their goal of putting Gospel literature in every home. When visiting homes on a large sugar estate near San Miguel, Tarlac, he happened to visit in one home there. To his surprise he saw about seven "Certificates of Completion" from the Bible School of the Air on the wall. This led to the discovery that several in that place had taken our courses and were also meeting together for Bible study. This contact was followed up by other visits beginning in September, 1964.

One Saturday afternoon I drove up to the barrio of Mapalacsiao on that sugar estate. Accompanying me to show the way was that worker, Eleazar Alfonso. Shortly after our arrival in the early evening we began a meeting. Eleazar and I took turns preaching and then in answering questions. About ten o'clock the folks there announced they had prepared some refreshments. So while we partook of rice cakes, cocoa, and other goodies, the conversation continued and went on until midnight. There was no doubt of their keen interest and desire to learn more about the Scriptures. At midnight we tore ourselves away for the three-hour drive home. We would get only a few hours sleep before being busy with the activities of the Lord's day. As we drove away, Eleazar remarked, "You wouldn't have got any more sleep if you had stayed—they would keep you up all night with their questions!"

Regular Sunday services were carried on with the help of visits from different missionaries and national workers. In those days there was a great deal of Huk dissident activity all through that part of central Luzon. One Sunday, Stimson Alviar couldn't understand why the folks didn't seem as cordial in their welcome as they usually were. However, the service began under the house as usual. While Stimson was speaking he happened to look up. Through the bamboo slats which were the floor of the home above he saw a man moving about and the man was heavily armed! There were no repercussions of that incident and that particular Huk at least heard the gospel that day.

Later on the group there received permission to erect a chapel and the work continued to grow. Now a second assembly has hived off from that first one. From there, trips were being made into Nueva Ecija, an adjoining province, where there are contacts in the towns of Aliaga and Talavera.

Just before our return to the Philippines in 1949, we learned of a young man studying at Moody Bible Institute who was interested in the work in the Philippines. During World War II he had been flying over the Philippines in a B-24 "LIBERATOR" (a flying fortress), and he would like to return there on

More Church Growth

a more peaceful mission. After correspondence, Kenneth Engle joined us in Manila in 1951. He had worked with WMBI in radio work while at Moody so he was a big help as we were resuming a radio ministry at that time. Later he was joined by his fiancee, Mary Lou Leonard, and they were married in San Juan. For some years they helped in the assembly in Binangonan. Then in 1967 they moved to Baguio for health reasons. Baguio is the beautiful mountain resort some 5,000 feet above sea level, where the climate is cooler than in the lowlands.

In Bagiuo they began to make contacts with neighbors with a view to establishing a work there. Among their neighbors with whom Mary Lou made friends was a Pakistani lady married to a Filipino professor. He had met her while he was studying on a grant in Lahore. She came from a mixed Eurasian background with nominal Christian contacts. Mary Lou got this lady, Evelyn Balanag, interested in studying the course "What the Bible Teaches." She took home the first two lessons and before very long was back again. Having finished those two lessons she wanted the rest and before the day was done had finished them all. The following day she was taken very ill with severe hemorrhages and was rushed to the hospital. In her extreme weakness through loss of blood, she thought she was dying. Opening her eyes she saw her husband sitting by the bed in obvious concern. Then she had a terrible thought—"If I had died, I would have gone to hell." Recalling what she had studied in the lessons, she accepted Christ as her Savior, even though still too weak to let anyone know what had transpired.

As soon as she was able, she told her husband and as she recovered began witnessing to others about her new-found Savior. She began memorizing Scripture and encouraged her husband to join her in this. However, she was a bit annoyed that he, who was not yet a believer, could memorize more quickly than she, a believer. She lost interest in the paperback novels which used to take so much of her time, but giving up smoking was harder. She once told her husband, "I could give you up, but not these cigarettes." But the time came, in answer to prayer, when she gave up smoking too. Her husband also trusted in Christ along with some of their friends. Many of these were Filipino servicemen connected with the Philippine Military Academy.

One day some Mormon missionaries called on two of Evelyn's

friends and tried to convince them of their beliefs. Evelyn didn't yet know enough of the Word to refute them, but she felt there was something wrong; so she got them to talk with Mary Lou who was able to show them the truth. Four of these people were baptized by Ken Engle in early 1970 and that was the beginning of the assembly there. While the Engles were on furlough from 1970 to 1972 we lived in Baguio and felt our ministry was particularly to strengthen these believers in their faith in Christ.

For a while the believers met in a home. Then permission was obtained to use a quonset hut which served as a guardhouse at the entrance to the military reservation called Navy Base. A Navy Base up in the mountains seems incongruous, but it got its name when used by the US Navy right after World War II. This guardhouse served as a meeting place for a few years. The folks used to say, "It is a guardhouse during the week, but on Sunday it is God's house." The Base had living quarters for Philippine Army personnel serving with the Philippine Military Academy. When martial law was declared in September 1972, we no longer had the use of this facility and went back to meeting in a home, or rather, in the carport of a home.

The Engles returned in 1973 and stayed until 1975, and during that time they got permission to meet in a Roman Catholic school building which had closed and the property was up for sale. Knowing this was only temporary, the assembly looked for land to build. They were able to purchase a lot and build a chapel quite close to the guardhouse where they had formerly met. There were then no other evangelical chapels in that part of Baguio. In more recent years two teams of workers from Gospel Literature Outreach (GLO) from Australia and New Zealand have helped in the building up of the work in Baguio. Periodic visits by different workers have helped the believers there carry on the work at times when there was no resident missionary there.

We had a number of contacts with the Philippine Military Academy, the West Point of the Philippines. At that time the Registrar, Lt. Col. D. Galia, was a fine Christian gentleman. At a time when they had no Protestant Chaplain we were invited to preach at their chapel service. The Cadets were obliged to attend church service in either the Roman Catholic Church or the Protestant Chapel on base. At the time we lived in Baguio

More Church Growth

there was a good deal of student unrest in the large cities. Although under military discipline the cadets were somewhat affected by this. At one point several objected to compulsory attendance at religious services. The Commandant arranged that those who didn't want to attend church should at that time listen to a lecture on good morals! The responsibility of arranging these lectures was turned over to our friend, Lt. Col. Galia. He invited me to give some of those lectures. This was a difficult assignment since I am a preacher, not a lecturer. To relax the atmosphere I tried to make it informal with opportunity for the cadets to participate. Yet at the same time I could not lose that opportunity to present the truth of the Gospel. No doubt when I was the lecturer, they got more religious truth than they would have heard in the church services! These young men were some of the smartest in the country; they had to be to pass the stiff requirements. They were polite and courteous but also quite frank. One of them said he thought I was an imperialist! When I challenged him to his definition of an imperialist, I was able to show him that I didn't fit in with his definition.

Beginning in 1970, Ken Engle was able to arrange for a Bible to be given to each graduate of the Philippine Military Academy. We were able to continue this until 1979 and were usually able to have this presentation included in the religious part of the graduation programs. The names of the graduates were printed in gold on the covers of the Bibles and a letter was enclosed. While the graduates usually expressed their thanks at the time, we never had any further word from any of them. It did afford us some opportunities to meet with some of the high military officials. However, in 1980, it was not possible for me to travel to Baguio to make needed arrangements. Also, we felt that the lack of response indicated that the money could be put to better use in other phases of the Lord's work. So this practice was discontinued. We have heard that another Christian organization is now donating Bibles.

For a time Dave and Ruth Harvey, along with national workers Rey and Norma Cervantes, lived in Baliwag, a large commercial center in the province of Bulacan. A good deal of evangelism was carried on in that area and a student center was carried on in the town. The Cervantes continued to work there after the Harveys left for furlough. There is now a company of believers meeting there and they have purchased a lot, but have not yet been able to build a chapel due to lack of funds.

A friend of Rey Cervantes became interested in fellowshipping with some of the workers in Bulacan. He was serving the Lord in a part of Malolos, the capital of Bulacan, and eventually decided to throw in his lot with us. The work at that place, Sumapa, has grown both in members and in outreach. The assembly there is active with a good number of young people. One Sunday afternoon when they were going out in groups to witness and distribute Gospel literature, one group was in a quandary. Coming to an intersection they couldn't remember whether they were supposed to turn right or left. Actually they turned in the opposite direction to what they had been told but it was of the Lord's leading no doubt. They encountered an older man who was already interested and whose heart had been prepared to receive the Gospel. Besides the first leaders, Oscar and Gloria de Leon, there have been others who have been commended by this assembly to full-time service for the Lord.

A family in San Juan came to know the Lord through the witness of the first Gospel Literature Outreach team. Later this family moved to Bicol provinces, and we thought there might be a possibility of starting a work there. However, before long they moved back to a barrio, Tuctucan, in the town of Guiguinto, Bulacan, a few miles north of Manila. Through the help of some from San Juan and from nearby Sumapa, souls have been saved and a work started in that place. For some time they met in the home of one of the believers, but as numbers increased they felt the need of acquiring a small lot and building a chapel.

Peter and Sue Booth are workers from assemblies in New Zealand. In their first term here they were associated with Open Air Campaigners, but on their return from furlough in 1979 they were commended to work more closely with the assembly work here. They rented a home on the compound of the Far East Broadcasting Company, north of Manila, in the town of Valenzuela. They were led to begin a work near there by distributing literature and having some home Bible studies. These led to the development of an assembly in an area called Malinta. This group of believers has been active in reaching out to nearby districts.

More Church Growth

In 1972, the senior national worker, Stimson Alviar went with Sgt. Resultan of the Basa Air Force to visit places in Pangasinan where Sgt. Resultan had some relatives. Pangasinan is a populous province about 150 miles north of Manila. The people there have their own language, Pangasinan which is related to Ilocano, an area just north of Pangasinan. In the early days of Bible School of the Air there were more requests each week for the free course from Pangasinan than from any other province in the country. The two men visited Urbiztondo and Basista in that province. While there have been some contacts in the former, it has been in Basista where the work has grown, specially in a barrio called Balaybuaya (crocodile's house). There being an open door for the Gospel, Ken Brooks and others visited there. Then two young women went to witness to the women and children. They were later followed by John and Gloria Paglinawan and in later years by Rod and Aida Miano. For some reason these workers all had health problems and were not able to stay long. Nevertheless, the work went ahead and quite a number were saved and baptized. Among them was a school teacher who later took leave of absence from his teaching to devote two years to the Lord's work there.

A few miles from there the first GLO team had made some contacts in the town of Asingan. Progress there was rather slow for some time. However, in 1982, Leonard and Mary Savill of New Zealand took up residence in Urdaneta, a large commercial town on the main north highway. Len and Mary had been here with the second GLO team and then had spent most of their time in Baguio. When they returned from their first furlough, they felt led to help in the work in Pangasinan. Largely due to their efforts, there are groups of believers in Toboy and San Vicente, both barrios in Asingan.

A flood control engineer working in Malauli, Pampanga heard the Gospel there and was saved. He too was concerned about his family and relatives in Mapandan, another town in Pangasinan. So with the help of workers Alex Lopez and Ben Manansala a work was begun in that town also. Some have been saved and a small assembly begun there also.

On the north shore of Manila Bay where the Pampanga River enters the Bay is the town of Masantol. Some of the barrios around Masantol can only be reached by "bangka" (canoe). In one of these barrios, called Malauli, there is a family which had been quite active in local politics and influential in the community. One of this family, Elpidio Manansala, also has a home in Pasig, the capital of Rizal province. He became interested in spiritual things through reading the Bible while still a Roman Catholic. While reading the tract "God's Way of Salvation," by Theodore Epp, he put his trust in Christ for salvation. The tract was published by Back to the Bible Broadcasters. One day Elpidio and a companion noticed the office of Back to the Bible as they were going to Manila from Pasig. They were interested in baptism and when the counselor at Back to the Bible heard their story, he suggested they talk with the elders at the San Juan assembly. The counselor was an elder from the assembly in Binangonan.

The elders in San Juan were convinced as to the visitors' salvation but suggested it would be a better testimony for them to be baptized in their own community of Malauli. Up to that point Elpidio thought of remaining in the Catholic Church to influence others of his fellow church members. It was arranged that two of the elders from San Juan and a missionary should spend a Saturday and Sunday in Malauli. Arriving in the afternoon, an evening service was arranged. One would preach the Gospel, another would speak on the Christian life, and the other would speak about the church and baptism. The meeting went on till after midnight so keen was the interest. They met again all Sunday morning and finished up with a baptism.

This was in September, 1975, and the work continued to grow. The baptism brought out some opposition so that they knew the Roman Catholics no longer welcomed them. The father of Elpidio was threatened with death because he no longer supported his former political position. On one occasion the opponents of the Gospel challenged the Christians to a debate. Filipinos love the excitement of a debate and some religious groups get involved to such a degree that violence sometimes results. The believers at Malauli called for help from some workers and elders in accepting this challenge. However, the workers said they would not debate but would welcome the opportunity to explain from the Scriptures what we believe. So this became a wonderful opportunity to proclaim the Gospel and to manifest the meekness of Christ in the face of opposition.

More Church Growth

The work grew remarkably as many more were baptized. So it was only a few years before as many as 150 would gather to remember the Lord. They built a chapel alongside the Manansala home. They have also reached out to another barrio nearby, a place called Nigue where there is now an assembly, as well as witnessing through home Bible studies in the nearby towns in Bulacan province, such as Hagonoy and Paombong. A brother of Elpidio, Ceferino, along with his wife, are active in San Juan assembly, where he is an elder. They have had children's classes and home Bible studies in their home also.

This church growth had reached out in three other parts of the Philippines. First, there were meetings held in Elpidio's home in Pasig and now there is an assembly meeting there. This was partly due to the fact that some from Malauli went to Pasig to work in factories there. In 1982 the group meeting there was too large to meet in a home and their plans are to build a chapel.

A family from Malauli moved to Dadiangas (renamed Gen. Santos) in the province of Cotabato on the island of Mindanao in the southern part of the Philippines. The Ducot family was a large one, but only a few were believers. In 1980, two of the national workers, Stimson Alviar and Nestor Dedel, responded to a call for help and went there to preach the Gospel. At first the people were a bit suspicious of the two preachers, but after hearing them they opened their hearts to the message. As a result several were baptized and meetings were commenced in the Ducot home. In 1981 Nestor and his wife Ligaya, who is a school teacher, were led of the Lord to move there and have seen the Lord's blessing upon their labors so that the work has grown. Also in that year, one of the elders from San Juan and some of his family moved to a ranch near there and have been a great help in that new work. The work there has continued to expand and in 1983 two other assemblies were started in Polomolok and Marbel. Plans are underway to have a camp in that area also.

Sometimes we make plans regarding church growth, and this is wise. Some of the workers, stirred by what has happened in some of these places, have had a vision to establish a line of local churches across the province of Bulacan. This started off with a zealous effort and some helpful contacts were made. Yet there have also been disappointments and difficulties. The work at Malauli and what has developed from it has not been because of a planned effort. It has been a thrill to see how the Holy Spirit came in and worked in the lives of men and women. So, while planning has its place, there needs to be above all else a dependence upon the guidance and working of the Holy Spirit. Without him there can be no real church growth.

Two activities have helped foster and establish this church growth. One of these has been the conferences that have been held over the years. In early years, conferences were held and hosted by different assemblies. At one of the conferences two elderly brethren were surprised to meet each other. One from Canlubang and the other from Dau, they had been schoolmates years before. Neither had known that the other had become a believer until they met that day. These conferences were precious times of fellowship together and also of profitable ministry of the Word. However, it was observed that the hosting assembly spent so much time in preparing food and serving it that they derived little benefit from the ministry and preaching.

Since obtaining the campsite, this has been a favorite location for conferences as it also provided accommodations for staying overnight. The conferences for elders and men in general have been very helpful. A topic is chosen for each occasion usually dealing with some phase of church life. In between the messages there are times for open discussion with freedom for questions and answers on the topic. In this way it has been possible to deal with church life in a practical way. A conference on the Lord's Supper dealt with the practical way of observing this, as well as the Scriptural teaching on why we observe it. The conference ended with an actual observance so that those who are from small groups would get a better idea.

Women's conferences have also been held at the camp. These give some of the women an opportunity to meet with women from other assemblies and spend a night away from home and its continual responsibilities. Practical ministry is also given by women concerning marital and family responsibilities from a Scriptural viewpoint. Also, there are opportunities for them to consider functions of women in the church, in their services for the Lord, and also being supportive of their husbands, especially if the latter are elders.

More Church Growth

The other factor in strengthening the churches is the publication of a bi-monthly paper called KAMANGGAGAWA (Co-worker). The first issue of this was published in June, 1968. Listed on the front cover were nine churches in three provinces, on Luzon (not those in Palawan). Fourteen years later the corresponding figures would be about 35 churches in nine provinces. There was a lapse of over three years before the second issue was published. This issue set forth some of the purposes of the project: to give news of the Lord's work in various places to foster fellowship between the believers in the different churches; to be a teaching tool, not only to teach the Word but also provide materials for others in their teaching; to stimulate the gifts among the Lord's people, both in writing and in ministering the Word. In that second issue I began a series of messages on church discipline. The first issue of volume 2 was very kindly dedicated to my wife and I on the occasion of our fiftieth wedding anniversary, September 20, 1922, and of our arrival in the Philippines on December 20 of that year.

For some years Miss Elvira (Bebs) Clavecilla had been editor of KAMANGGAGAWA in spite of severe health problems. She needed to have open-heart surgery and some thought was given to having her fly to the United States for this. However, it was decided this operation could be done in Manila in the University of Santo Tomas Hospital. The Lord wonderfully supplied the great needs for this expensive operation and she entered the hospital at the end of January, 1974. The operation seemed to be successful, but she developed lung congestion and, due to her weakened condition, this proved fatal. She went home to be with the Lord on February 2, 1974. In spite of her frailty she was deeply devoted to the Lord.

Beside the Bible teaching and ministry in this paper are reports about the Lord's work in different parts of the Philippines. This helps to foster fellowship and stimulate prayer among the Lord's people. Those in small assemblies don't feel quite so alone as they learn of others, and those who may not be seeing much fruit for their labors are encouraged by knowing that God is working in other places.

While foreign missionaries are sometimes invited to provide articles the editorial work is carried on by the national brethren and sisters. Occasionally significant articles from magazines like

INTEREST are translated into Tagalog (with permission). Local brethren and sisters are being encouraged to develop their ability they have for writing articles or poems.

For several years KAMANGGAGAWA was mimeographed in the office of the Bible School of the Air. In recent years, it has been typed on an IBM machine and thus prepared for printing. Many have commented on the blessing they have derived from this magazine.

23

THE BIBLE SCHOOL OF THE AIR

"Their voice has gone out into all the earth, their words to the end of the world." (Rom. 10:18)

The Apostle Paul was quoting from Psalm 19:4 the words of David of how God's creation, visible in the heavens, declares the glory of God. Through creation God speaks to all mankind. The apostle uses these words to describe the spread of the Gospel of Christ throughout the world. He himself had a large share in the dissemination of the Gospel. "So from Jerusalem all the way around to Illyricum, I have fully proclaimed the Gospel of Christ." As he wrote those words he had the urge to go on further to Spain. In the earliest of his epistles he described the far-reaching effect of the testimony of the Thessalonian Christians: "The Lord's message rang out from you not only in Macedonia and Achaia—your faith in God has become known everywhere."

Yet neither David nor Paul could have possibly imagined the modern means of universal communication. It is a challenging concept that by means of radio and television one man's voice may reach around the world. One day we received a letter from a listener in what was then British Guiana, now Guyana, who had heard the program of Bible School of the Air. Looking at a globe we realized that was halfway round the world from Manila and wondered which way the signal travelled! What privilege to send the Gospel around the world—what a great responsibility.

At the Guelph Summer Bible School in Ontario in 1948, we had some talks with Dr. Edward Harlow regarding Bible schools. While a missionary in Africa, he sent a gift towards starting a Bible school in Canada. That was a seed that lay in the ground for some time. When he came home from Africa, the seed sprouted and with the help of other brethren led to the start of Emmaus Bible School. Dr. Harlow was interested in the formation of Bible schools on the mission fields as a means of training nationals for the Lord's work. I too was interested since for several years I had taught at the Manila Evangelistic Institute.

Yet as we contemplated returning to the Philippines at that time, it did not seem feasible for us to start any such project then. There did seem to be a potential for a correspondence Bible school, however. Some feeble attempts had been made by others in this direction before World War II. These had failed, largely because they used correspondence courses from the United States and it took too long to return the test papers. There needed to be a closer contact between the staff and the students of a correspondence school. Also, such a venture needed to be adapted to the local situation.

On our return to Manila in August, 1949, we were interested in resuming a radio ministry, since we had been involved in such before the war. In June, 1948, the Far East Broadcasting Company (FEBC) had set up their radio station and begun operations. Max Atienza who had been one of my students at the Manila Evangelistic Institute was then on the staff of FEBC. Knowing of my previous radio ministry, both he and Mr. Robert Bowman approached me about having a program on FEBC. This was attractive to me, but time and prayer were needed before making a decision. Just then other things had priority, such as getting settled and helping the church at San Juan get re-established. Another consideration was the relative value of a Christian program over the commercial station such as we had before. This would involve more expense in paying for air time but would also mean a wider audience of unsaved people. On a Christian station the bulk of the listeners are those who have some interest in religious matters.

The Bible School of the Air

Another factor to be considered was what type or format the program should be. A largely musical program was definitely out; we didn't have the resources for that within our own group. Early in 1950 we were still praying for the Lord's guidance. We felt strongly inclined towards a radio ministry of Bible teaching. It was then that Emmaus Bible School sent us a copy of their new course "What The Bible Teaches." In twelve simple lessons this course presents some basic Bible truths along with a clear presentation of the truth of the Gospel. Upon reading this course, the Lord's leading seemed to crystalize. We would have a program of simple Bible teaching and offer this course for home study. We would combine the ideas of a radio program and a correspondence course.

Without losing any time, we wrote to William MacDonald, then President of Emmaus in Chicago, to ask his permission to use the course and also asking for advice and suggestions. We envisioned printing the course locally in looseleaf form so we could send out two lessons at a time. When students returned the first two tests, they would receive other lessons. Also, we looked forward to having the course translated, first into Tagalog and then later into other Philippine languages. We soon received the desired permission and some helpful advice from Emmaus.

Then we were ready to present our proposal to Robert Bowman of FEBC. His response was a striking confirmation that this project was the Lord's will. He said their staff had recently reviewed the different types of program they already had. They felt there was a need for a program which would offer helps in Bible study. He was quite enthusiastic about our proposal of a weekly half-hour program. He offered to give us time on Monday evenings which had been a part of his own nightly program which was quite popular. Also he offered to help us with the first two or three programs to introduce our program. We discussed a name and ruled out "Emmaus" for two reasons. It was not a name which would be familiar to most hearers and it would probably not be pronounced correctly. We decided on "Bible School of the Air" and launched the program in April, 1950.

When I told a Baptist missionary friend about this project, he remarked, "That sounds good! But it could turn out to be a full-time job." That proved to be true though we had thought of it as a sideline to our other work. Furthermore, we were not aware that we were sort of pioneering this type of evangelistic approach, though the Seventh-Day Adventists had been using a similar method. It has been a source of thanksgiving that others have been inspired to adopt this method in other places. While on furlough, a missionary from the West Indies said, "We would like to do something like that, but we couldn't afford it." I replied, "Neither could we when we started!" Blissfully ignorant of what this would amount to, we stepped out in faith. Had we known all that would be involved, we probably would not have had the faith to start. The Lord knew and he led us on step-by-step. He has not failed us but has supplied every need.

At the beginning all the requests for the free courses came from radio listeners. I still remember our thrill when we were able to tell Bob Bowman that we had received a thousand requests. When "What the Bible Teaches" had been translated into Tagalog, our friend Max Atienza used this one evening a week on his program "Bukas na Aklat" (Open Book). This added to the interest and to the number of enrollments. Later on, translations were made into three other Philippine languages. However, on an average 60% of the requests have been for the course in English. This is due to the fact that English has been the basis of education in the schools. For a time we offered this course in Spanish, but this was later discontinued. The few that asked for the course in Spanish were students trying to improve their skills in that language. Years ago Spanish was the means of communication among the upper classes, a hang-over from the Spanish regime. That is no longer the case.

Translation often presents many problems. On the lesson on "salvation" the word "deliver" is frequently used. Evidently the brother who translated into Tagalog must have been depending on his dictionary for this word. He used a word which means to deliver a package or a message. It was no problem for me to check over the Tagalog translation, but in other languages it was necessary to depend on others.

The Ilocano translation was done by a man who had an interesting story. During World War II he served as an officer in the guerilla movement opposing the Japanese. He attended a Methodist church and was the adult Bible class teacher. Some American G.I.'s went to this church after the Liberation. One of

The Bible School of the Air

these later returned as a missionary and visited his former friends in that church, though he was a Baptist. Through his testimony the pastor was saved, after having been a pastor for 12 years. When he asked the missionary how he would help the members of his church, he was advised to write to the Bible School of the Air. A number of names were sent and God began a work of grace in many hearts. The pastor's wife was saved, and also a high school teacher of literature. The two high schools in which she taught were private schools and the parish priest was on the school board. He became quite upset when he learned that this teacher was recommending reading the Bible as the best of English literature. She would tell her pupils, "If you want a correspondence course to help you understand the Bible, you can get it from the Bible School of the Air, free of charge."

One Saturday evening, the former guerilla leader, Mr. Lamagna, was preparing his Sunday school lesson for the next morning. In his hand was a cigarette as he turned to a reference in the lesson. He read, "Having therefore these promises, dearly beloved, let us cleanse ourselves from all filthiness of the flesh and spirit, perfecting holiness in the fear of God" (2 Cor. 7:1). At that moment, for the first time in his experience the Bible became a living Book. God spoke to him; the cigarette in his hand and the liquor in his cupboard were "filthiness of the flesh." He went before his class the next morning a different man. He said, "Something happened to me last night. God spoke to me. His Word is alive."

Shortly after he studied the lessons on the new birth in the Emmaus course, "This is what happened to me! I was born again and I didn't know what it was." He was often invited to speak at Methodist conferences and from then on his favorite topic was, you guessed it, the new birth. People would ask him where he learned that, and he would recommend the Bible School of the Air. After such conferences we would receive a list of names of a hundred or more asking for our course.

Mr. Lamagna wrote to ask for advice as he was starting a Bible class on Sunday afternoons (in addition to his regular classes). Could we recommend a topic or series of lessons? We suggested the course "Lessons for Christian Living" or "Guide to Christian Growth." In the former is a lesson on baptism, and

Mr. Lamagna asked us how to teach that under his circumstances. We replied that the lesson presented what we believe is the teaching of the New Testament. It would be his responsibility to decide if this was right or not. Soon after that he showed up at our home. When I inquired why he had come to Manila, he said that he wanted to be baptized by immersion. So we had the joy of baptizing him in Manila Bay.

There were about forty in his Bible class, so when they had finished the course he asked if we would be willing to go to San Nicolas and present the certificates in a sort of graduation. We drove up there on Saturday afternoon and I preached in the church service on Sunday morning. I was interested to see in the pastor's study a set of J. N. Darby's "Synopsis of the Bible." That afternoon in a special service we presented the certificates. As we were about to leave Mr. Lamagna's to return home, he brought out half a sack of rice and put it in our car. I remonstrated that we didn't expect anything from them but were glad to serve freely. He related that the previous year he had decided to tithe his harvest. He reaped 75 sacks and gave seven and a half to the church. He said, "You know the pastor can preach better when he gets enough to eat!" The following year from the same rice land he reaped 175 sacks and after giving 17 to the church, he had the half-sack for me. He was the one who translated "What the Bible Teaches" into Ilocano.

When we commenced the Bible School of the Air, tape recorders were not available so each program was done live at the studios of FEBC. At first Anna had a part in reading letters or in asking questions. When Ken Engle arrived, having radio experience at WMBI, the Moody station, he helped in the program. He stayed with us until he was married and was very much like a son to us. Strangely, many people mistakenly supposed he was our son-in-law! A year later our own son Ken arrived and had a part in this ministry.

Answering the student's questions with a personal letter was an important part of this ministry. Many of these related to matters in the lessons. Others perhaps were prompted by curiosity. My secretary used to be a bit disgusted with those who asked run-of-the-mill questions like "Where did Cain get his wife?" We tried to impress upon students the importance of reading and studying the Bible so they could answer their own

The Bible School of the Air

questions. One man would send in lists of questions and I suppose over a few years I must have answered at least a thousand of his questions. At times I continued by trying to impress upon him the importance of salvation. I don't know whether he ever came to know the Lord.

Over the years the radio program has had different formats. For a time the actual message took about seven minutes and then after a hymn we would have a forum time when three or four would sit around the mike and discuss some things in the lesson. Then it became possible to record the program ahead of time. This was much more convenient because we could select a recording time. In the early days we had to go out to the radio station each Monday evening. In those days there was a great deal of dissident unrest around Manila. We frequently heard rifle fire in the distance when we drove out to the station, a 13 mile drive each way. We were thankful for the Lord's preserving care. With the opportunity to record in the daytime, we dropped the forum and had a longer message. In that way it was possible to prepare a month's worth of programs in one morning. For a while we also had three 15 minute programs each week in English taking up different courses than those being used on the half-hour programs. Since 1981, one of the gifted Filipino missionaries has been reading scripts that I prepare. He is so occupied with other work he doesn't have time to prepare scripts (though he is quite capable of doing so), and I was finding it too tiring to drive out to the station.

In recent years the direct response from the English radio program has been meager. However, there has been a good response from the Tagalog program carried on by Rey Cervantes, another of the national missionaries; but he too has been faced with the problems of finding time to prepare for the programs, especially since he has been finishing his studies in a Bible institute.

Soon after we started the Bible School of the Air we noticed that students would ask for the course to be sent to their friends or classmates. So to facilitate this we sent forms on which they could enroll six others when they sent in their test papers. We also occasionally put advertisements in local papers. These greatly boosted the numbers being enrolled. After enrolling a student's friends, we would send the list back to them with a letter asking them to encourage their friends to respond. Soon we were getting as many as 3000 names a week. It was just a coincidence that we reached our peak of 4000 plus in the week Dr. and Mrs. Harlow visited us in 1962. In May, 1967, we held a public rally and presented a Bible to five students from the Manila area who were enrolled when we reached a total of one million. In March, 1976, the total enrollment reached one and a half million.

We were enrolling more than in any other Emmaus center around the world, but our percentage of completions was about the lowest. It was obvious that many who received the first two lessons did not proceed further. Our completion rate was only about 10%. Followup letters were sent to those who had not responded, which brought a few results. At that time we were sending the first two lessons to anyone whose name and address was given to us. In recent years we have been sending a letter asking if they really want the course, along with some Gospel literature. While this method has reduced the number of enrollments, it has raised the percentage of completions. Another factor in this was the increasing cost of postage. When BSA began, a two-centavo stamp was sufficient to send a letter (one cent U.S.); now it takes forty centavos! While that is only five cents U.S. at the present exchange, it has added considerably to the postage bills.

It was soon evident that the course was an excellent means of evangelizing in all parts of the Philippines, from Batanes in the north to Tawi-tawi in the south. More than once some missionary would go into an area where he thought there had been no previous Gospel witness. Then in some home he would see a Certificate of Completion proudly displayed in a frame on the wall. Since there were those who did not return the first tests, it was important that they be given a clear presentation of the Gospel. At first, R. A. Laidlaw of New Zealand kindly sent us a supply of his excellent booklet, "The Reason Why." Other booklets were used and we received some grants of "Here's How" from Life Messengers in Seattle. There were other booklets that we preferred to this one, but we found that "Here's How" seemed to be more effective. As we analyzed the reason for this, it was our conclusion that since it was written in the form of a dialog, the readers put themselves into the part of one in that dialog. This helped them in understanding the message.

The Bible School of the Air

As a result of this study, we came out with a booklet "What's the Answer?" It presents a couple in a local setting asking this question. Through a Christian neighbor with a Bible, they learned the answer to a number of questions commonly raised here. The neighbor explains the way of salvation, and the story ends with the couple on their knees accepting Christ as their Lord and Savior. This was translated into the four languages in which our course is distributed locally. Our intuition proved correct for many have written to tell how they accepted Christ, even to getting down on their knees just as that couple did.

A man in the Visayan Islands wrote that one day he was visiting in the home of his relatives and saw a booklet on the table. Out of curiosity he started to read it, but as it made him feel uncomfortable, he put it down. The same thing happened on subsequent visits but the third time he decided to read all of the booklet. As he finished the booklet, he too accepted Christ as his Savior.

A missionary from the Far East Broadcasting Company told of visiting a tribe of Sea Gypsies in the remote southern islands, just a few miles north of Borneo. To his surprise he encountered a Christian in that part of the country which is largely Moslem. When he inquired of this man how he became a believer, he was told it was through courses from the Bible School of the Air.

During one of our visits to Baguio we visited a crippled Chinese girl in her home there. Her father was a businessman who had a large store in the city. She had been wonderfully saved through studying the course "What the Bible Teaches." Though crippled and getting around in a wheelchair she had a radiant testimony for the Lord, even though most of the family were not sympathetic. On a subsequent visit to Baguio, we learned that she was then staying in a barrio up in the mountains where her parents had a business. We found out that there was a bus which went out that way in the morning and returned in the afternoon. Leaving Baguio about eight we arrived in the barrio about eleven and thus were able to have about two hours for visiting before the return trip. Most of the way the road was unpaved, winding alongside the mountains and deep in dust. When we boarded the bus we were the only white people, the rest were brown Filipinos. When we got off we were all the same color! Those buses have open sides and afford no protection from dust! At prayer meeting that evening, I remarked on

God's Word to Adam, "For dust you are and to dust you will return." We didn't particularly relish returning to dust in that way! Nevertheless, it was worthwhile to offer some encouragement to that girl. Later the Lord led her into full-time Christian service in spite of her physical handicap.

In earlier chapters, I have related how assemblies have been formed in Tarlac and in Bahay-pare, Pampanga as a result of contacts with the Bible School of the Air. From time to time we have heard of other groups formed into local churches through this contact. In a place called Nahapay in the province of Iloilo is a small assembly that came into being through some being saved through the courses. We have been able to have some fellowship with this group through visits of national workers. We could go on to tell about men and women now serving the Lord in various capacities who were helped or who were saved through their studies. Mr. Fred Magbanua, managing director of the Far East Broadcasting Company, is one of these.

For some years the half-hour English program was aired over several commercial stations. In some of these Back to the Bible Broadcast would sign a contract for air time seven days a week. We would take the Sunday time and reimburse them for it. When martial law was declared in September, 1972, all radio stations were temporarily ordered to stop activities. The stations of the Far East Broadcasting Company were among the first permitted to resume activities, largely because of their non-political status. I think we only missed one week's broadcast on that account. For some of the commercial stations, it took longer to resume broadcasting. When they did, most of them charged much higher rates than before. We re-evaluated the situation, and since the response from these stations was slim, we decided it was not worth the added expense.

Soon after commencing operations it was evident that we would need some clerical help. Miss Luz Lazaro from the San Juan assembly came to work for us and is still faithfully serving in the office after more than thirty years. A number of others over the years have worked with us for longer or shorter periods. Misses Letty and Nelly Licera have rendered valuable help for many years. When Mr. and Mrs. Glynn Dean left for the United States, brother Elino Aragon who had been working for Glynn, came to the Bible School of the Air as office manager in

The Bible School of the Air

1974. He is an elder in the Binangonan assembly and is involved in many other activities in the Lord's work, particularly in the camp work. Thus the entire operation of the office of BSA is now in the hands of these nationals. A committee of three missionaries and Brother Aragon meet occasionally to discuss major matters. The staff are on a salary basis.

This phase of the Lord's work has been a venture of faith and we do praise the Lord for His faithfulness in supplying the needs. Some of the Filipino brethren and sisters give regularly, but the bulk of the finances comes from abroad. Some years ago I was laying before the Lord the needs for this work. A rough calculation showed that $500 was needed particularly for printing and postage. As we sat down to breakfast after my devotions, Ken Engle stopped by. For some reason he had to be out early that morning and stopped by the post office to pick up our mail. To our delight (and amazement, I must confess) one letter contained a check for $500. The funds didn't usually come in such a spectacular manner, but we can testify that God has not failed us.

24

CAMP WORK

"But thanks be to God, who always leads us in triumphal procession in Christ and through us spreads everywhere the fragrance of the knowledge of him." (2 Cor. 2:14)

In a few words the Apostle paints a wonderful picture of victory. Christ has triumphed over all His foes and leads us who are His redeemed in His triumphal procession. Roman triumphal processions were accompanied by the burning of incense. In Christ's victory parade the incense is the fragrance of the knowledge of Him. For the surpassing greatness of knowing Christ Jesus his Lord, Paul was willing to lose any gain this world could offer. But we are not only to know Him; we are to make Him known. The fragrance of that knowledge needs to be spread everywhere. One of the ways by which that knowledge has been spread has been through camps.

Mention has been made in an earlier chapter of the Philippine Keswick Camp. At the first such camp, held at Montalban from December 26, 1931, to January 2, 1932, there were 85 young people. It proved to be a time of rich blessing in spite of really inadequate facilities. In those days it was not so easy for students to attend high school or college in the provinces. Also, those who studied in Manila were often not able to go home for the Christmas holiday. So it was the idea of one missionary to have a camp at that time for students. At the fourth camp in

1934, 136 attended. Just prior to the 1937 camp a bad typhoon washed out much of the gorge at Montalban where previous camps were held. A new location was found in the hills below Antipolo.

Preparations were well in hand for the eleventh Philippine Keswick Camp at the end of 1941. The work party planned for December 8 was cancelled as the word came of the Japanese attacks on Pearl Harbor and places in the Philippines. Much of the camp equipment was stored at our house. The camp cots were turned over to the American committee at the Santo Tomas Internment Camp. Later in the war, a Christian Chinese family asked for the use of the tents. They were evacuating to a small island north of Luzon. It may have been those tents which attracted the attention of U.S. bombers, probably thinking they were being used by Japanese. Unfortunately, some of our Chinese friends were killed and injured in those attacks. Naturally there was no possibility of holding camps during the Japanese occupation. Nor were we in a position to resume such activities when we returned to the Philippines in 1949.

Later on, Ray Kalback and Ken Brooks with some others began the Highland Bible Camp. Their first camp was held in 1954 in Tagaytay, and it was a time of blessing for the young people who gathered there. One day at this camp, the director Ray Kalback happened to go around the back of the kitchen just in time to see a carabao (water buffalo) sampling the soup for dinner. The carabao was hastily shooed away though apparently the soup met with his approval. The soup was well-boiled after that and none of the campers were any the wiser. The facilities there were not ideal, so the next year the camp met on the grounds of Far Eastern Bible Institute and Seminary (FEBIAS). There was room enough for the campers, but the buildings were hot as camps are held during the hot season. Nevertheless there was sufficient interest and blessing to warrant continuing this effort.

For the years 1956 to 1961 they were able to rent facilities at the Nazarene Bible School which overlooks Trinidad Valley near Baguio. This broad flat valley is famed for its vegetable and fruit farms and has been called "the salad bowl." Situated in the mountains the climate is cooler; in fact, some lowlanders felt it was a bit too cool at camp. Different camps for Filipinos and

Camp Work

Chinese were held over a period of six weeks. Many have testified of the lasting blessings they received at those camps and some who attended are now in full-time service for the Lord.

One of these is our brother Elino Aragon, an elder in the Binangonan assembly and also office manager for the Bible School of the Air. He writes, "I grew up attending Sunday School so I knew the way of salvation by heart. Even though I cannot remember the time I came to the Lord and accepted Him as my Lord and Savior, I considered myself saved. However, it was not until I attended camp that I became aware of doubts I had regarding my salvation. I was in my early teens then and was so interested in the activities at camp. One of my favorite times was the Gospel Hour where we studied the First Epistle of John. When we came to 1 John 4:20, I was puzzled. The verse said that if a man says he loves God and hates his brother, he is a liar. At that time I always disagreed and quarreled with my older brother. I went to the speaker afterwards and asked him about my predicament. Is it possible for me to be saved and yet hate my brother? He counselled me, and I rededicated my life to the Lord. When I went home I tried to have a new attitude with my brother. After a few years, I realized that the verse does not refer to brothers in the flesh but to fellow Christians. Anyway that verse became the turning point in my Christian life."

In 1962, Milton Haack arranged for a camp at Valdez, beside the river close to Floridablanca. This was primarily for believers in that area of Pampanga. Some of these folk could not afford the expense involved in travelling to Baguio. It has always been the aim of the camp committee to keep the costs as low as possible so poor students could attend. In subsequent years camps were held at Cabcaben and at the New Tribes camp grounds in Dinalupihan. Both of these places are in Bataan where the Filipino and American troops held out against superior Japanese forces in 1942. In 1974, the last year before using our own campsite, there were 69 campers from 15 churches at the Christian Training Camp in Dinalupihan along with 26 staffers. Elino Aragon was director for that camp. The young people returned home with a burden to help in the work in their different assemblies. That same year 48 attended the Pampanga Youth Camp at Floridablanca and ten of these professed faith in our Lord Jesus Christ. Stimson Alviar was the director for that camp. In all of these camps, believers were strengthened in their faith and a number of unsaved came to know Christ as their Lord and Savior.

In all of these locations there were problems because camps had to be scheduled at times that were convenient to the owners of the camp property. It would be much more satisfactory to have our own camp, but where would we get the money to buy the suitable property? For some time the committee looked at different possibilities and some of the available sites. There did not seem to be any clear guidance from the Lord about any of these. Only when they were in the will of the Lord could they expect Him to supply the needs.

In 1974 one of the national workers learned about a piece of land near Malolos, the capital of Bulacan. Through a friend who was a real estate agent he found that there were two hectares (a little more than five acres) of riceland but also with some fruit trees, mostly mangoes. The price of the land was quite reasonable compared to the prevailing prices in that area. It would be necessary to buy a small strip of land for a right of way, but otherwise it was quite accessible. Being close to the main highway north from Manila, it could be reached from Manila in an hour by car. Furthermore, it was fairly central to most of the assemblies on Luzon.

After much prayer and consideration, along with calculation of available funds, it was decided to proceed with negotiations. The owners were not believers but proved to be quite reasonable to deal with and suitable terms were arranged. Money for the downpayment was either available or became so through the gifts of the Lord's people and assemblies locally. Workers Together in the U.S. was able to stir up interest among the Lord's people in the United States and Canada. These and other channels were what the Lord used in supplying the needs so it was possible to make all the payments on time. It was a demonstration to the Lord's people in the Philippines of how the Lord does supply the needs for His work. Since only part of the land is presently needed for camping purposes, it was the aim to make enough off the rice crops and fruit to pay for the operating costs of the property itself.

For the first two years (1975-1976) on our own property,

Camp Work

tents were borrowed for dormitories. While these served the immediate purpose, they were uncomfortably hot. So the following year, it was possible for two dormitories of a temporary nature to be erected. These were made mostly of palm thatch roofs and sides and it was estimated that they would serve for some five or six years. It was thought by that time it would be possible to build permanent dorms. Two small houses were put up for the caretaker and the farmer and their families. Experiments in raising chickens and rabbits unfortunately did not prove successful on account of sickness and thefts at night. One of the first projects was the dining room and kitchen. It was a great advantage when these were finished and screened all round. However, at this writing (1982) these facilities are very crowded when more than a hundred are enrolled in camp; so plans are being made to enlarge these. The dining hall often serves as a meeting place, though in good weather classes are held under the shade of the trees. Also at this time several dormitory rooms of hollow block have been built with double bunk beds built in. In the next few years they hope to add to these and also build a chapel, possibly some day even a swimming pool. Electricity has been available, which has made it possible to have a pump to raise water from the well to a water tower. We do praise the Lord for His provision of all these facilities.

Naturally the question would arise as to whether the camp is used enough to justify the expenditure of the money for land and buildings. Obviously, we cannot expect the returns on this investment to be in material things. There are two ways of looking at this. First, the actual use of the property, and second, the results in the lives of men and women and children.

In this tropical climate camps don't need to be winterized; there is not much variation in temperature throughout the year. During the worst of the rainy season (August to October) it was usually too wet underfoot. The regular camping season is in the hot season (which is also school vacation) in April and May. For some years a two-week Christian Training Camp has been a most profitable time. Mostly young people, but also some older ones, attend this camp. It is run like a "short-term" Bible school with a curriculum spread over a four-year period. Bible studies take up some books of the Bible and some doctrinal studies.

There are also classes dealing with practical phases of Christian service. The objective is to instruct believers in Biblical truths, along with methods of service, so that this knowledge may be used in their home assemblies. Along with this is the desire to enrich their spiritual lives and establish them in the faith so there will be a spiritual motivation for serving the Lord.

Camps for young people are also held each year for high school age and also for others who are older. In these camps there are a mixture of believers and unbelievers, so there is more of an evangelistic outreach. Each year there are reports of some being saved and brought into a personal relationship with our Lord Jesus Christ. As much as possible these are followed up so they may become involved in young people's activities in the local churches.

About 1969, Miss Tessie Castro, whose conversion led to the beginning of the work in Bahay-pare area, had a vision of a children's camp. During the Christmas vacation time children from that area were invited. Tessie's father, in previous years, had an egg business and kept the laying hens in structures on his land. After the business had been given up, they cleaned up the hen houses and used them as temporary dormitories for the children's camp. The facilities were far from ideal, and the resources were meager; but it was an opportunity to bring some of the children under the influence of the Gospel. In recent years the children's camp has been transferred to the new camp-site and has a wider outreach and better facilities.

At one time we had to rent camp facilities but now we are in a position to rent the camp to approved evangelical organizations at times that are convenient to our own group. This brings in a little revenue to help with upkeep and improvements. During the year the camp is frequently used for overnight or weekend conferences. Each year a men's conference is held over some public holiday. Men from different assemblies gather for a time of fellowship and instruction in the Word of God. The topics chosen are often practical to help in the life of the local church, such as The Choice and Function of Elders; Discipline in the Local Church; or the Lord's Supper, what it means and how it is to be observed.

In recent years there have been women's conferences. The husbands are exhorted to take over the care of the home for a couple of days so their wives can be free to participate in these conferences. It is not only a great time of fellowship as they gather together from different places but also a time of learning. Here too the teaching is along practical lines about the place of sisters in the local church and in the home. Other groups such as Boy's Brigade, Pioneer Girls, and young people's fellowships use the camp for some special gatherings. After a lapse of some years, in 1982, a name was chosen from among several suggestions. It is now known as "Emmaus Bible Camp." It is the prayer of all concerned that this camp will indeed be like the Emmaus road, a place where people learn to walk with Christ and listen to His teaching.

Ever since the camp property was acquired the brethren have had a vision of using it also for a Bible school. There are many good Bible schools and seminaries in the Philippines. However, whether denominational or nondenominational, they are not in a position to teach New Testament truth as we understand it. Moreover, it has been our experience that some of our young people who have attended such schools have been attracted to other groups. When offered the choice of a regular salary or trusting the Lord for their needs, the former sometimes seems more appealing. The first Bible school was held from January to March, 1982, with 15 students. Some of these were commended workers who felt the need to add to their knowledge of the Word. Others came from different assemblies, the eldest among them being a retired army man from Baguio. Since the basis of education in the Philippines is in English, many Bible schools use that language. One of the reasons for this is that their students come from different language areas. A problem resulting from this is that often students have difficulty expressing theological concepts in their own language. There have been occasions when preachers have said something in English and have turned to me, "How do you say that in Tagalog?" So in our small school the teaching has been in Tagalog. Later on, it is hoped to develop the school into a full term school, using the camping facilities when it is not the regular camping season.

Yet all of these activities avail for nothing unless there are spiritual results in the lives of men and women. Indeed there have been such results for which we praise the Lord. In the May-June 1973 issue of KAMANGGAGAWA, we find testimonies like this. From a young lady in San Juan: "This camp has been a great blessing to me. When I came, I came with a hungry heart for real Christian fellowship. I had some questions that were troubling me. My questions were answered here and I got what I wanted—fellowship among Christians my age. It was satisfying because it was shared in Jesus' Name."

Here is a translation of a Tagalog testimony by a young man from Sumapa which is the nearest assembly to the camp: "Here I found true assurance of my salvation. I yielded my life to Him and I know that if I will be faithful, I will have victory in my faith all the time."

A young lady from Caloocan City gives this testimony: "I came from a Roman Catholic background, so I knew nothing about salvation. Through the personal witness of my counsellor and the messages given, I came to know Jesus Christ and surrendered my life to Him who is now my Lord. I am so happy! Thank God for camps like this."

There can be no doubt that the camp ministry has been and will continue to be a valuable contribution to the furtherance of the work of the Lord and the building up of God's people in their most holy faith. This, of course, leads to spiritual growth and the development of local churches.

25

FELLOWSHIP IN THE GOSPEL

"God, who has called you into fellowship with his Son Jesus Christ our Lord, is faithful." (1 Cor. 1:9)

That great devotional writer and speaker of a former generation, Dr. F. B. Meyer, once wrote, "Whilst willing to devote my energies to those with whom my belief necessarily allies me, yet I refuse to be a mere denominationalist and I glory most in being the brother of all who love the Lord Jesus Christ in sincerity." Sentiments like that probably are more attractive to those in the mission field where by force of circumstances we are brought into direct contact with those in other Christian groups. While we are not prepared to give up those truths we find taught in the Scriptures, we can fellowship with God's children who may not always accept some of those truths. The truth of separation can be carried too far when it leads us to refuse any fellowship with those of God's children. Such fellowship does not mean that we necessarily approve of all their methods of service or their interpretations of Scripture. They are the Lord's servants and to Him they will give account, not to us. The Apostle Paul was aware that some preached the Gospel with false motives, yet he rejoiced that the Gospel was preached (Phil. 1:15-18).

It is in the spirit of the foregoing that it has been esteemed a privilege to serve in some capacity with a number of other organizations through the years. For longer or shorter periods I have had the privilege of serving on councils or advisory boards of such groups as Christian Literature Crusade, Open Air Campaigners, and Back to the Bible Broadcast. For some 15 years it was my privilege to be associated with the latter organization, first as a member of the Philippine Advisory Council, then when the Philippine Bible Broadcasters were incorporated I met with them, first as a member and then as a consultant until I resigned in December, 1979. By then, at the age of 81, it was necessary to cut back on some of my activities. Our son Kenneth is now a member of that board.

One activity from which I have not yet resigned is the advisory board of Overseas Christian Servicemen's Centers. In an earlier chapter mention was made of the servicemen who came to our home in the years prior to the outbreak of war in the Pacific. Contact has been made with some of these men who survived the war, including prisoner of war camps in some cases in the Philippines and in Japan.

Jessie Miller was one of those, and he wrote his story in a tract, "Nine must die." After the Death March from Bataan he was in camp in Tarlac where they were divided into squads of ten. "If one escaped, the nine would be shot," said the Japanese. One of Jessie's squad did escape and the nine found themselves lined up before a firing squad. With all the misery of starvation, malnutrition and illness, Jessie wished they would get it over with. Then his sufferings would be over—at home with the Lord. Just then the Lord spoke, "Jessie, are you willing to come back here as a missionary?" That seemed like an impossibility but Jessie replied, "Yes, Lord, I am." He said that at that moment he knew the Japanese couldn't shoot him! For some unknown reason (that is unknown to all except Jessie) they marched the men back to barracks and said "Tomorrow." That tomorrow never came!

After years of prison camp and hard labor in Japan, J-Day came at last. Back home Jessie went to Biola and eventually came back to the Philippines as a missionary. After a few months he was off to Japan to claim as his bride a tall, blonde beauty, Netty, who was a missionary there. Soon after their return to Manila, a call came for an auxiliary chaplain to hold services for a detachment of the U.S. Air Force in Manila Port Area. This

Fellowship in the Gospel 235

became an opening for a work among servicemen which the Lord abundantly blessed in the salvation of a number of men.

We became closely associated with the Millers in this new venture and helped find locations for a servicemen's center and also in conferences that were held for servicemen. This work was at first under the wing of Far Eastern Gospel Crusade with which the Millers then served. However, since this kind of effort was not within the planned outreach of this mission, it was mutually agreed that this ought to be a separate work. While we were on furlough in 1953-54, I was invited to go to Chicago for a conference with the Millers and some of the servicemen who had been saved. Through the courtesy of the OMF we were allowed to meet in their home there for a few days. This time was spent in defining objectives and drawing up a constitution for Overseas Christian Servicemen's Centers, Inc.

Through the years this work has been greatly blessed by God. Some of the men first saved through this work have had a large part in its growth. Dick Patty who had formerly been at a center in Oxnard, California, came to open a center in Olongapo and later to build a center near the gate of the Subic Naval Base. Later on, a home was opened up near the Clark Air Force Base. Many are the men whose lives have been changed through coming to know Christ in these centers. One man was a typical old-time soldier whose face showed the effects of his dissolute life. His drinking, bad habits, and foul language all changed when he trusted Christ. His wife was not a believer, and when he went back home to her in the U.S., she left him. He was "too good" for her!

The Manila Center was closed but another was opened in Cavite near the Sangley Naval Base. When that facility was turned over to the Philippine Government, that center was closed. But during the years it was open, many were blessed. One man there professed to be a believer from an assembly in the Eastern U.S. He had been in Sunday school, and attended summer camp where he professed his faith in Christ. He was later baptized and received into the fellowship before going overseas. One night in Cavite, he was sick. Lying on his bunk he thought of the verse, "That which is born of flesh is flesh, that which is born of the Spirit is spirit." He came to a realization that though he had a Christian upbringing, had made a profession of faith, been baptized and received into church fellowship, actually he had never been born again. He settled that issue that night, and the subsequent change in his life was very evident.

Work among servicemen overseas is a fluctuating work in two ways. For one thing the military personnel have limited terms of service overseas, usually about two years. Centers catering to the Navy feel this more acutely as the ships come and go. With such mobility it is not possible to build up a work with the same people. On the other hand, political changes and war change the movements of the military. During the Vietnam War, OCSC opened centers in Vietnam, Thailand, and Taiwan; but these were all closed at the time of the military pull-out from these places. Centers have been maintained in Japan and Korea aiming to provide "a home away from home" for servicemen and women. In the early years of this work it was mostly men who were being reached but now there are a number of women.

It was with considerable regret that the Hospitality House at Clark was closed late in 1981, shortly after they had celebrated 20 years in that location. The rented facilities were sold by the owner and efforts to find another suitable location proved ineffective. Another factor was that some church-oriented groups around that Air Force base were catering to the Christian fellows. In the early days of this work the main thrust was in the far east, but now it is in the European countries and to some extent also in the United States. We count it a joy and privilege to have had some association with this effort which has been used by God in the salvation of many men and women.

After World War II a number of young missionaries came to the Philippines. Many of the pre-war missionaries did not return. These new missionaries with young families were soon concerned about the education of their children. A few tried sending their children to the Philippine public schools but there were problems in this. There were cross-cultural and language problems, even though English is the basis of education. Furthermore, the local curriculum made it difficult for the MK (missionary kid) to fit in at schools at home during furlough times.

Others tried teaching their children at home with the help of correspondence courses. For a few years we had used the Calvert system which was quite satisfactory, but it does take a lot of

Fellowship in the Gospel

the parent's time, and there is a lack of cooperation or competition with other children. Some of the missions had teachers for the children in their own mission, but it is difficult for a teacher to supervise and teach children in several grades and children miss much in the way of sports, music, and other extra-curricular activities.

Many years ago some missionaries, especially among the British, would send their children home to attend private boarding schools. This assured the children of a good education in their own culture, but it deprived them of the essential home life with their parents. In this way it was often an unsatisfactory arrangement because the children lost contact with their parents. A son of missionaries who had been educated in this way in later years asked us what we were doing about this problem. He advised us by all means to endeavor to keep our children with us. Being aware of the instability in his own spiritual life, I felt he had been speaking out of his own experience.

In 1955, a number of missionaries met together to discuss this vital concern of their children (or, in our case, our grandchildren). There was no doubt as to the need for such a school, but the big questions were: Who would operate it, where would the finances come from, and where should it be located. As to the last point, it was noted that such schools in tropical countries are generally in mountain resorts where the climate is cooler and healthier. Some therefore suggested the school should be in Baguio, the mountain resort, 150 miles north of Manila. It was noted that the Brent School was there, a private Episcopalian school. The final decision was to locate somewhere in the Manila area. A deciding factor was that many missionaries lived in the great Manila area and so many of the children could live at home. One result of this has been that only about one-third of the pupils have been boarding.

Many missionary schools are operated by one mission or by a group of cooperating missions. This means that a lot of the basic decisions are controlled by the offices or headquarters of these missions in the homelands. It was rather a momentous decision that the new school would not be mission-operated but missionary operated. There would be a self-perpetuating board of men (and later would include women) who would be chosen from various missions who had children in the school. Along with this was the decision to ask missions represented in the student body to supply qualified teachers who would be supported through their own groups.

As to finances, there would, of course, be tuition and boarding fees and also fees for transportation. There would be an additional fee to help provide for expanding facilities. The needs were made known and gifts began to flow in for the school. I don't know who first suggested the name Faith Academy, but it certainly has been through faith in God that the needs of all kinds have been supplied. Even the obtaining of a sizable loan to build the school was an act of faith, for it is rather remarkable that a large insurance company would lend such a sum to a bunch of missionaries.

It was my privilege to serve on the first Board of Trustees and as one of the first original incorporators in 1956 and 1957. The school was able to locate an old, large house on V. Mapa Street in Manila. Considerable renovation was needed but by July, 1958, it was ready to serve as a school for 47 students and a boarding home for 12. The large yard with some acacia trees sufficed as a playground, though not suited for many sports activities.

We were home on furlough from the fall of 1958 until 1959. During this year the school grew and a separate home had to be rented for boarding. During that time the search was on for land which could be purchased for the school. Leonard was very much involved in this search. Land was located a few miles east of Manila on higher ground. The owner told Len, "Go and look out what you think you will need in that area." Len marked off some 12 acres and when he returned to the owner with his proposal, he replied, "What have you left me? Nothing but hills and gullies!" Some thought it was too far out and too inaccessible. However, the Board decided to purchase that land and in response to faith the Lord supplied that need.

Right after our return from furlough, a few missionaries climbed one of those hills and in a simple prayer service informally dedicated it to the Lord's service. Soon the bulldozers came in and cut down that hill. Thus, it was possible to provide a level area for school buildings and campus. The latter was down to hard rock, and the Board begrudged money for even a thin layer of top soil for growing grass. Would anything ever

Fellowship in the Gospel

grow there? It didn't seem likely then. Those who view the plants and trees growing there now would have a hard time visualizing what it once was. But isn't this an illustration of what God is constantly doing in the lives of men and women and even children, like those attending Faith Academy? The seed of God's Word planted in hard stony hearts watered by prayer and tended by tender, loving care produces a harvest to the glory of God.

Two factors played a part in our getting a sizable loan from an insurance company. First, one of the Board members was a highly respected insurance actuary. He was known by officials of the insurance company. Also, that their president had been in Los Baños internment camp with us.

Accessibility to the property was provided when the surrounding country was developed as a high class residential area, along with a golf and country club. Faith Academy was able to purchase a right to the use of their private road. At the time the price seemed high but over the years has proved worthwhile. During those years the Board elected me to be treasurer, but that was certainly not on the basis of experience. It meant a lot of extra work for me as the building was progressing. Thanks to a very efficient bookkeeper, I survived that ordeal. The Board was then estimating a possible enrollment of 300, double those who were then enrolled. In recent years the enrollment has been in excess of 500, so through the years there has been considerable expansion.

Transportation was provided for day students, and one of the first buses was a jeepney like those so common on Manila streets. Faith Academy couldn't afford to buy new buses so acquired secondhand buses, some from U.S. armed forces surplus. Inevitably such buses would break down at times. The telephones of missionaries would ring early in the morning asking help to take children to the school. During those early years we had located a used bus which seemed to be in fairly good condition. The Board was undecided whether they could afford that expense. Among other things at that time, I was working several days a week on a committee for the revision of the Tagalog New Testament. One morning a mission treasurer stopped by the Bible House to hand me a check for Faith Academy from their mission. It was for a good amount and on the way home for lunch I was praying for guidance about what recommendations I would make to the Board for its use. Reaching home I told Anna about the check; I was quite elated. She startled me by saying, "Oh, that's for the bus!" How could she make such a decision—she wasn't even a Board member! Then I learned the dealer had called about the bus. They were desperately in need of cash *that day*. If we could come up with cash that same day, he would let us have the bus at a much lower figure, a real bargain. Lunch had to wait while I contacted some Board members and got their consent, then call the dealer and accept his offer. Another answer to prayer and faith.

Another concern and matter for prayer those days was finding water. A well digger had tried, but the holes he dug were all dry. Meantime we were hauling water in a small tanker for cement mixing and building needs. Geologists were consulted about the rock formation. They reported that a strata of hard rock of unknown thickness lay under our property, so the prospects of finding water were slim indeed. Had God led us that far and supplied the needs for building, only to lead us into a stalemate about water? There was much prayer going up to God from all the missionary community. Some people interested in the property around said to one Christian businessman, "Do those crazy missionaries think they can sit up on a hill and get water by just praying for it?" Well, we didn't expect God to send a Moses and tell him to smite the rock, but we did believe the Lord would answer our prayers.

Just at that time some friends from the U.S. visited us. This brother, who had a keen interest in missions, was a successful builder and contractor. When Ken and Elaine took him up to the operations at Faith Academy, he was a bit concerned about the methods used by Filipino workmen. When he learned that there was still no certainty about water, he too began to think we were "crazy missionaries." He thought we should have been sure of the water supply before beginning to build. This brother also had some experience in well drilling, and he suggested boring a hole near the northwest corner of the property. It became the Lord's provision for water at that time.

Several years later, that first well was not producing enough water for the growing needs. So again water was an urgent prayer request. For a time the children were asked to bring

Fellowship in the Gospel

drinking water each day for their own needs. Another hole was drilled. Some water was found but of uncertain amount. It was decided to dig deeper but soon ran into hard rock. When the hole was enlarged to develop what was there, it proved to be more than originally expected. Faith had again triumphed at Faith Academy.

When we returned to the Philippines in 1970, after furlough, we went to Baguio for two years to help care for the work there. Ken and Mary Lou Engle who had started that work were going home for a protracted furlough. There were young Christians who needed to be nurtured. While there, in November, 1970, a very strong typhoon swept across the Manila area. We could not contact our folks by telephone as lines were down. From the news, we learned that the television tower near our house was down; then we got word through missionary radio contact that our folks were all right though some trees were down at our house. Also, that there had been extensive damage at Faith Academy. This was confirmed by a picture of the school in a newspaper which reached us a couple of days later.

Later we learned that the gymnasium roof was blown away and two walls collapsed. Also part of the roof of the academic building was gone and library books were soaked with rain, besides other damage. Schools are automatically closed when typhoon signal #2 and #3 go up, so it was only the boarding children who were at the dorms. The home where Len and Esther were house-parents sat on the side of a hill. A porch extended the full length of the house overlooking the garden and the swimming pool. The strong wind lifted the roof of the porch, along with the heavy beams supporting it, and tossed the whole thing over the house on to the driveway at the back. The force of the wind was almost incredible. Two pickups with chains could hardly budge those beams off the driveway. One of the plate glass doors on to the porch was shattered. In the goodness of God, Marilou, our granddaughter, turned her back just as the door struck her. She was badly cut but it would have been worse had she been hit face-on. With trees and poles down, it was difficult to get her to a hospital for care.

Usually destructive typhoons pass quickly. So the next day was bright and sunny as the missionary community rallied to help. Children spread library books out to dry while adults began to clear away the debris. As news spread about the extensive damage, material and financial help poured in from local donors and from abroad. The U.S. Navy sent relief materials and workers from the Subic Navy Base by helicopter. This help enabled the school to be rebuilt with some features that would make it less vulnerable in the future.

It is easy to assess material gains but difficult to measure all the spiritual benefits. Nevertheless, there is no doubt that the latter have been considerable. There have been times of revival and blessing in the history of the school. Lives have been challenged and changed. Faith has been stimulated, and fellowship between missionaries of various groups has been fostered. Many of the high school graduates have in later years been involved in full-time Christian service, some of them coming back to serve at Faith Academy. We have counted it a privilege to have had a small part in this venture of faith.

26

FELLOW-WORKERS IN CHRIST

"Therefore, my brothers, you whom I love and long for, my joy and crown, that is how you should stand firm in the Lord, dear friends." (Phil. 4:1)

There is no doubt that the Apostle Paul deeply appreciated the fellowship of others serving with him in the Lord's service. Frequently he wrote about his "fellow workers," "fellow servants," and "fellow soldiers." When he travelled he was seldom alone, nor were his co-workers usually Jews like himself; more often they were Gentiles from various places. On one occasion the team was made up of men from some five or six communities (Acts 20:4). When he was left alone at Athens, we sense his loneliness as he sent word for Silas and Timothy to join him as soon as possible. The Scriptures do not envisage a man working alone in the Lord's work, except under unusual circumstances. We cannot afford to be so individualistic in our service for the Lord. When Christ sent out the Twelve and the Seventy, they went out two by two (Mark 6:7; Luke 10:1).

So through the years we have been deeply grateful for our fellow workers. Of course, to be honest, we must admit at times there have been misunderstandings and disagreements. Now with the benefit of hindsight it is easy to see how things could have been handled more tactfully. But keeping things in perspective, we acknowledge that the fellowship and cooperation have far outweighed any difficulties.

Mention has already been made of some of our fellow missionaries, and if some names have been omitted that is not to be construed as lack of appreciation on our part. Often we have praised the Lord for the fine cooperation among the missionaries of our group here in the Philippines, but now it is time to make mention of another group of fellow workers; namely, those national brethren and sisters whom the Lord has called into full-time service for Himself. Like Paul, we love them and long for them.

In the years before World War II we sometimes had help from students at Bible school as they did their practical work assignments. These were often a valuable help, but in the main any expenses involved were carried by the missionary. This is not an ideal situation. There were not yet any full-time commended workers as the work was still in a pioneering stage in the San Juan area. However, all the time we had before us the concept of a truly indigenous work which could be carried on by nationals. This concept involved three requirements: the establishing of strong local churches, men and women called by God to give themselves fully to the Lord's work, and the commendation and support of such workers by the local churches.

Much teaching along these lines was needed based on the Word of God, which would be new in many of the local churches. Here was a concept that was quite different from the prevailing practices in Christian work. The usual thing was for a young person to go to Bible school or seminary if they had a desire to go into Christian service. Some were sincerely desiring to do something for the Lord while others were not even sure of their salvation but thought Bible school was a less onerous path towards education. Some were following the wishes of their parents, but few had the backing of their own church. So the Bible schools became a recruiting station for missions or churches needing workers. It was presumed that a graduate from such schools was adequately equipped for Christian service. So, three lines of teaching have been needed.

First, the local churches need to be taught that only those whom God has clearly called should involve themselves in full-time service for the Lord apart from any secular occupation. Besides the personal conviction of the individual of such a call from God, and clear guidance from the Holy Spirit, there needs

Fellow-Workers in Christ

to be some evidence of this in his life as a Christian. He should show some indication of a gift from God with this gift being exercised in the local church. Unless he thus commends himself to his own home assembly, he should not expect to be commended by them as a servant of God.

There is a prevalent idea that missionaries and full-time workers are in some way on a higher plane spiritually, that they are specially privileged to be fulfilling the will of God. That if a believer is fully surrendered to the Lord, he will give up secular employment in order to devote his time to the Lord's work. This is not necessarily so. The most important factor in any believer's life is that he do God's will for him as an individual. Undoubtedly for some it is the will of the Lord for them to remain in their profession or occupation, whatever it may be (1 Cor. 7:20). Obviously it would not be the Lord's will for anyone to remain in a situation where his Christian testimony would be affected adversely. The Lord Jesus was just as much doing the will of His Father when He lived in obscurity as a carpenter in Nazareth, as when He carried out His redemptive work. If He had not lived in the Father's will in Nazareth, He could not have accomplished the greater objective of His will at Calvary.

Second, a prospective worker needs to have the fellowship and commendation of the elders and believers in his own local church. If they have spiritual discernment, they will recognize not only the potential capabilities but also the leading of the Lord in the life of that prospective worker. In some cases they may be guided by the Lord to take the initiative in encouraging such. On the other hand, they will also discern any lack of fitness or any possible mistake as to the imagined guidance of the Lord. There must be close fellowship between elders and candidates so there will be a mutual understanding of the Lord's will.

This spiritual discernment by the elders has to be developed through prayer and knowledge of the Scriptures. Some have been discouraged because elders lack discernment and consequently are hesitant to commend a worker. However, more often such lack of discernment has resulted in commending those who were not yet ready or who have not been called by God. There is still need for teaching on this subject of commending workers. This is a topic which has been discussed and taught in some of the men's and elder's conferences in the Philippines.

Third, there has to be a teaching about the support of workers, and there are two aspects to this. For the worker, he must clearly understand that he will be depending upon the Lord for his support. While the assemblies and the Lord's people will be the channels the Lord uses, yet he must constantly look to the Lord as the source. Sometimes, it is true, the channels are clogged and the needed support doesn't arrive as it should; but the Lord has promised to supply our needs and He will not fail when our trust is in Him. Nor should the national worker depend upon the foreign missionary. The work will never be truly indigenous if his support is provided by funds from abroad. This is not saying that the foreign missionary will not be aware of the national's needs, nor that he will not give towards these needs. Nor is this to say that gifts from abroad should never be sent to help national workers. However, as a general rule, it is better that such gifts, whether from the missionary or from those in other lands, should be channelled through the local national churches or else through a fund managed by national elders to distribute gifts, either as designated or as directed by the Lord.

Along with this phase of teaching, there is its counterpart, the teaching of the believers and assemblies to give. While the worker is looking to the Lord for his support, money does not come showering down from heaven like the manna in the wilderness. It has to come out of the pockets of the Lord's people. While the worker *lives* by faith, believers must *give* by faith. Many of the assemblies are small and composed of people with small incomes. As a result there is a tendency to shirk the responsibility of giving, hoping that someone else will shoulder the burden. Yet it has often been experienced that when an individual or an assembly begins to give, even if only in a small way, they have been surprised to find that they can do more with the Lord's help than they had ever anticipated. Theoretically, if ten families would each give a tenth of their income, that would be sufficient to support a worker on the same scale of living. Yet we do need to recognize that for a poor family raising and educating children, to give even a tenth is a real venture of faith.

In this matter of support there will probably always be some difficulty regarding the disparity between nationals and foreign workers. There does not seem to be any easy solution to this problem. In one way the foreigner has an advantage over the national brethren. Back in the homelands are many assemblies besides the one which commended him. Through letters and missionary periodicals the missionaries become known over a wide area. The national worker does not have that wider range of supporters, nor are most of these as well off as those in the missionary's homeland. The disparity in the support creates problems for the missionary and dissatisfaction on the part of the national. Admittedly this has sometimes been aggravated by some degree of ostentation on the part of the missionaries. He is accustomed to a higher standard of living and has equipment and vehicles which the national worker cannot afford to purchase or maintain. Few national workers realize that the missionary may be living more frugally than he would at home in a secular occupation. They can only see that the missionary has a higher standard of living than do many of the nationals. Of course, even among national Christians there are differences. It is usually not wise or feasible for health and family reasons for a missionary to live entirely as do the nationals. There have to be some adjustments in food, hygiene, and housing.

It was after our return to the Philippines in 1949 that Eleazar Alfonso decided to go to Bible school. Eleazar had grown up in San Juan and was a grandson of Timotea who has been mentioned in earlier chapters. She had often prayed that her grandsons would devote themselves to the Lord's service. Eleazar told me that he wanted to help me in serving the Lord because at that time we had so much to do. While in Bible school he met and fell in love with another student, Aurora Valdez. After graduation, they were married and spent some time at her home in Cotabato on the island of Mindanao. In 1957, they returned to San Juan believing it was the Lord's will for him to serve Him there. The elders were happy to commend them as the first full-time national workers, even though what they had to offer as financial support was inadequate. Nevertheless, it has been observed that from that time the level of giving at the San Juan Chapel has steadily risen. The Lord's people responded to the challenge. This has continued through the years as the responsibility to help more workers has increased. There have been years when 75% of the total giving there has been given for the support of national workers.

It is not unusual for Filipinos to speak two or three languages, especially if they live in an area where languages overlap. Many also speak English, depending upon how far their education has gone. Eleazar could speak Tagalog, Pampangan, and Ilocano besides English. The Lord gave him a gift in preaching and this was particularly evident in his preaching of the Gospel. It was a joy to hear him preaching in the open air to a crowd of people. For a time he also helped Every Home Crusade in literature distribution. It was while engaged in this ministry that he came upon the group in Tarlac who had become believers through the courses from the Bible School of the Air. We felt it was a real loss to the Lord's work in the Philippines when, in 1968, Eleazar decided to go to the United States and later was joined by his family there.

Zaccheus overcame the difficulty of his short stature by climbing a tree. Stimson Alviar may have climbed some trees, too; I don't know. But I do know he has overcome the problem of his short stature in other ways. In his unsaved days he was a boxer, featherweight probably, and also took care of riding horses for a wealthy landowner! Perhaps his slight build made him look like a jockey! These days Stimson is senior among the national workers and highly respected and beloved by his fellow workers and other Christians. They call him "Tatang" (Daddy) a term of both respect and affection. He was commended to the work of the Lord by the assemblies in San Juan and in Pampanga. His growth in grace and knowledge has been aided by his study of many of the Emmaus courses obtained through the Bible School of the Air. Much of his labor for the Lord has been in his native province of Pampanga where he and his wife make their home. They have five children, and the eldest son and his wife are also devoting themselves to the Lord's work caring for an orphanage under the auspices of the Philippine Faith Mission. While Stimson is a short man, almost hidden behind the pulpit when he preaches in San Juan, there is power in his preaching. Stimson has helped in teaching at Christian Training Camp and Bible school, but most of his ministry has been in establishing and building up small local churches in different places in Central Luzon. This has involved a lot of travelling and being away from home.

Fellow-Workers in Christ

Nestor Dedel was brought up in a Roman Catholic home and was without God and without hope. As a young man his life was in a turmoil which was not relieved by his desire for liquor. One day he was given a New Testament by a friend and read it through in one week. It was in Mindanao that he then also gained peace of heart, assurance of salvation, and a new way of life. Two months after his conversion, he felt that the Lord was calling him into His service and enrolled in a short-term Bible institute in Mindanao. From there Nestor went to the mountains to preach the Gospel to the Manobo tribespeople. After a year of such pioneering work he felt the need for a deeper knowledge of the Scriptures. So he came to Manila and enrolled at the Far Eastern Bible Institute and Seminary (FEBIAS). During his time there he became acquainted with the Castro family at Bahay-pare and eventually fell in love with and married Ligaya Castro, a public school teacher. In this way he learned about the brethren assemblies. After his graduation from FEBIAS he served the Lord in Pampanga and in 1969 was commended as a full-time worker by the San Juan Gospel Chapel. For some years they helped build up the work in San Juan. Nestor's gift is not so much in the realm of teaching but as an evangelist and pastor. When a new work opened up in Cotabato in 1981, Nestor and Ligaya spent some time there helping to establish the believers.

Working with our brother and sister Milton and Marjorie Haack in Pampanga are a couple by the names of Simeon and Tessie Susi, Jr. As is the custom of this country, Simeon is more often spoken of as Jun or Junior. His testimony was given in the November, 1971, issue of KAMANGGAGAWA and I take the liberty of condensing this:

> "My parents were Protestants and my grandfather was a Protestant minister, so I heard about the teaching of the Lord Jesus Christ from childhood, but I never really understood what it meant to have faith in Christ. When I attended school in Manila, friends enticed me to go to nightspots and join in worldly pleasures which soon led me to habitual drinking. Often I was convicted of this, but my efforts at self-reform were always in vain. I prayed that God would lead me to the truth, and I believe God did just that. I remembered meeting a missionary, Mr. Milton

Haack, a couple of years earlier, so I determined to find him. When I saw him with his wife in San Fernando I asked how to be saved. As Mr. Haack explained verses to me from the Bible, I knew this was the wonderful plan of God's salvation. That same night I kneeled in prayer and thanked God for our Lord Jesus Christ who I accepted as my Lord and Savior. A few days later Mr. Haack taught the subject of baptism. I decided I wanted to be baptized. After I was saved I told my wife Tessie, and she too received the Lord as her personal Savior. My brother too trusted Christ. All three of us have been baptized at the Basa Air Base Chapel and after the baptism we joined the Christians at the Lord's Supper. In my unsaved days, besides drinking, I was a chain smoker. Today, God has given me the victory over it, too."

Brother Susi also relates how he gave up politics and how he had a bonfire in his yard when he burned the literature of Herbert Armstrong and the Mormons. Several assemblies have been established in Pampanga through the labors of the Haack's and Susi's and other workers. This too in an area where Roman Catholicism has been very strong.

When Ken Engle and others began a Christian Service Brigade group in San Juan, one of the boys was Rudolfo Ponce de Leon. His parents who formerly lived on the island of Cuyo in Palawan were friends of Sandy and Maisie Sutherland. Mr. Javier Ponce de Leon was for many years active in the Boy Scout movement and was a most gracious Christian gentleman. Before I give you Rudy's own testimony, I want to mention one thing which he, in his modesty, does not mention. The highest award in the Christian Service Brigade is "Herald of Christ"— like being an Eagle Scout. Rudy was the first one outside the continental United States to earn this award. A few years later, his nephew Pete Barotilla also earned that award. But here now is Rudy's testimony:

"I came under the influence of the gospel through San Juan Gospel Chapel's Sunday school and Christian Service Brigade programs in 1952. Although I could not now point to the exact moment of my conversion to Christ, it was sometime in November of 1956 that I gained full assurance of salvation.

"Through the influence of godly men, missionaries in particular, my spiritual and social development was enhanced. Through service and leadership opportunities I grew in my capacity to be useful for the Lord. When I was finishing my college studies in Commercial Art, conviction came to me regarding total dedication of my self and my ambitions, my future to my Lord and Savior. This was followed almost immediately by employment as staff announcer with Far East Broadcasting Company. During my four or five years with FEBC I continued to be active in church, in Sunday school, in youth fellowship, and especially in the Brigade where I had taken over the leadership.

"As the challenge to expand the work of the Brigade to other churches throughout the country increased, I felt called of God to resign from FEBC in order to devote fulltime to Brigade. This I did in 1965. As I resigned from FEBC, I let the elders know of my exercise before the Lord to serve him full-time and to trust Him for meeting my needs. Sometime later, within a few months, the church through the elders commended me to the Lord's work with boys. My ministry was to be both with our church's local chapter as well as to the national headquarters as the Brigade office was called. For ten years I served as executive secretary seeing encouraging fruit in all the 25 local churches where Brigade clubs had been formed.

"In 1975, with inflation as well as inadequate local church support making it extremely difficult to maintain a national office, it was decided to close up the national effort and to put all information we had on boy's work into a book that churches could buy and use to organize their own clubs. I then met with the elders to let them know that at this stage I was inclined to go into the ministry of the assembly as a whole and not just for young people.

"In 1977, I took advantage of an opportunity to study at the Bible College of New Zealand with my wife simultaneously taking further studies as a doctor in the medical field. We returned in 1980 to resume work at the chapel and in other ministries connected with the assemblies."

It would be too tedious to write about all of our valued national fellow-workers, but I would like to mention three other couples. The young people in the region of Bahay-pare held rallies under the name of the Bulacan Youth Fellowship. Some from other groups were invited to share in this fellowship. Through this Rey Cervantes from Plaridel became acquainted not only with the assembly work at Bahay-pare, but also with Norma Castro. Both of them also attended camp and studied at the Philippine Missionary Institute. Following their studies there they were married and were commended to the Lord's work by the assemblies in Bahay-pare and Baguio. For some time they worked along with Dave Harvey in Baliwag, particularly in student work. Baliwag is an important commercial town in Bulacan, the focal point of a large farming area. When the campsite was purchased, Rey and Norma moved there to oversee that work. Later on they went back to Baliwag and then took time out to complete their studies at the Philippine Missionary Institute. Now they are back in Baliwag endeavoring to see the work there built up. In addition to this they accepted the responsibility of preparing the radio program for the Bible School of the Air in Tagalog. This has been a most acceptable ministry bringing in good response.

In Plaridel, Rey had a friend who was also a believer, Oscar de Leon. He was an insurance underwriter; and he married a girl, Gloria, who was from Sumapa, a section of Malolos, the capital of Bulacan. Through attending camps, conferences, and other meetings with Rey, Oscar became interested in serving the Lord with the assemblies. He was convinced of the Scripturalness of their position. He was commended to the work by the assembly in San Juan and has been working in the province of Bulacan, principally in Sumapa where there is an active assembly. This assembly has grown and has also commended others to the Lord's work. It was through Oscar's contacts that we learned about the property which was purchased for the camp. This is not far from Sumapa, so Oscar and Glo have been near at hand to help in camp activities. Oscar has also given a great deal of help in teaching at camp and at the Bible school there.

John Paglinawan and Gloria Latagan met at one of the Christian Training Camps held in Bataan before we had our own camp site. John was from Basa Air Force base in Pampanga and Gloria from San Juan. Later they attended Philippine Missionary Institute and as man and wife were commended by the assembly in San Juan for the Lord's work, working initially in a

Fellow-Workers in Christ

new work in Basista, Pangasinan, and later in San Juan. They had a burden for missionary work overseas. Several Filipinos with other groups have gone to other countries as missionaries. John and Glo applied and were accepted by the Overseas Missionary Fellowship. This mission has the policy of accepting nationals from different countries for missionary work outside their native land. The assembly in San Juan recommended them for this service and pledged to continue to minister to them as they had done previously. However, the support from local assemblies was not sufficient to meet all their needs. After a time of language study in Malaysia, John and Glo left their two children in the missionary school there and went to Thailand. During their first four-year term they learned many lessons. With their trust in God, they were reaching a people of entirely different culture, language, and religious background. In spite of the difficulties they gained a good command of the Thai language. The Lord blessed their labors, and they had the joy of seeing a young church established. At this time, they are back in the Philippines for further studies and to serve as representatives for the Philippine Council of the Overseas Missionary Fellowship. They would like to return to the work in Thailand in the Lord's will.

Needless to say, it was a great joy to us to see those first missionaries going forth from our fellowship to another land, to see that the Philippines is not only a land where missionaries from other lands are received but from where missionaries are sent forth. But what of the future in this direction? There are no doubt other young people here who would be willing to respond to the challenge of missionary work overseas. Thousands of Filipinos go overseas every year in pursuit of secular employment. There are many of them today in the Middle East among the oil-rich countries. They earn good money, much of which is sent back here to support their families. With missionaries the flow of money would have to be in the opposite direction and that's where the rub comes. The assemblies here are too few, too small, and too poor to be able to adequately support foreign workers. Supporting the national workers at home base is difficult. No doubt there are some who would glibly say, "Let them go forth in faith, trusting in God to supply their needs." Such people often quote Philippians 4:19, forgetting this was written by a missionary and addressed to a local church, a church which was already giving liberally and whose needs would be supplied as they could give more.

In the Third World today there are young people who are a potential source of foreign workers. They have some advantage in that they are not identified with nations who were formerly colonizers. They are not white-skinned, fair-haired Europeans or Americans. Already they are familiar with a multi-lingual situation in their own countries. But how could such Third World missionaries be supported, not only in their own living expenses, but also those involved in their service for the Lord? It would be neither wise nor practical for their names to be included in lists of workers from Western lands. There would be problems involved in making known their work through mission magazines, like Missions or Echoes. From experience we know it would not be wise for such workers to be directly supported by churches or individuals in Western lands.

It seems little thought has been given to the possibility of encouraging this phase of missionary endeavor. Yet it is high time it should be considered. If the Lord does not come soon, this may be the way missions will go in the near future. One possibility would be for some responsible elders and leaders in a country such as the Philippines to form a committee which could function like the CMML or MSC. Then foreign funds could be channelled through that committee to further their objective of missionary outreach to other lands.

27

THE PROGRESS OF THE GOSPEL

"Finally, brothers, pray for us that the message of the Lord may spread rapidly and be honored, just as it was with you." (2 Thess. 3:1)

No doubt most will be more familiar with the older translation, "That the word of the Lord may have free course." They will also be aware that the more literal translation is "that the word of the Lord may run." In making this prayer request, Paul remembered how the Gospel spread so quickly in Thessalonica, as he had written in the first epistle, "The Lord's message rang out from you, not only in Macedonia and Achaia—your faith in God has become known everywhere." It was a remarkable example of the rapid spread of the Gospel. In that early Apostolic age the message of the Lord has indeed spread rapidly and widely. In these last days we need to be reminded that the Word of the Lord can only *run* as we give it legs and feet. When the Prophet Habakkuk was looking to see what the Lord would say to him, he was told; "Write down the revelation and make it plain on tablets so that whoever reads it may run with it" (Hab. 2:2, NIV marg.). God's message is so urgent that, having read it, the herald must run to proclaim it. So the head cannot say to the feet, "I have no need of you." Our Head needs us, his feet, to run His message.

Some years ago my brother-in-law, George Gibson, in Buffalo

had to have both legs amputated. To get to the meetings he was dependent upon others to take him in their cars. One day, explaining to me why he was not at a certain meeting he said, "Cyril, if I had my legs, I would have been there." After nearly two thousand years there are still people who have not heard the Lord's message. Is our Lord saying, "If I had the use of my people's legs, I would have been there?" Is it any wonder then, that Paul quotes Isaiah in saying, "How beautiful are the feet of those who bring good news!"

Praise the Lord for all those who yield themselves to Him to be heralds carrying the glad, good news of salvation. In recent years some of these have been young people serving in the mission field for short periods of time. Some have gone as a team, at their own expense, giving a few weeks of summer vacation to help as they may in some mission field. This has given them opportunity to see the mission field firsthand, to know what the conditions are, to be challenged by the need, and to fellowship with those of another race. In former times this was not possible because most of their time would have been spent in travelling by ship. However, I do think that this type of short-term effort needs to be re-evaluated. Are the results commensurate with the expense involved?

Others have served for two or three years on some mission field but not with any specific commitment to a longer stay. There has been much discussion about the pros and cons of short-term service. Years ago missionary service in a foreign country was thought of as a life-time commitment, unless it was interrupted by health or family concern. Some have a tendency to think short-termers are not quite so fully committed. Undoubtedly there is room today for both short-termers and those who can stay for a longer period. Modern travel means that almost any part of the mission field can be reached in a matter of hours, whereas it used to take days if not weeks. In general terms we might say that the short-termers can supplement what is being done by those who are more permanent. With a firsthand knowledge of the work, they are better able to discern the will of the Lord and their own suitability for longer terms of service. They will have learned some lessons of acculturation and gained some knowledge of another language.

In 1965 a team from International Crusades (then Literature

The Progress of the Gospel 257

Crusades) came to the Philippines. They placed a heavy emphasis on distribution of literature and much of this was done in markets and around schools and colleges. Seeing that so much English is spoken here, especially in cities like Manila, it seemed unnecessary to spend time in language school as was the case with later teams. After about a year some of this team moved on to Korea, namely Warren and Flo Dunham, Stuart Mitchell, and William Roller. Later they returned there for a longer period of time. After two years here James and Gerrie LeValley and Steve and Dot St. Clair returned on a more permanent basis, the latter couple being involved with Faith Academy.

The Australian and New Zealand counterpart of International Crusades is known as Gospel Literature Outreach (GLO). This group has sent two teams at different times. These teams concentrated on house-to-house distribution of literature, following this up with home Bible studies wherever there was an interest. This was done in areas near to existing assemblies so the follow-up work could be channelled into those assemblies. The methods of the first IC team resulted in a greater distribution of literature but follow-up was more difficult because contacts were more scattered. Some of the follow-up work in all of these efforts has been done through the courses offered by the Bible School of the Air. Unfortunately, some of the single ladies on these teams had to return home early because of health or emotional problems. After two years here the two couples in the first team returned to Australia. Of the two couples in the second team, one came back again. Len and Mary Savill were commended by their home assemblies in New Zealand and have been working in the province of Pangasinan. Two of the three assemblies in that province were fruit of the first team. Both teams spent some time in Baguio and were a great help to the assembly there.

In 1980, a second team of six came here from International Crusades. After a few months in language study they moved to the town of Morong in the province of Rizal. (There is another Morong in Bataan where there is a refugee camp for boat people escaping from Vietnam. They remain there until they can be processed to proceed to some other receiving country. Some relief workers are helping there.)

Another team of four from IC came in 1982 and after their

language study moved to Morong to help and take over when the first team left in 1983. Whereas the GLO teams worked around existing assemblies, these later teams decided to move into a place where there was no assembly and endeavor to establish one during their stay in this country. Through house-to-house visitation, home Bible studies, film showings, and use of puppets, they have had the joy of seeing some saved and baptized. With the help of some from the assembly in Binangonan and other missionaries, regular meetings were begun and in a little over a year the new believers along with the team were meeting for the observance of the Lord's Supper.

Since the Lord called Rose to serve him in Pakistan in 1966, it has been our privilege to visit there three times. The first visit was in 1969 when we stopped off for a week. Heading home for furlough, we had earlier decided to go by way of Europe. At that time we spent a week in Multan where Rose was working in a Women's Christian Hospital. Multan is a very old city. Supposedly Alexander the Great, going through the Khyber Pass, extended his conquests as far as that city. Though on the edge of the Sind desert, the country around is quite fertile because of the irrigation canal system that was developed by the British in Punjab. Our visit was in May which was the beginning of the hot season and the daytime temperature was up to 110°F or above 40° Celsius. One evening as we sat at supper with the hospital foreign staff, everyone suddenly left the table, leaving us sitting there to imagine what the emergency was. Soon it was evident that it was a dust storm and every door and window needed to be closed. Even so some dust penetrated. I remarked to the lady doctor in charge that when I left I would not shake the dust off my feet, I would still be spitting it out from my throat. She replied, "Oh, you won't get rid of it that easily. You'll be shaking it out from your suitcases for weeks."

Bethel, the Brethren chapel, was a short walking distance from the hospital. So we enjoyed the fellowship of the believers there, though hardly any spoke English. Everyone sat on carpets spread on the floor, leaving their shoes at the door. For my wife and I they kindly provided chairs. On one occasion I was glad to yield my chair to an aged Pakistani brother who was not at all well. Baba Hashim had given himself to serving the Lord, and his ministry was well received, even though he was illiterate. He had members of his family read the Bible to him and became well versed in the Scriptures. We were told that there were occasions when someone reading from the Bible would make a mistake and be corrected by Baba Hashim. One afternoon we visited the Brethren workers who carried on a clinic for women and children at Mumtazabad, a suburb about four miles out.

After a week there, we flew from, Karachi to Beirut where we stayed overnight. Since it was not possible to fly from Beirut to Tel Aviv, we had to fly to Cyprus and from there to Tel Aviv. Our stay in Jerusalem was limited to two days, but we shall not easily forget those memorable scenes—Mount of Olives and Gethsemane, the Wailing Wall and the Temple site with the Dome of the Rock. The Via Dolorosa and David's Tomb. Vivid in our memories remains Gordon's Golgotha and the Garden Tomb, as well as a visit to Bethany, Jericho, and the Dead Sea. Leaving Jerusalem we spent a night in Rome and then on to Britain. After a long weekend in London, we had a nice visit with my niece, Rue Hatton, and her family who lived just north of London. From there we travelled north, visiting in Yorkshire with Miss Jennie Coxon who had been with us during Japanese occupation days. Then to our old friend David Shepherd in Paisley, Scotland, and to Miss Lois Stephen in Aberdeen. Her parents were missionaries in north China and she had been born in Lingfield on one of their furloughs. Not aware of our link with Lingfield, she had started corresponding with Anna some years before. A couple of nights were spent with friends in Edinburgh before driving south through the Lake district to Lingfield. In a meeting in the Mission Room there I was introduced by a brother whose father had been a close friend of my father's. Next morning we stopped to see the house where I had spent the first seven years of my life. Then on to Dorking to visit the two sisters of my late brother-in-law, Richard Weller. They had lived in the same house since childhood, and it didn't seem to change much since I visited there as a little boy. Later on we drove down to Devon for a few days with my other niece, Beryl Heggadon and her family. When we first planned this trip we had hoped to see my brother George after a lapse of fifty years but in the Lord's will he was called home to be with the Lord before we went that May.

Our second visit to Pakistan was in the latter part of 1973.

Ken and his family were on furlough so we decided to spend Christmas with Rose. October to January is the cooler time of the year. Arriving at Multan airport in the evening, there was no one to meet us. Our letter about our arrival time had not reached Rose. Seeing our predicament, a Roman Catholic priest very kindly offered to take us out to Mumtazabad where Rose was then living. She had by then been commended to serve with the workers there. During their prayer meeting the door bell rang. Supposing it was a call for one of the midwives to go for a home delivery, she was surprised to learn she had visitors from Manila!

Rose wanted us to see more of Pakistan than just dusty Multan, so she planned an itinerary including a couple of days of Lahore and Rawalpindi which are more advanced cities than Multan. Then a drive up to Murree in the mountains at the western end of the Himalayan range. The hotel at which we had reservations neglected to inform Rose they would then be closed for the season, so we had to find a second-class hotel. There was little heat provided so we spent a cold night. However, there was compensation in the wonderful views of the mountains. The next day we visited the school for missionary children at Murree and had lunch there. They were sending some pupils to the dentist in Rawalpindi that afternoon and there would be room for us in the van. Our hotel reservations in Pindi were for the following night, but we anticipated no difficulty. On the way down the Pakistani driver of the school van was travelling rather fast for a narrow, winding mountain highway, so rounding a curve he collided with an army jeep. There was not too much damage though some of our party were badly shook up. As always in the Orient, a crowd quickly gathered and, seeing foreigners, was not exactly friendly. One man averred that one of the foreigners was driving, which of course was not true. Since most of us didn't know what was being said, we could only sit quietly and pray. It was a relief to finally get a car which would take us the rest of the way.

At the hotel we were informed they had no vacancy that night and calls to other hotels were all negative. There was some kind of convention ending that night. We were all discouraged as well as weary, especially dear Anna who still had some shock from the accident and the ensuing unpleasantness. The desk clerk went out of his way to find some accommodations for us and finally announced he had found a vacancy at the New Comrade Hotel. With the Soviet influence in that part of the world, I had some misgivings about a hotel with that name. Just as we were making our way to a taxi, the clerk approached me. He said he didn't like to see us going to that hotel. If we were willing he would put up cots in a room downstairs, but we would have to get up early as the waiters would need to get in there to set tables for breakfast. We accepted this gratefully and though inconvenient it was worth a good tip.

We got into a room next morning for a weekend stay but were not able to look up the assembly there because I had a stomach upset. On the Monday we were able to fly to Peshawar where we had nice accommodations. In the late afternoon we went out for a walk and to our surprise saw Mr. and Mrs. Dennis Clark, missionary friends, just leaving their home. Rose hadn't been sure they were in Peshawar then. We had dinner with them the following evening. We engaged a car to take us the next morning to the famous Khyber Pass, the road that leads into Afghanistan. We could not visit Kabul because we had a single-entry visa to Pakistan. That was very rugged mountainous country. Huge cement blocks beside the road showed how quickly a road barrier could be set up. Standing by the gate on the road leading into Afghanistan, the guard permitted me to take some pictures there. It seemed that every man in the area carried a gun and looked quite warlike. Means of travel for many of them was in old sedans from which the roof and trunk lid had been removed. Every available spot was occupied by men standing with the bumpers almost dragging on the ground. It didn't seem possible that tires and springs could stand such a weight of humanity.

The city of Peshawar was quite old and interesting with high wooden houses jammed close to each other. In the stores at street level, various trades were being carried on. In one "chapatis" were being made, the flat pancake type of wheat bread so widely eaten there; in another, a tailor squatting on the floor was operating his sewing machine by hand; then there were those making items of brass. For less than two dollars we bought a brass calendar good for forty years by turning a center part. Peshawar has a long history in its relation to the Khyber Pass.

There was modernity too as we saw American young people, fellows and girls alike with long hair, shabby clothes, and a back pack, wandering like gypsies and many with a drug problem.

It was a pleasure to get to know Robbie Orr and his wife Dr. Jean in Multan. Robbie had pioneered missionary work in Multan, often mobbed by angry Moslems as he proclaimed the Gospel. He is a fluent speaker and able writer in Urdu and a student of Scriptures. During the Christmas season that year, his brother Willie from Winnipeg was visiting Multan. The two brothers have a keen sense of humor so there was many a hearty laugh in our time together.

During that time we made a trip with Robbie and his brother to the mountains east from Multan to the area of Baluchistan which borders on Iran. This involved crossing part of the desert and the Indus river. Since the river was low at that time of the year, we travelled for two or three kilometers across the dry sandy river bed until we reached the river itself. This was crossed by the Bridge of Boats. The number of boats used was determined by the width of the river at any time. From there we climbed up the narrow mountain road to Ft. Monroe where there had been an old British outpost. In the old graveyard were gravestones dated in the 19th century. We could only speculate about women and children who died from illness or of soldiers killed in battle—all of them lying in lonely graves so far from the land of their birth in Britain. In one of the old buildings there was a resthouse where we spent the night, shivering with the cold. How glad we were for a fire in the fireplace as we cooked some food we had brought with us. Anna was reluctant to leave the warmth of the fire to go out in the cold night air, but we finally persuaded her that she must not miss the unusual sight of the sky. It was a clear night, not a cloud in sight and no moon. With clear mountain air, far removed from the smog and glare of any city, there was a view of the stars that will stand out in our memory. It seems incredible that those dots of light which shone so brightly could be millions or billions of miles away! It seemed as if we could have reached up and touched them if only our reach was a bit longer! God's words to Abram seemed more meaningful then—"Look at the heavens and count the stars—if indeed you can count them."

Travel on some of the Pakistani highways was a hair-raising

experience. Many of them are only asphalted in the center, the width of one vehicle. There was no such thing as a white center line! Naturally everyone drives in the center until passing an oncoming vehicle. It was an awesome sight to see a multicolored, highly decorated bus or truck barrelling down the highway towards us. Then just at the last moment each driver would yield half of the pavement and pass with two wheels on the unpaved section.

Traffic in Multan is not noted for its speed so much as its variety. Besides buses and trucks, there are three-wheeled vehicles for taxis and horse drawn carts for hire. Strings of camels laden with large bundles of cotton lumber along at a leisurely pace. Beside these are bull carts, donkey carts, bicycles darting about amid the stray sheep and goats plus pedestrians who expect the drivers to avoid hitting them. Oh well, one thing we could be sure of—there were no stray pigs!

Our third visit to Pakistan was in 1977, and by that time the assembly, the clinic, and the missionary residence were newly built on their own property in Mumtazabad. It was time for their annual convention at which I had been asked to speak, of course, by interpretation. Large tents had been erected beside the new chapel and mats spread on the ground. When the space seemed filled the chairman would call on everyone to stand and move forward into a closer formation. Thus, there was no difficulty in providing space at the back for latecomers. The singing is all in Urdu with local tunes and accompanied by lively music—a small type of organ which is played by the right hand while the left hand operates the bellows at the back; a drum, castanets, and a clapper keep up the rhythm. A number of hymns are translated psalms.

Another speaker at the convention was Alex Smythe, a missionary who has been in India for many years. He understands Urdu, but didn't feel sufficiently fluent to preach in it so spoke in English. One illustration he used proved embarrassing for him but quite amusing to other missionaries. Speaking of the evil of gossip he told of the gossipy woman who was told to shake the feathers from a pillow abroad and then pick up all the feathers. In Pakistan they don't have feather pillows for their pillows are filled with kapok. Also there didn't seem to be any definite word for feathers. The interpreter seemed to have the right idea and was substituting something else for feathers. It would have been wise to let it go at that. But Brother Smythe knew what he was saying and insisted it must be feathers. The poor interpreter spoke about a pillowcase full of chickens and then of chicken wings but still no feathers. Oh, the hazards of speaking through an interpreter!

After the convention the missionaries went for a few days retreat at which I again shared the ministry with Brother Smythe. Here we were on firmer ground so far as the language was concerned for we could speak directly in English. This retreat was held on the grounds of a Roman Catholic training institute. We took our meals along with the staff of priests and nuns in a very friendly atmosphere despite our theological difference.

Our return to Manila was an ordeal rather than a pleasure. Unknowingly we had made reservations for the time when Moslem pilgrims were returning from their annual pilgrimage to Mecca. In addition to many Philippine pilgrims were Filipino workers returning from the Middle East. Flush with money they were loaded with radios, stereos, and gifts for their families. The plane was late leaving Karachi so we had a weary wait in the airport there and then some eight hours of flying in a plane where every seat was occupied. How thankful we were to be greeted by Ken at the Manila airport.

Some years ago missionaries of different groups used to meet for prayer breakfast one Monday morning a month. One Monday our good friend Dr. Edwin Spahr was to be the speaker and it seemed like a bigger crowd than usual. We thought it was due to Dr. Spahr being loved by so many and being called "The missionaries' pastor." To our surprise we discovered that we were being honored on our 40th wedding anniversary! The fulsome praise in Ed's talk prompted one lady to remark afterwards that she would want him to speak at her funeral!

Ten years later our fellow missionaries arranged for a banquet to celebrate our 50th and again Dr. Spahr was invited to be the main speaker. Another celebration then was at the San Juan Chapel as our Filipino friends gathered to express their affection. At that time, Mr. Hahn Browne of the Far East Broadcasting Company arranged an interview for us with President Ferdinand Marcos in his office at Malacañang. We had a pleasant 15-minute chat with him only a few days before he declared martial law.

Another ten years sped by and another banquet celebrated our 60th anniversary. At the head table we were flanked by our family, Leonard and Esther, Ken and Elaine, and also Rose, along with Leonard's son, Dave and his wife Lois as representative of the grandchildren and great-grandchildren who could not be there. It was also a pleasure to have my great-niece Miss Ruth Shannon from Taiwan with us for that happy occasion, when some two hundred friends gathered with us to thank the Lord for His faithfulness and goodness. These celebrations have had a double significance because our arrival in the Philippines was just three months after our wedding. We are especially grateful to the Lord for His goodness to our family. The immediate family are all engaged in the Lord's service and all the grandchildren in the family of faith with those who are married bringing up their children in the nurture and admonition of the Lord.

The prophet Isaiah depicted some one calling to him from Seir, "Watchman, what is left of the night?" In his urgency the caller repeats his question. The prophet as a watchman replies, "Morning is coming, but also the night" (Isa. 21:11-12). The question is appropriate for us to ask in these days. Scientists, statesmen, and men of the world say we are almost at the midnight hour, the hour of doom. Yes, indeed, for the world the darkest hours are ahead—"but the night is coming." For us who know the Lord, it is time to lift up our heads in expectancy. "Morning is coming." Surely soon the Bright and Morning Star will appear. There is a verse in Anne Cousin's hymn based on writings of the saintly Samuel Rutherford which is not found in most hymnals:

> "I have wrestled on towards Heaven,
>   'Gainst storm and wind and tide:
> Now, like a weary traveller,
>   That leaneth on his guide.
> Amid the shades of evening,
>   While sinks life's lingering sand
> I hail the glory dawning
>   From Immanuel's land."

But waiting time is not to be wasted time! While the doors are open and there is still liberty for the spread of the gospel, we need to press on in our service for Him who loved us and gave Himself for us.

And all the way it has been for us "Grace Triumphant."